Advanced Information and Knowledge Processing

Series Editors

Professor Lakhmi Jain
Lakhmi.jain@unisa.edu.au

Professor Xindong Wu
xwu@cs.uvm.edu

Also in this series

Ajith Abraham, Lakhmi Jain and Robert Goldberg (Eds)
Evolutionary Multiobjective Optimization
1-85233-787-7

K.C. Tan, E.F.Khor and T.H. Lee
Multiobjective Evolutionary Algorithms and Applications
1-85233-836-9

Nikhil R. Pal and Lakhmi Jain (Eds)
Advanced Techniques in Knowledge Discovery and Data Mining
1-85233-867-9

Amit Konar and Lakhmi Jain
Cognitive Engineering
1-85233-975-6

Miroslav Kárný (Ed.)
Optimized Bayesian Dynamic Advising
1-85233-928-4

Yannis Manolopoulos, Alexandros Nanopoulos, Apostolos N. Papadopoulos and
Yannis Theodoridis
R-trees: Theory and Applications
1-85233-977-2

Sanghamitra Bandyopadhyay, Ujjwal Maulik, Lawrence B. Holder and Diane J. Cook (Eds)
Advanced Methods for Knowledge Discovery from Complex Data
1-85233-989-6

Marcus A. Maloof (Ed.)
Machine Learning and Data Mining for Computer Security
1-84628-029-X

Sifeng Liu and Yi Lin
Grey Information
1-85233-995-0

Vasile Palade, Cosmin Danut Bocaniala and Lakhmi Jain (Eds)
Computational Intelligence in Fault Diagnosis
1-84628-343-4

Mitra Basu and Tin Kam Ho (Eds)
Data Complexity in Pattern Recognition
1-84628-171-7

Samuel Pierre (Ed.)
E-learning Networked Environments and Architectures
1-84628-351-5

Arno Scharl and Klaus Tochtermann (Eds)
The Geospatial Web
1-84628-826-5

Ngoc Thanh Nguyen
Advanced Methods for Inconsistent Knowledge Management
1-84628-888-3

Amnon Meisels

Distributed Search by Constrained Agents

Algorithms, Performance, Communication

 Springer

Amnon Meisels
Department of Computer Science
Ben-Gurion University, Beer-Sheva, Israel

British Library Cataloguing in Publication Data
A catalogue record for this book is available from the British Library

AI&KP ISSN 1610-3947
ISBN: 978-1-84996-710-5   e-ISBN: 978-1-84800-040-7

9 8 7 6 5 4 3 2 1

springer.com

To Sari with love
My wife and best friend

Preface

Distributed search by agents is an important topic of distributed AI and has not been treated thoroughly as such. While the scope of work on multi-agent systems has grown steadily over the last decade, very little of it has spilled into distributed search. In conrast, the constraints processing community has produced a sizable body of work on distributed constrained search. Paradoxically, a community that concentrates on search algorithms and heuristics has created a distributed model for agents that cooperate on solving hard search problems. Traditionally, this field has been named *Ditributed Constraints Satisfaction* and lately also *distributed constraints optimization*. The present book attempts to prompt deeper response from the MAS community and hopefully to give rise to cooperative work on distributed search by agents. In order to achieve this high goal, the book presents the large body of work on distributed search by constrained agents. The presentation emphasizes many aspects of distributed computation that connect naturally to multi-agent systems, especially measures of performance for distributed search algorithms and the impact of delays in communication.

Distributed Constraints Satisfaction Problems (*DisCSPs*) have been studied over the last decade, starting with the pioneering proposal by Makoto Yokoo [18]. The first distributed search algorithm for DisCSPs - Asynchronous Backtracking (ABT) - was first published in complete format in 1998 [64]. The first book on Distributed Constraints Satisfaction Problems has appeared as early as 2000 [61]. The book includes most of Yokoo's early work - distributed search algorithms, both complete and stochastic, and some experimental evaluation of the algorithms. It took five more years for the extensive form of *ABT*, including three well-defined versions and a correctness proof, to be published. In total, 10 years elapsed between Yokoo's original proposal of Asynchronous Backtracking, to the final extended form in the AI Journal in 2005 [9]. This gives a clear demonstration of the intricacies of distributed search algorithms, which form the heart of the field and of the present book.

In the last six years, since the year 2000, the community of researchers in the field have had at least one yearly workshop. These activities have helped the field mature into one of the recognized disciplines of both Constraints Processing (CP) and Multi-Agent Systems (MAS). In fact, the yearly workshops have been taking place alternately within the CP conferences and the AAMAS conferences (and the general AI conference, IJCAI). The series of Distributed Constraints Reasoning (DCR) workshops served as the forum for a community of more than 50 researchers worldwide and has published more than 20 papers yearly on DisCSP.

The field of distributed constraints search now includes two main families of problems - Distributed Constraints Satisfaction Problems DisCSPs and Distributed Constraints Optimization Problems (DisCOP)s. With the rapid rate of published work on DisCSPs and DisCOPs a book is very much needed, to present in detail the accumulated body of work of all researchers. While preparing my tutorial talk for CP-2004 in Toronto, I first noticed that a short presentation of the field must include three parts. These three parts form the backbone of this book. The first and most important part introcuces in great detail search algorithms for DisCSPs and DisCOPs. Quite a number of search algorithms have been proposed in recent years for both DisCSPs and DisCOPs and an in-depth exposition of all algorithms is long overdue. The algorithmic part of the exposition has also grown to include ordering heuristics. Both asynchronous heuristics and sequential ones have appeared in the DisCSP literature in the last three years. Asynchronous heuristics are accompanied by an innovative algorithm that enables ABT to include dynamic ordering of agents [74].

The second part of the presentation of Distributed Search by Constrained Agents includes a comprehensive study of distributed performance measures for all algorithms. Based on the resulting coherent and asynchronous scale of performance, an extensive experimental evaluation can be constructed. In the present book this part is in Chapter 10 and Chapter 11.

The third part of our presentation of current research on DisCSPs and DisCOPs relates to their inherent distributed nature and addresses potential problems. These can relate to potential delays in communication, or to a variety of other agent topics, such as privacy of information used during search. This book addresses communication problems like message delays in detail in Chapter 12 and measures the impact of delays on the performance of families of DisCSP search algorithms in Chapter 13. The first few steps in the direction of privacy preservation have been taken in the last four years, for example, investigating means of preserving privacy [10, 42]. However, this topic is left for a later addition when more work will have accumulated.

The book starts by describing the problems and by giving motivation for their great usefulness in today's distributed world. In order to solve DisCSPs one needs distributed search algorithms. The first asynchronous algorithm in the field was introduced a decade ago by the pioneering work of Makoto Yokoo [62, 64]. The asynchronous backtracking algorithm (ABT) is presented in its modern form, as in [9]. *ABT* continues to be a central DisCSP search algorithm and will be used in two forms in the book, first, as a reference for all performance evaluations of other algorithms, second, as a basis for enhancement, regarding ordering heuristics.

The distributed nature of the search problem that is at the center of this book makes it a natural selection for a graduate course on this topic. Distributed search algorithms that are run by all agents and find a global solution can serve as a solid demonstration for distributed AI and multi-agent systems (MAS). A short introduction on Constraints Satisfaction Problems is needed, perhaps a bit more extensive than the one given in the first chapter. Part of the material in this book has been presented by me in the graduate course on Constraints Processing that I have been giving over the last four years in both my department at Ben-Gurion University and at the computer science department of the Open University. Emphasizing the distributed nature of DisCSP algorithms I have routinely focused all final projects of the students on my course on implementing and investigating distributed search algorithms.

This book focuses on the main research results in distributed constraints satisfaction and optimization over the last decade. Thus it can serve as a research asset to researchers and to graduate students that focus on distributed search by agents and in particular on DisCSPs and DisCOPs. It is my hope that this complete text can serve as a basis for a course on distributed search in AI. I believe that the accumulated work on search by constrained agents is an excellent algorithmic and clearcut example of the cooperation of agents in search.

The present book is the result of six very intensive years of research with my wonderful group of graduate students. My sincere thanks go to all of them, without whom the great research on Distributed Constraints would have not been possible. My deepest thanks to my students - Amir Gershman, Arnon Gilboa, Eliezer Kaplanski, Oz Lavee, Michael Orlov, Igor Razgon, Moshe Zazon, and Roie Zivan. The theses of Oz, Michael, and Amir have also been used extensively within the text of the relevant chapters. The chapter on *ADOPT* (Chapter 15) is completely taken from Amir's thesis. The extensive study and wonderful implementations of *ADOPT* by Amir have made him in my eyes the world's expert on the *ADOPT* algorithm. The contents of the outstanding thesis of Roie Zivan (which is still not written) are present in most of the book, from our papers on search algorithms (Chapter 6, Chapter 7), through our work on concurrent performance measures (Chapter 10), and to his briliant work on asynchronous ordering heuristics (Chapter 9). I look back in appreciation on the great research road we have covered together and in excitement on what's yet to come.

Beer-Sheva, July 2007   *Amnon Meisels*

Contents

List of Algorithms

List of Figures

1

Introduction

The investigation of Distributed Constraints Satisfaction Problems (DISCSPs) started only a decade ago. It focuses on constraints satisfaction problems (CSPs) that are distributed among multiple agents. Imagine a large university that includes many departments. The weekly schedule of classes is generated by each department, scheduling its classes and teachers for the whole semester. A weekly schedule is a typical constraint satisfaction problem. Class meetings are variables and the timeslots of the week are the domain of values that have to be assigned to classes in order to generate a schedule. The fundamental constraints of timetabling require that two classes taught by the same teacher have to be assigned different timeslots. Another common constraint is to require that two meetings of the same class will be assigned to different days of the week. In the university as a whole, the departments can be thought of as agents that generate their departmental weekly schedules. The weekly schedules of different departments are constrained by the fact that there are students that select classes from these departments. This generates constraints between departments and the generic scenario of a *distributed CSP*. Agents own parts of the global problem (e.g., departmental schedules) and cooperate in search of a global solution in which the constraints between departments are satisfied. In order to solve such a distributed problem, all agents must cooperate in a global search process. Search algorithms for a distributed problem operate by agents performing assignments to their variables and exchanging messages in order to check their assignments against those of constraining agents.

Much research has been performed over the last 20 years on search algorithms and heuristics for solving constrained search problems. All of this work needs to be widely adapted, in order to become suitable for distributed constraints. When a distributed set of agents run the search for a globally consistent solution (or a global optimum, in *distributed optimization* problems in Chapter 14) they need to coordinate their operations by distributed means. Even when the global search algorithm resembles simple backtracking, problems of concurrency pop up. Is the distributed algorithm complete (e.g., does it return a solution if one exists)? Is it free of deadlocks? Does it necessarily terminate? All of these are typically complex problems that relate to the distributed nature of distributed search algorithms.

This book is dedicated to the presentation of distributed search algorithms, to their analysis, and to a comparative study of their performance and behavior under a variety of distributed conditions. It includes work on distributed constraints satifaction problems and on distributed constraints optimization problems (DISCOPs). Problems of constraints optimization (COPs) arise in cases where constraints have costs (values or weights) and the goal is to find a minimal-cost solution. An important class of COPs is that of unsolvable CSPs, where the goal is to find a complete assignment that has a minimal number of constraint violations (conflicts). This family of problems has been termed MAXCSP [33] and has been studied extensively as an example family of COPs [36]. The centralized problems and algorithms for their solutions will be described briefly in Chapter 3.

Moving to the distributed scenario, when agents hold parts of the COP, we arrive at distributed constraints optimization problems - DISCOPs. Chapter 14 introduces DISCOPs and the methods of search needed for their solution. In general, complete search methods for COPs are Branch and Bound algorithms (BnBs). A simple extension is the *distrbuted* BnB, or *DisBnB*, algorithm in Chapter 14. Three years ago an asynchronous branch and bound algorithm for DISCOPs was proposed - the Asynchronous Distributed Optimization algorithm (*ADOPT*) [47]. *ADOPT* performs assignments and distributes information among agents in a completely asynchronous manner. It turns out that, similarly to the case for DISCSPs, it is interesting to investigate the potential of asynchronous processing. In other words, to explore algorithmic options that use asynchronous distributed processing combined with sequential assignments. This ensures the processing of consistent partial solutions and avoids redundant (asynchronous) computations relating to intrinsically inconsistent partial solutions [22].

Let us try to get some feeling of the distributed nature of search. Consider a 4-queens problem in which the four queens are independent agents. The 4-queens problem is quite well known. It requires one to put four queens on a 4x4 chess board, so that none of the queens threatens any other. In searching for such a solution (four nonthreatening positioned queens) one needs to go over all possible positions of all queens over the 4x4 board. Let us try to imagine a distributed scenario, one of many possible. Each agent/queen can position itself at any square. Queens check for the compatibility of their positions with the positions of other queens by exchanging messages. For the sake of simplicity let us assume that each agent only selects positions in one specific row. This will simplify the search and will enable a partial search space, where each agent has only four possible positions, which still contains all solutions. Let us assume that each agent positions itself initially as in Figure 1.1. Next, each agent starts to exchange messages with the other agents in order to check its compatibility with all agents' positions. When conflicting positions are encountered, agents change their positions and attempt to achieve compatibility.

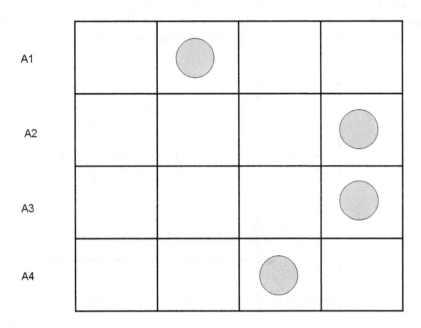

Fig. 1.1. Starting positions for the distributed 4-queens problem

This example is extremely naive in that it does not consider an *algorithm* for achieving a solution (e.g., a distributed search algorithm). Instead, it tries to play around with a distributed scenario in order to ger some feeling for the behavior of such scenarios. Assuming no specific algorithm, we'll just continue for a few steps. Let us take the case that each agent sends messages informing all relevant agents about its position. For the 4-queens problem every agent is constrained by every other agent. So, each agent sends a message to the other three informing them of its position. After all messages have been sent and received, all agents know the positions of all other agents.

Observe agent A_1. It finds out that it is involved in a single conflict, with agent A_3. Agent A_2 is involved in a single conflict with agent A_3 and this is also the number of conflicts discovered by agent A_4. Agent A_3 is the only agent that finds out that it is involved in two conflicts - with agents A_2 and A_4. Each agent has to decide what to do in this situation. Remember that this is only an ilustrative example of a *distributed search problem* and not of a *search algorithm*. Therefore, we are just exploring possible actions of agents. Let us assume that agents that are involved in a conflict decide on the party that changes its position by giving priority to the agent that has more conflicts. Among each pair of conflicting agents it is agent A_3 that has more conflicts than its conflicting partner. So, agent A_3 decides to change its position and it finds a position that has no conflicts for itself. It moves its position to that conflict-free square and the result is the state in Figure 1.2. This is actually a solution and none of the agents needs to change anything.

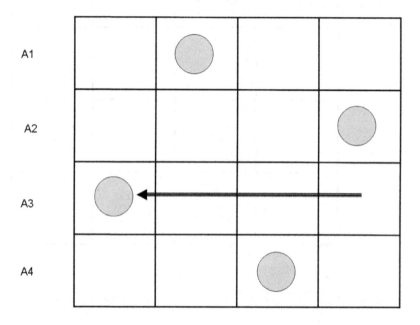

Fig. 1.2. The resulting move of agent A_3

Please note that there are very many different ways to construct the protocol of the agents during search. Agents could exchange messages about their *intentions* to select a value, to give one extreme example. They could wait for all others to select values and then choose their own. All of these would be different distributed search algorithms. The present book presents several approaches to design such search algorithms and we show that such algorithms use protocols that have important features. A distributed search algorithm must terminate. It must return a solution if such a solution exists and otherwise return a no-solution message. These features and additional ones are essential to distributed search algorithms and will be discussed in detail for all the presented algorithms.

In the above very simple example there were exponentially many ways to *describe* the run of the agents. We could have thought about agent A_3

making its decision after it received the message from A_2, after it received message from A_4, before all messages arrived, and many more possibilities. All of these options form the many ways in which a distributed computation can be performed. Analyzing the *behavior* of distributed search algorithms is therefore complex. Since any design of search algorithms needs tools for measuring their performance and for comparing their behavior, we will dwell on methods for measuring distributed search algorithms in Chapter 10. The resulting measures will be used for comparisons of many algorithms that are described in this book, in Chapter 11.

Another interesting question relates to the behavior of different distributed search algorithms in the presence of communication problems. Communication problems can take a wide variety of forms - from total disconnection (i.e. *lost messages*) to false or added messages and partially incorrect messages. In order to remain in an area where the main focus is on the search algorithms and not on methods for immuning or correcting messages, it is customary to consider only delayed messages. In other words, the routine assumption of all distributed search algorithms is that all messages arrive at their destinations in finite time. The importance of studying the behavior of distributed search algorithms under message delays, in addition to the simple fact that message delays are common, can be understood as follows. All complete distributed search algorithms (the vast majority of which will be presented in this book) assume asynchronicity of operation. They guarantee the finding of a solution if it exists, independently of the exact manner in which information is exchanged among all agents (as long as messages arrive at their destination in finite time). All search problems are NP-Complete and consequently the worst case run-time of distributed search algorithms is exponential in the number of variables in the worst case. The acceptable way of comparing different distributed search algorithms and heurstics for these algorithms is to evaluate their performance empirically. But, empirical evaluation depends on the set of problems used, on the implementation of algorithms, and on the particular runs of the distributed simulator (cf. [45, 72]). It is therefore extremely interesting to perform the empirical evaluation of distributed search algorithms also in distributed environments that include message delays. Incorporating message delays into the experimental setup of distributed search algorithms is presented in Chapter 12 and experimental results of algorithms in the presence of message delays are described in Chapter 13.

Constraints Satisfaction Problems - CSPs

Constraints Satisfaction Problems (CSPs) have been studied intensely since the early 1980s, as a paradigm on their own. The first important papers on certain fundamental properties of Constraints Networks were by Montanari and by Freuder [21]. Papers on search algorithms were published by Elliot and Haralick [26] and later by Pearl and Dechter [15]. The body of work accumulated during the 1980s has driven a community of researchers and a special track on constraints-based reaoning in all important AI conferences. The field became known as CSP and the next milestone was a paper by Patrick Prosser, which formalized a large family of search algorithms for CSPs [51]. Several search algorithms that fall under the term *Intelligent Backtracking* were proposed early on. These include ideas like Lookahead [26] and BackJumping. Some of these algorithms were proposed in the general AI search context. As we will see, CSPs provide a well-defined search space definition, which enables exact formulations of all search algorithms. This makes the field an excellent laboratory for formulating new and complex ideas for search strategies. For the same reason, *distributed* CSPs are a fundamental formalism for advancing the whole field of distributed search.

The paper by Prosser [51] succeeded in defining a uniform structure for the different algorithms that were proposed in a variety of forms during the previous decade. The main result of [51] was a large set of hybrid algorithms that were combined from fundamental ones by using the uniform structures of the paper. The main core of search algorithms for CSPs are termed nowadays on the basis of the terminology of [51]. These are the Backjumping (BJ) algorithm and Conflict-based Backjumping (CBJ), and Forward-Checking (FC), which is the simplest lookahead algorithm (cf. [26, 51]) and their best combination, FC-CBJ. In the following sections we will present these algorithms briefly, to set up a basis for the distributed algorithms that use versions of the same ideas.

2.1 Defining CSPs

Introductory texts on Constraints Satisfaction Problems (CSPs) can be found in [16, 58] and the basic papers are [15, 51]. A CSP is a well-known NP-complete problem [16], which is often used to represent and solve problems such as timetabling [41, 43], meeting scheduling [60] and a variety of other scheduling problems [12]. Formally, a CSP is a tuple $< X, D, R >$, where X is a finite set of variables $X_1, X_2, \ldots, X_m$, and D is a set of domains $D_1, D_2, \ldots, D_m$. Each domain D_i contains a finite set of values which can be assigned to variable X_i. R is a set of relations (constraints) that specify for each value $v_j \in D_i$, the set of allowed combinations for it to be assigned to variable X_i. More formally, constraints or **relations** R are subsets of the Cartesian product of the domains of the constrained variables. For a set of constrained variables $X_{i_k}, X_{j_l}, \ldots, X_{m_n}$, with domains of values for each variable $D_{i_k}, D_{j_l}, \ldots, D_{m_n}$, the constraint R is defined as $R \subseteq D_{i_k} \times D_{j_l} \times \ldots \times D_{m_n}$. A **binary constraint** R_{ij} between any two variables X_j and X_i is a subset of the Cartesian product of their domains - $R_{ij} \subseteq D_j \times D_i$.

An assignment (or a label) is a pair $< var, val >$, where var is a variable and val is a value from the domain of var that is assigned to it. A *compound label* is a set of assignments of values to a set of variables. A **solution** P to a CSP is a compound label that includes all variables, and which satisfies all the constraints [16, 58].

Constraints can be either explicit, in the form of a listing of all forbidden assignments combinations, or implicit. An implicit constraint can be, for example, a set of rules that the assignments must follow. For example, $X_1 > X_2$ can be such a constraint if the value domains are numeric. The most commonly used constraints are binary constraints. A CSP with only binary constraints is called a binary CSP. A CSP can have more than a single solution. A CSP may also have no solutions at all, in which case it is declared to be unsolvable.

In Figure 2.1 we have two CSPs. Each CSP has four variables X_1, X_2, X_3, X_4. The domains of values of all variables contain the three values: r, g, b (not shown). Constraints are represented by lines connecting variables. As we can see, all constraints are binary. All constraints are inequality constraints ($\neq$). The CSP on the left-hand side is solvable. The assignment ($X_1 = r, X_2 = g, X_3 = b, X_4 = r$), for example, is a solution. There is more than one solution to this CSP, for example ($X_1 = g, X_2 = r, X_3 = b, X_4 = g$) is also a solution. In contrast, the CSP on the right-hand side (RHS) is unsolvable. There does not exist an assignment of values to all variables that satisfies all constraints. One can say that the CSP on the RHS of Figure 2.1 is overconstrained.

The size of the search space for solving CSPs is exponential in the number of variables, in the worst case. The base of the exponential is the domain size of variables (e.g., the number of possible assignments per variable). This led researchers to propose methods that have the potential to find equivalent versions of the problem that have smaller domains of values. The general idea is to check values of the CSP and remove those values that can never be

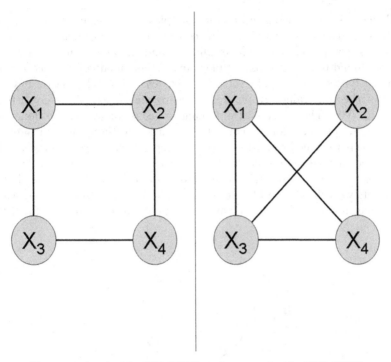

Fig. 2.1. A solvable CSP (LHS) and an unsolvable CSP (RHS)

part of a complete assignment that is a solution to the CSP. If such values
are removed from the domains of their variables, one achieves two goals. On
the one hand, the number of solutions to the problem remains exactly the
same. On the other hand, some of the domains of values become smaller and
thus the search space is reduced. The operation of removal of values that
are inconsistent (e.g., cannot participate in any solution) is termed achieving
local consistency. It is important to note that during a process of achieving
local consistency the domain of a variable may become empty. In such a case
the problem has been proved to be unsolvable [16]. One can say intuitively
that in such a case a real saving of computation has been achieved, instead
of exponential in the number of variables just exponential in the number of
variables in a local neighbourhood (related to the specific local sonsistency
that was used).

Consider the problem in Figure 2.2. There are three variables, each with its
domain of values and all constraints are inequalities (e.g., a coloring problem).
The value R of the variable A at the top of the graph is not compatible with
any of the values of the variable B, at the bottom left of the graph. One
can say that if the value R is removed from the domain of A, the resulting
problem will have exactly the same solutions as the original problem. The
process of removal of values that do not participate in solutions of a CSP is

based on checking consistencies. In our example the consistency is that of pairs of values in constrained variables. The constrained pair of variables (A, B) is checked for compatible pairs of assignments and (as we explained) the value R in A is found to have no compatible value in the domain of variable B. This particular type of check is called *Arc Consistency*, as it checks consistency over "arcs" of the constraints graph (for extensive discussion of arc-consistency see [6, 16, 58]). The process of enforcing arc-consistency can be done as a preprocessing phase, before a search for a solution to the CSP is initiated. It can also be performed at multiple stages during search. Consistencies can also be of higher degree than a single arc. One could check, for example, triplets of variables for consistent assignments [16]. In our description of distributed constraints we will refer to ideas of enforcing local consistency during search in a similar manner in which they are used in centralized CSPs (cf. [31, 51]).

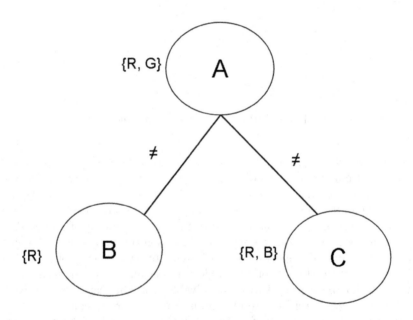

Fig. 2.2. A graph-coloring (solvable) CSP that is not arc-consistent

2.2 CSP Algorithms and Techniques

Practically all complete search algorithms for CSPs are based on the *backtracking* algorithm. In the backtracking algorithm, there are two possible steps, an assignment step and a backtrack step. In an assignment step, the algorithm assigns a value to one of the variables, and checks that no constraint is violated (broken) due to this new assignment. If this is true, then the next step is another assignment step, or termination if all variables are assigned (a solution was found). If a constraint was violated, a backtrack step undoes the last assignment made and the next value in this unassigned variable's domain is assigned instead, if such a value exists. If the domain of the current variable is exhausted and there is no next value to try to assign, another backtrack step is taken. The backtracking algorithm is a depth-first search, on the search tree of possible value assignments to all variables. In the worst case, the algorithm requires exponential time in the number of variables, but only linear space [16, 31, 58].

Backtracking algorithms can be improved in two general ways. One way is to select a variable to backtrack to, that is not necessarily the last variable to have been assigned [31, 51]. The other way is to prune the search space by the use of lookahead methods. Lookahead methods were proposed by Haralick and Elliot in [26], categorized by depth, and will be described in more detail below.

Other methods of selective backtracking involve the maintenance of No-GOODs and explanations [23]. The family of algorithms that prune the search space by selective backward moves is commonly termed *backjumping*. These algorithms include simple backjumping (BJ), conflict-based backjumping (CBJ) [51] and Dynamic Backtracking (DBT) [23]. They have been shown by [31] always to visit no more nodes in the search space than simple backtracking.

The simplest form of lookahead, as analyzed by Haralick and Elliot, was later termed Forward Checking (FC) [51]. When the search process performs an instantiation (assignment) of a variable, it looks ahead towards the future (unassigned) variables, and removes from their current domain values that are incompatible with the tested instantiation. If the current domain of some future variable becomes empty, the combination of the assignments made so far would conflict with all value assignments of that variable, and thus the current state is inconsistent, and a backtrack is performed [51]. The current partial assignment cannot be extended to a solution of the CSP because the domain of some variable became empty and no assignment of this variable is compatible with the current partial assignment (cf. [31]). The current partial assignment is called a NOGOOD and the notion will be used extensively in all DISCSP algorithms.

When backtracking, it is important to undo all the value eliminations that were performed because of the trial instantiation. This is an immediate overhead of all lookahead algorithms (such as FC). The goal of the FC algorithm is to fail early by detecting inconsistencies as early as possible, thus saving exploration of dead ends. Forward checking performs more computation per assignment than the standard backtracking algorithm. The hope is that this will pay off by performing less assignments overall during the search.

Forward checking is the simplest method of *maintaining local consistency* (i.e., checking that the current state of the unassigned part of the search space is consistent). Exactly what is consistent is defined by the method used. Besides FC, many other methods for maintaining local consistency of the unassigned part of the search space exist. One can define two types of local consistency that can be used to induce a stronger lookahead than forward-checking.

- **Arc consistency**. The assignment $X_i = a$ is arc-consistent with respect to constraint C_{ij} (the constraint between X_i and X_j) if there is a value $b \in D_j$ such that $X_i = a, X_j = b$ satisfy C_{ij}. Such a value b is called a support of a. Variable X_i is arc-consistent if all its values are arc consistent with respect to every binary constraint involving X_i. A CSP is arc-consistent (AC) if every variable is arc-consistent.
- **Directed arc consistency (DAC)**. A variable X_i is DAC if all its values are arc-consistent with respect to every binary constraint involving X_i and X_j where $j > i$. This is a directed consistency and the check for existence of support values is only performed in one direction of the constraints. A CSP may be DAC for one ordering of the variables but not for another. Obviously AC is a stronger property than DAC.

Arc-inconsistent values can be removed, because they cannot participate in any solution. Enforcing AC or DAC does not guarantee that the CSP contains a solution. However, if a CSP is not AC or DAC, then it can be transformed into an equivalent CSP that is AC or DAC and that contains all the solutions of the original CSP [16]. AC (or DAC) can be achieved by removing arc inconsistent values until a fixed point is reached. If enforcing AC (or DAC) yields an empty domain, the problem is proven to be unsolvable. A major advantage of transforming the CSP into an equivalent AC (or DAC) CSP is that the resulting equivalent CSP may be of smaller size (e.g., its domains contain fewer values). There are several AC-enforcing algorithms. Two well-known algorithms are: AC3 [1] and AC2001 [5].

It is important to note that stronger methods for maintaining consistency do not always produce better performance. A tradeoff exists between the number of assignments performed, and the computational effort following each assignment. Enforcing stronger consistency may lead to fewer assignments done, as fewer dead-ends will be explored. However, to check and maintain consistency, some computational effort is required following each assignment.

We will refer back to these methods later on, when discussing how to maintain local consistency in optimization problems. Obviously the present exposition does not come near to summarizing all CSP algorithms. We choose to mention only what is most relevant for distributed search. For more information, one can consult the books by Dechter and Tsang [16, 58].

2.3 Behavior of CSP solving algorithms

CSPs are NP-complete problems. Therefore, evaluating the performance of algorithms by theoretical measures will not be of much use. In order to evaluate CSP solvers, empirical evaluation is often used. Performance is measured over a predefined set of problems. In order not to rely on implementation details that might influence results (such as implementation efficiency, processor speed, background processes running, etc.) performance is evaluated using a logical measure. The number of constraint checks (CCs) is one such measure that is frequently used. Another is the number of assignments made [31, 52].

The above two measures relate to the search process and search space, rather than to the specific implementation. A search algorithm that belongs to the backtracking family is a depth-first procedure. It assigns variables sequentially, checking each assignment in turn for consistency with former assignments [16]. Algorithms differ in their decision of how to backtrack (e.g., of forms of *backjumping*) or in their forms of checking the consistency of unassigned variables (e.g., *lookahead*). The main part of computation that is common to all search algorithms is to check consistency against the current partial assignment. This computation is composed of a series of checks of pairs of assignments (for binary CSPs). Each such check can be thought of as an $O(1)$ operation, accessing the constraint matrix to find whether a pair of values are compatible. By counting these operations all CSP search algorithms can be measured on a uniform scale.

The number of assignments performed by a search algorithm is also an implementation-independent measure. Here one considers the trajectory of the algorithm in the search space. Assigning variables one by one, any search algorithm checks for consistency and then proceeds to the next variable. When it gets to a dead-end it backtracks and each reassignment of a variable is counted by this measure. It is clear that the number of assignments will be lower for algorithms that prune the search space efficiently. However, if pruning the search tree is based on additional computations at each node visited, the resulting procedure does not necessarily perform fewer computations. In other words, it is an interesting question whether a lookahead CSP search algorithm will be faster. It has been shown theoretically that forward checking (FC) performs no more assignments than simple backtracking [31]. Independently, it has been shown *empirically* that FC outperforms BT on randomly generated CSPs.

It is of interest to investigate the dependency of a random problem's difficulty on the parameters of the problems. The number of variables and the domain size obviously influence the problem difficulty, as the search space grows exponentially with these two parameters. However, even for a fixed number of variables and a fixed domain size, the problems vary wildly, due to the nature of the constraints. For a fixed-size problem, one problem can be extremely easy to solve, if there are almost no constraints, while another may be highly constrained and require more effort until a solution is found. Over the last decade a uniform set up for testing CSP algorithms has been established. Experiments are commonly performed on randomly generated binary CSPs. The problems are randomly generated using four parameters: $< n, k, p_1, p_2 >$, where n is the number of variables, k is the uniform domain size, and p_1 is the probability of a constraint existing between any two variables X_i and X_j. If X_i and X_j are constrained, any two value assignments $a \in D_i$ and $b \in D_j$ are forbidden with probability p_2 [52]. p_1 is called the **constraint density**, and p_2 is called the **constraint tightness**.

When evaluating algorithms on such randomly generated problems, it was discovered that one of the four parameters is a critical parameter. When three of the parameters n, k, and p_1 are held fixed, the critical parameter is p_2 (the *tightness*). When p_2 varies between 0 and 1 the problem difficulty exhibits a **phase transition**. The average difficulty of problems goes from easy, to difficult, to easy. When measuring the run time of the algorithm by counting the number of constraint checks, the run time varies with the value of the tightness p_2 through three regions - low-high-low. All algorithms finish their execution very fast for very low values of p_2 (only a handful of value combinations are forbidden and most full assignments are in fact solutions). Run time increases exponentially with increasing p_2 up to some peak, after which it starts to decrease. Figure 2.3 shows the phase transition for $n = 20$, $k = 10$, $p_1 = 1.0$ (presented in Prosser [52]). Figure 2.4 presents the phase transition for similar random problems with a density of $p_1 = 0.5$, the phase transition peak is at roughly $p_2 = 0.4$ (for these parameters).

To the left of the left vertical bar in Figure 2.5 ($p_2 = 0.35$) all problems are solvable, to the right of the right vertical bar ($p_2 = 0.41$) all problems are unsolvable. The area between the two vertical bars contains both solvable and unsolvable problems, this area is also called the "mushy region" by [52, 56]. It is in this region that the average search effort is maximal. The algorithm used, for Figure 2.5 is an enhanced variation of the forward-checking algorithm.

The existence of the phase transition is explained intuitively as follows. For low values of the tightness p_2, the constraints are very loose and the problems are easy. Increasing the constraint tightness naturally increases the difficulty. As fewer full assignments become solutions, it becomes increasingly hard to find a full assignment that is consistent (a solution). When the value of p_2 is high enough, the problems become easier, in that the algorithm does not need to search the entire exponential search space. The problems are overconstrained and have no solution. The algorithm reaches an inconsistent state higher up the search tree, thus pruning more of the search space.

The phase transition (mushy region) at the center of the peak contains a mix of solvable and unsolvable problems. Intuitively these are problems with either few solutions (so they are hard to find and require searching through most of the search space to reach), or unsolvable problems (that are consistent up until a very late stage of the assignment process, thus forcing the search process to explore most of it before declaring there is no solution).

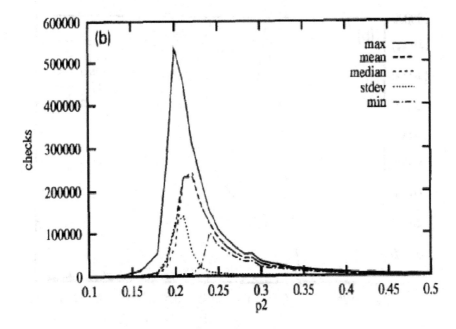

Fig. 2.3. The phase transition for $p_1 = 1.0$ (from [52]).

The phase transition of problem difficulty is very important. It was also discovered for distributed CSPs and can serve as a very good feature for checking the validity of performance measures in the distributed domain. Furthermore, the exponential growth in difficulty of finding the first solution to a CSP is an excellent differentiating criterion among search algorithms. In order to achieve a substantial gain in efficiency, algorithms need to be tested on hard problem instances. For randomly generated CSPs these are at p_2 values that are near the critical value (e.g., near the peak). Throughout this book when the performance of algorithms is compared we will use random CSPs and observe the different behavior of the algorithms being compared for hard problem instances. It is for these problems that one wants to design a more-intelligent algorithm and a better heuristic (see Chapter 11).

It is also important to mention that a similar phenomenon has been also discovered for some constraint optimization (COP) and distributed constraints optimization (DisCOP) *algorithms*. The important difference is that a phase transition exists for CSPs for all algorithms. For constraint optimization problems (COPs) a phase transition was found only for certain lookahead search algorithms [33, 36]. Chapter 3 describes constraints optimization problems (COPs) and algorithms for finding an optimal solution. These algorithms belong to the Branch and Bound family, but use additional lookahead tech-

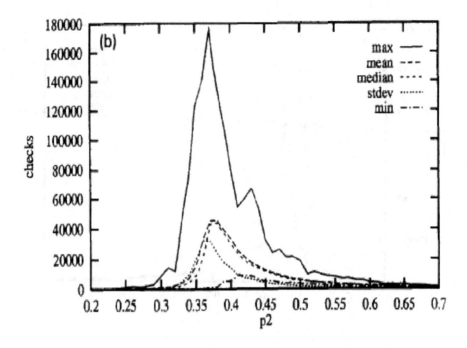

Fig. 2.4. The phase transition for $p_1 = 0.5$ (from [52]).

niques. The deeper methods of lookahead turn out to produce a specific form of a phase transition for COPs [33]. Chapter 3 presents the latest results on COP algorithms. Chapter 16 presents the first distributed optimization algorithm that demonstrates a phase transition for *Distributed COPs* [22]. As will be shown in Chapter 18, standard asynchronous distributed optimization algorithms do not produce a phase transition for hard instances of DISCOPs [22].

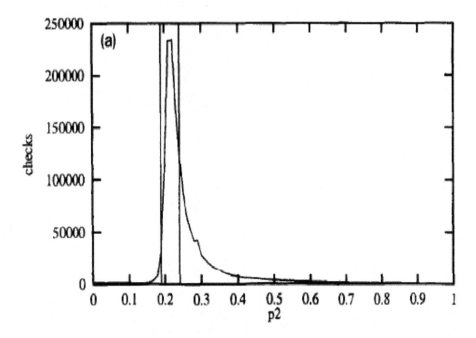

Fig. 2.5. The phase transition region for $p_1 = 1.0$

Constraints Optimization Problems - COPs

Formally, a COP is a tuple $< \mathcal{X}, \mathcal{D}, \mathcal{R} >$. $\mathcal{X}$ is a finite set of variables $X_1, X_2, ..., X_m$. $\mathcal{D}$ is a set of domains D_1, D_2, ... , D_m. Each domain D_i contains the finite set of values which can be assigned to variable X_i. $\mathcal{R}$ is a set of relations (constraints). Each constraint involves some variables and defines a non-negative *cost* for every possible value combination of these variables. A *binary constraint* refers to exactly two variables. A *binary COP* is a COP in which all constraints are binary. An *assignment* (or a label) is a pair including a variable, and a value from that variable's domain. A *partial assignment* (PA) is a set of assignments in which each variable appears at most once. The *cost of a partial assignment* is computed over all constraints that involve only variables that appear in the partial assignment. Each such constraint defines some cost for the value assignments detailed in the partial assignment. All these costs are accumulated, and the sum is denoted as the cost of the partial assignment. A *full assignment* is a partial assignment that includes all the variables. A *solution is a full assignment with minimal cost*.

Intuitively, the optimization problem is harder than the satisfaction problems (but both are NP-complete). One can gain some intuition into these two problems along the following lines. The solving of a satisfaction problem can be achieved by modeling the problem as a COP combined with the assignment of some positive cost to all constraints defined by the CSP. Solving this problem by using a COP solver would return some solution. If this solution has a cost of zero, it is also a solution to the CSP, otherwise the CSP has no solution. In the other direction, observe the following. Both CSP solvers and COP solvers can stop once they find a full assignment that has no conflicts (a cost of zero in the COP case). However, a CSP solver can maintain local consistency during the search. Like the backtracking algorithm, it can ensure (at the very least) that the partial assignments made so far have no conflict among themselves. A COP solver cannot stop at this point, since it is possible that the current conflicting assignments are part of a solution (which has a cost greater than zero). So a COP solver may need to search more of the search space.

It is important to mention a specific problem that can be solved as a COP, because many of the COP and DISCOP algorithms are evaluated on this family of problems. MAXCSPs are standard CSP problems, where a solution is a full assignment with the least amount of violated constraints (e.g. conflicts). A MAXCSP is equivalent to a COP with all costs being either zero or one. A common special case of MAXCSPs is the **graph-coloring** problem. The input is a graph G and a number k. The satisfaction problem is to color each vertice in G with a single color out of the k possible colors in such a way that no two neighboring vertices have the same color. In the optimization problem, the goal is to minimize the number of vertex pairs connected by an edge that are colored by the same color.

Graph coloring problems are often characterized by three parameters: n, k, d. n is the number of vertices, k is the number of colors, and d is the link density (the average number of neighbors per vertex). Since-graph coloring problems are a subfamily of CSPs, one can use these these parameters to infer the parameters of the equivalent constraints satisfaction problem. The problem density (p_1) and tightness (p_2). The number of constraints (e.g., edges or links) is $nd/2$. Divide that by the maximal number of possible constraints $n(n-1)/2$ to compute the problem density - $d/(n-1)$. The problem tightness is determined by the number of colors k, since between two neighboring vertices, all k^2 possible color assignment combinations are good, except for exactly k of them. Therefore, $p_2 = 1/k$ and $p_1 = d/(n-1)$. This simple calculation is useful because many times in the literature graph coloring-problems are used for evaluating search algorithms. Bearing in mind this simple calculation, one can immediately see into what region of difficulty these problems fall. For example, take 3-coloring of graphs with 50 nodes and link densities of $d = 5$. The equivalent constraint density is $p_1 = 0.1$. The tightness of these graph coloring problems is $p_2 = 1/3$ and we know that for CSPs with density of $p_1 = 0.1$ problems with such low tightness are relatively easy (i.e., far away from the peak of hard instances). Still, many experimental evaluations of both distributed CSPs and distributed COPs in the literature use 3-coloring.

In order to achieve a basic understanding of COPs and methods for their solution, some of the algorithms and techniques developed for COPs are presented next.

3.1 Branch and Bound (BnB)

Branch and Bound (BnB) is the basic COP solver, similarly to the backtracking algorithm - the basic CSP solver - it can be extended into more sophisticated algorithms.

The general scheme of the algorithm is presented in Algorithm 3.1, and is based on the pseudo-code given in [36]. X is the set of all variables, D is the set of all domains, C is the set of all constraints, $PA(t)$ is the current partial assignment, LB is the lower bound, and UB is the upper bound. In the first call to the function *BranchAndBound* the parameter LB is set to zero and UB is set to infinity.

A lower bound (LB) for a current partial assignment is an admissible estimation of the lowest-cost full assignment extended from the partial assignments made so far. Admissible means that it is always smaller than or equal to the true cost of such an assignment. In the BnB algorithm, the LB equals the accumulated cost of the assignments made so far, which is of course always smaller or equal to the cost of any full assignment extended from these assignments. Consider the COP in Figure 3.1. There are a total of four variables ordered by $V_1, V_2, \ldots V_4$. The first two are assigned and their assigned values are circled. The partial assignment is $< V_1, b >, < V_2, a >$. Each value of the example COP has a value associated with it. The cost of the first assignment in Figure 3.1 is 1 and of the secnd assignment is 2. In order to compute the total cost of the partial assignment we need to know the cost of the constraints. Let us assume for simplicity that all constraints have a uniform cost of 3. All values connected by a line are constrained and all disconnected values are not constrained (i.e., their assignment incurs a cost of 0). The total cost of the partial assignment in figure 3.1 is therefore $1 + 2 + 3 = 6$. This value can also serve as the lower bound on any complete assignment that extends the partial assignment in Figure 3.1.

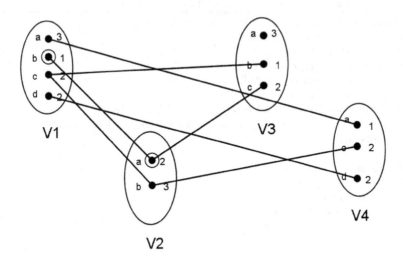

Fig. 3.1. A COP example with four variables the first two are assigned

An *upper bound (UB)* equals the cost of the best (lowest-cost) full assignment found during the search. Initially, before the search begins, no full assignment was found, and so this bound is set to infinity. As search progresses and full assignment combinations are explored, this bound decreases.

A partial assignment, for which $LB > UB$ cannot lead to a solution, as any full assignment extended from it would cost at least LB (and a lower cost full assignment was already found, costing UB). A partial assignment for which $LB = UB$ should not be extended since any full assignment extended from it would cost at least LB. Extending it cannot lead to a better full assignment.

The algorithm traverses the search tree in a depth-first manner. After picking an assignment for the current variable X_i, the new subproblem is constructed. The procedure *LookAhead* transforms the current problem into a new subproblem that includes the assignment $X_i = a$. If that subproblem is locally consistent, the search continues by recursively trying to solve the sub-problem. The algorithm returns the cost of the solution to the problem. The best full assignment found for the subproblem is set as the new upper bound in line 7. The procedure *LocalConsist* returns true if the given problem is consistent (should be explored) or false if there is a dead-end. This is done by checking if the accumulated cost of the partial assignments made so far exceeds the upper bound (line 14).

Algorithm 3.1: The Branch and Bound Algorithm

Function BranchAndBound($PA, LB, UB, X, \mathcal{D}, \mathcal{C}$):
1. if ($X = \emptyset$) then return LB
2. i ← ChooseVar(X)
3. foreach $a \in D_i$ do
4. $\mathcal{DD} \leftarrow \mathcal{D}$; $\mathcal{CC} \leftarrow \mathcal{C}$; $nPA \leftarrow PA + (X_i = a)$; $nLB \leftarrow LB + UnaryCost(a)$
5.   LookAhead($i, a, \mathcal{CC}$)
6.   if (LocalConsist($nLB, UB, X - \{i\}, \mathcal{DD}, \mathcal{CC}$)) then
7. $UB \leftarrow$ BranchAndBound($nPA, nLB, UB, X - \{i\}, \mathcal{DD}, \mathcal{CC}$)
8. return UB

Procedure LookAhead($i, a, \mathcal{C}$):
9. $\mathcal{CC} \leftarrow \mathcal{CC} - \{C_i\}$
10. foreach $C_{ij} \in \mathcal{CC}$ do
11.   foreach $b \in D_j$ do
12. $C_j(b) \leftarrow C_j(b) + C_{ij}(a, b)$
13. $\mathcal{CC} \leftarrow \mathcal{CC} - \{C_{ij}\}$

Function LocalConsist($LB, UB, X, \mathcal{D}, \mathcal{C}$):
14. return ($UB > LB$)

3.2 Branch and Bound + Arc-Consistency (BnB-AC)

In the past decade Larrosa and others investigated methods for solving COPs (sometimes refereed to as Weighted CSPs - WCSP - and MaxCSPs) [33–36]. The main result of this research takes the form of a framework for maintaining local consistency during branch and bound search. Several methods for local consistency were proposed, and their performance evaluated. The most basic form of maintaining local consistency, is the one used by the Branch and Bound algorithm (in Section 3.1), which checks that the cost of the assignments made so far does not exceed the upper bound.

A stronger form of maintaining local consistency during BnB search is to maintain arc consistency. Arc consistency as defined in Chapter 2.1 does not fit COPs, since two conflicting assignments can still be part of a solution. An extension of the definition was proposed by Larrosa et al. [36]. The paper by Larrosa et al. refers to binary COPs that may also include unary constraints. Such a constraint simply defines a cost for every value of a variable. If the variable is assigned a value, the unary cost of that value is added to the global cost of the current partial assignment. The algorithm in [36] uses a process called *projection of constraints*. This *projection* involves transferring costs between unary and binary constraints. If a binary constraint between variables X_i and X_j assigns a cost greater or equal to c for some specific value $a \in D_i$ and every value $b \in D_j$, it is possible to project this cost on a unary constraint involving X_i as follows. From the binary constraint, c is reduced from the cost of all assignment pairs including $a \in D_i$, and in the unary constraint of X_i the cost c is added to the cost assigned to the value a. An intuitive explanation is the following. If X_i assigns a, then no matter what X_j assigns, the constraint between them would cost at least c. This process can also be applied from unary into binary constraints. If a value $a \in D_i$ has a unary cost of c, then we can remove this unary cost, pick some other variable X_j and add c to the binary constraint between the assignment $X_i = a$ and every value of X_j.

Larrosa et al. [36] define *node consistency* for constraints optimization problems. A COP with an upper bound UB is *node-consistent* (NC) if the unary cost of every value of every variable is smaller than UB. A COP with upper bound UB is *arc-consistent (AC)* if it is NC and, for every two variables X_i and X_j, and every value $a \in D_i$, there exists a value $b \in D_j$ such that the binary cost of assigning a and b equals zero (b is called the support of a in such a case). These definitions are reduced to the classical CSP definitions if we set $UB = 1$.

If a COP is not NC, we can remove all values with cost greater or equal to UB. The resulting COP will contain all full assignments with cost lower than UB. This is trivially correct since values with unary costs of UB or more cannot be part of assignments that cost less than UB. If a COP is not AC because of a value $a \in D_i$ that has no supporting value in D_j, then by projecting the costs of this binary constraint onto the unary cost of a, we can reach an equivalent COP that is hopefully AC (it is still possible for it to be not NC [36]).

These ideas are implemented in [36] by the W-AC3 and the W-AC2001 algorithms. These algorithms enforce arc consistency in COPs by replacing the *LocalConsist* method in the BnB algorithm. Arc consistency is achieved by pruning node-inconsistent values and projecting binary constraints over unary constraints until the property is satisfied. It is important to note that there are several arc-consistent problems that can be obtained from an arc-inconsistent problem. The result will depend on the order in which values are pruned and the constraints are projected.

The experimental evaluation reported in [36] shows that a BnB algorithm that maintains this form of AC has a far superior performance to that of a BnB that only enforces NC (or none at all as in Algorithm 3.1). These important results, from *centralized* COPs, will later be used for an innovative *distributed* optimization algorithm that will be described in Chapter 16. It is based on distributed methods for maintaining bounds consistency during DisCOP search and exhibits a large improvement over all *DisCOP* solvers.

3.3 Branch and Bound + AC* (BnB-AC*)

A stronger form of maintaining local consistency is also presented in [36]. The intuition behind it is as follows. Suppose all values of a variable have a unary cost greater than c. Any assignment to this variable would therefore cost at least c, but this cost is not known by the search process until it actually performs the assignment. It is possible to add this cost to the lower bound even before an assignment is made, and potentially prune subspaces of the search tree sooner. A global constraint is constructed, and this constraint assigns a cost to be added to any full assignment performed. Initially this cost is zero, but once a variable such as the above is discovered, the cost c can be added to it, and subtracted from the unary constraint of all values of that variable.

More formally, a COP with an upper bound UB is NC*, if the unary cost of every value plus the cost of the global constraint is smaller than UB and every variable has a value with unary cost zero. A COP with upper bound UB is AC* if it is both AC and NC*.

To transform a COP that is not NC* into one that is NC*, one needs to project costs from unary constraints to the global constraint until the variables all have a value with unary cost zero. Then, values with too high a unary cost are removed (similarly to maintaining NC). This produces the W-NC* algorithm [36].

To enforce AC*, we have the W-AC* algorithm [36]. First the problem is enforced to be NC*, then projections from binary constraints onto unary constraints are performed (enforcing AC). This may cause re-enforcing NC* by projecting from the updated unary constraints to the global constraint.

If the global constraint was increased, then NC* may be violated at other variables, and so they must be checked for NC* again.

The experimental evaluation reported in [36] shows that BnB that maintains AC* slightly outperforms the BnB version that maintains AC.

3.4 Phase Transition in MaxCSPs

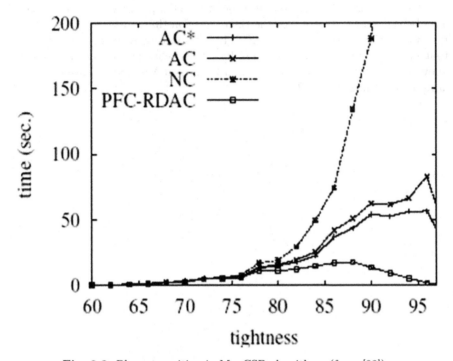

Fig. 3.2. Phase-transition in MaxCSP algorithms (from [33])

Constraints optimization problems behave very differently than CSPs when the tightness of randomly generated COPs is varied. As the tightness increases, so does the problem difficulty as realized by the total number of constraints checks (CCs) or the run time. This measure keeps increasing with problem tightness in an unbounded way. In fact, for problems with $p_2 \geq 0.9$ the run time for problems with reasonable size typically gets too large to insert into the graph for all p_2 values [33]. In other words, unlike CSPs, the basic algorithms for COPs do not produce any phase transition in their performance. From experiments on MaxCSPs it appears that only some algorithms produce a behavior that resembles a phase transition. Larrosa and Meseguer found that, when a *BnB-AC* algorithm is used, the search effort decreases for ever growing problem tightness [33]. The behavior of simple algorithms for solving *MaxCSP*s, such as Algorithm 3.1, is the following. As the tightness is growing, so does the average difficulty of solving problem instances. For simple algorithms like *BnB* (or even NC in figure 3.2), the run time of the algorithm diverges. Surprisingly, when deep lookahead methods are used the run time of the "smarter" algorithms reaches a peak and then decreases. This is evident for all three lookahead algorithms in figure 3.2 (from [33]).

According to [36], only algorithms which enforce a strong enough method of local consistency (include the costs of constraints between pairs of unassigned variables in their lookahead computation of bounds) produce this phenomena. This behavior was reported for the BnB variation that enforces AC as well as the BnB variation that enforces AC*. It is important to mention that BnB that enforces only NC does not produce this behavior (as was mentioned above for the figure). The experimental results on MaxCSP reported in [33] are presented in Figure 3.2.

4

Distributed Search

Distributed constraint satisfaction problems (DisCSPs) are composed of agents, each holding its local constraints network, that are connected by constraints among variables of different agents. Agents assign values to variables, attempting to generate a locally consistent assignment that is also consistent with all constraints between agents (cf. [57, 61, 64]). To achieve this goal, agents check the value assignments to their variables for local consistency and exchange messages with other agents to check the consistency of their proposed assignments against constraints with variables owned by different agents [8].

Distributed CSPs are an elegant model for many everyday combinatorial problems that are distributed by nature. Take for example a large hospital that is composed of many wards. Each ward constructs a weekly timetable assigning its nurses to shifts. The construction of a weekly timetable involves solving a constraint satisfaction problem for each ward. Some of the nurses in every ward are qualified to work in the *emergency room*. Hospital regulations require a certain number of qualified nurses (e.g., for emergency room) on each shift. This imposes constraints among the timetables of different wards and generates a complex Distributed CSP [30, 57].

An example of a large-scale DisCSP started as a defence agency advanced research project (DARPA) problem presented publicly on the web in 2000. The description here is from [3]. The problem has n sensors and m targets, where a target is tracked if k sensors are tracking it at the same time. The major constraint is that a sensor can only track one target at a time. Bejar et al. formulated this problem as a DisCSP as follows. Each sensor is represented by an agent. Each agent has variables for every target that is in range. Variables are assigned the value 1 if the agent selects to track them and 0 otherwise. Each agent is constrained internally to have only one variable with the value 1. Constraints between agents are such that for every target, there are at least k agents that have assigned 1 to the value of their variable that corresponds to that target. Bejar et al. termed this distributed constraints problem SensorCSP [3].

A search procedure for a consistent assignment of all agents in a distributed CSP (DisCSP), is a distributed algorithm. All agents cooperate in the search for a globally consistent solution. The solution involves assignments of all agents to all their variables and exchange of information among all agents, to check the consistency of assignments with constraints among agents. An intuitive way to make the distributed search process for DisCSPs efficient is to enable agents to compute concurrently. Concurrent computation by agents can result in a shorter overall time of computation for finding a solution.

Concurrency of computation during search for DisCSPs is perhaps the most important research topic in the field. The present book focuses on DisCSP search as a model for distributed search in general. In this regard one can delineate several aspects of concurrency that hold center stage in the field of distributed search. First and foremost is the efficiency of the distributed search algorithms. The next important aspect is the analysis and design of concurrent measures of performance for all algorithms. Due to the distributed nature of the computation, these measures must be general enough to include the impact of communication problems, such as message delays. Last but not least, one must deal with purely distributed aspects of DisCSP search - the privacy of agents' data and the dynamic nature of the problems.

An interesting way to describe the advancement of DisCSP research in the last six years, which is very much at the center of the present book, is the following. Search algorithms have been central to Artificial Intelligence (AI) over the last 30 years. Certain aspects of search have been used extensively in AI and compose an important part of any search algorithm. Taking the field of CSP as an example for the rest of AI, one can describe these essential parts of searches as they appear in CSP. One important component is a set of methods for pruning the search space. The main examples are BackJumping and Lookahead methods [51]. These methods are based on the concept of visiting nodes on the search tree [31]. Other methods are based on heuristic ordering of the search, which in CSP is the ordering of variables and of values [13].

This book presents research on distributed search that explores the above aspects of search in AI in general and in CSP and COP in particular. The main goal of many of the distributed search algorithms is to exploit the *distributed counterparts* to known search strategies. It presents all complete search algorithms by looking at their strategy of concurrency and its consequences over the different aspects of distributed search. It points to aspects that can be enhanced by certain strategies such as concurrent processing of sequential assignment algorithms, by all agents (cf. Chapter 6 and Chapter 16). The bottom line of research of the last six years is that *all aspects of centralized search can be designed into distributed search and all of them work well*, though sometimes in surprising new forms of heuristics and concurrency. This is for example the case for ordering heuristics, where they turn out to be as important for distributed search as they are for standard search. However, asynchronous heuristics (Chapter 9) behave differently than synchronous heuristics (Chapter 8.1). They also need totally different distributed methods.

A major point of the present exposition of Distributed Constraints Search and Optimization is the emphasise on the inherent concurrency of all algorithms and computations. Concurrency of computations introduces many additional aspects to the investigation of search algorithms and heuristics. The intricate topic of measuring the performance of distributed search algorithms is introduced in depth in Chapter 10. Based on measures of distributed performance, one can start to investigate the impact of communication on the behavior of DISCSP search algorithms. A preliminary study includes the design of a model for message delays, within a concurrent simulator for distributed constraints search algorithms. The overall approach and design is described in Chapter 13.

Similarly to distributed constraint satisfaction problems, constraints optimization problems also have a distributed counterpart. A COP has values attached to every pair of assignments of constrained variables (in a *binary* COP). A *distributed* COP is composed of a set of agents that own nonintersecting parts of the variables of the COP and together own the whole COP. Constraints among variables that belong to different agents are valued each pair of value assignments has a value (or cost) associated with it. A partial assignment of values to variables owned by a set of agents has a cummulative cost that is the sum of all assigned constraints. A solution to the DISCOP is a complete assignment of all variables, by all agents, that has a minimal global cost. Clearly, DISCSPs are a special case of DISCOPs where all constraints are either 0 or 1. Many researchers believe that the natural formulation of real-world problems is by a DISCOP. Take for example the Meeting Scheduling Problem (MSP). A set of agents have meetings in which various subgroups of the agents need to participate. Agents need to participate in several meetings each and need to have enough time to travel among the meetings they are attending (*arrival constraints*).

Initially, this problem was formulated in the literature as a DISCSP [59, 60]. The problem is for the agents to search cooperatively for a schedule of all meetings that satisfies all arrival constraints [59]. Another view of this real-world problem is to take into account the fact that not all meetings can be scheduled in a conflict-free way (i.e., a solution to the DISCSP does not exist). Moreover, different meetings usually have a different utility for the participants. So, a realistic alternative to the above is to formulate the MSP as an optimization problem that minimizes the costs/penalties of all participating agents [38]. This way, the problem becomes one of finding the optimal assignment of time slots to meetings, such that the global sum of all agents' penalties (costs) is a minimum.

In the following sections distributed search algorithms for DISCSPs will be introduced. The aim is to try and provide an intuitive understanding to distributed search, before it is presented in full detail in Chapter 5, Chapter 6 and Chapter 7. An introduction to distributed search for an optimal solution of a DISCOP, as well as to DISCOP algorithms, is left to Chapter 14.

4.1 Distributed search algorithms on DisCSPs

A DISCSP can be thought of as a CSP in which the variables are divided among a set of agents $A_1, A_2, ..., A_n$. Each agent knows only the constraints of its local variables. It is often assumed that each agent holds exactly one variable because multiple-variable agents can be represented by single-variable agents in two general ways. One way is to define a composite assignment state for multiple-variable agents. Each such state is composed of assignments to all of the agent's variables. This will make agents have a large number of values, all combined assignments of an agent's variables. However, it clearly generates a single variable representation. The other form of generalizing a multiple-variable agent is to define "virtual agents", each holding one of the variables of the agent. Thus, each agent in the distributed problem is a single-variable agent. If the original problem had n multiple-variable agents, each holding m variables, then the new version of the problem has $n \times m$ "virtual agents" each holding a single variable. This representation enables any ordering of the "virtual agents" and is a little more general than the composite-variable representation. The bottom line of the above methods for representing multiple-variable agents by single-variable agents is that it is enough to deal with the simpler kind of agents. Those that hold only a single variable. This has been the practice of all researchers in the field (cf. [9, 61]).

Agents communicate by messages, trying to find a solution to the DISCSP. The common assumptions of DISCSP algorithmic research are the following:

- Messages arrive at their destination in a finite time
- Messages arrive in the order in which they were sent
- A total ordering of the agents and variables is known to all agents
- The constraints are at most binary

These assumptions are commonly used for DISCSP and DISCOP algorithms [47, 61]. We will assume that each agent owns a single variable and thus use the term "agent" and "variable" interchangeably.

The simplest distributed search algorithm for a distributed constraints satisfaction problem can be described as follows. Imagine a special type of message that we will term a *Current Partial Assignment (CPA)*. The CPA starts empty at the beginning of the run of the algorithm. There is only a single copy of the CPA (e.g., it is a *token*) and it passes all agents in order to accumulate a complete assignment to all variables of all agents. Each agent that holds the CPA adds to it assignments to its variables. Added assignments must be compatible with all former assignments. If no compatible assignments can be found, the agent holding the CPA returns it to former agents, requesting them to revise their assignments on the CPA. This is an operation of backtracking. It is easy to see that the algorithm that has been described is a standard backtracking algorithm that is performed by all agents in a distributed manner. It is also clear that all assignments are performed sequentially because the CPA is held by a single agent at a time. Tradition-ally, this algorithm has been termed *Synchronous BackTracking (SBT)* by Yokoo et. al [63, 64]. One can try to improve the performance of SBT by using standard techniques from centralized CSP search, such as backjump-ing. It is interesting to note that this idea appeared quite late in DISCSP research and has indeed improved the performance of sequential assignments distributed search algorithms (cf. [11, 71]). However, in order to understand the improvement in performance, one needs to learn first about concurrent performance measures (Chapter 10) and than investigate the behavior of a variety of algorithm types in a concurrent environment (Chapter 11).

One method for achieving concurrency in a single backtrack search on a distributed CSP is to try and avoid the waiting time of agents, for the arrival of a single CPA. In order to avoid this waiting time, agents may compute as-signments to their variables asynchronously. In asynchronous backtracking al-gorithms, agents assign their variables without waiting to receive information about all relevant assignments of other agents [53, 64]. To ensure the correct-ness and completeness of asynchronous backtracking, all agents share a static order of variables and the algorithm keeps data structures for NOGOODs that are discovered during search (cf. [8, 9]). Asynchronous Backtracking (*ABT*) is undoubtedly the flagship of distributed search algorithms for DISCSPs. In the next chapter the ABT algorithm will be described in great detail, in its improved version of NOGOOD storage [9]. In Chapter 9 advanced versions of ABT that enable dynamic ordering of agents during search are described. Not surprisingly, these versions of asynchronous backtracking have a much better performance than statically ordered ABT.

The next three chapters present the state of the art of complete distributed search algorithms for DISCSPs. The first and most important algorithm is *Asynchronous Bactracking (ABT)*. The main design principle of ABT is to exploit the option of performing multiple assignments concurrently [64]. Its great virtue stems precisely from that feature - performing multiple assign-ments concurrently (by multiple agents) and still maintaining a correct asyn-chronous backtracking procedure over the complete search space.

A very successful family of classical search algorithms, on centralized CSPs, uses different versions of lookahead [26]. These algorithms span a wide range of lookahead methods. From *forward-checking (FC)* [51] to maintenance of deeper forms of lookahead. A major focus has been on the maintenance of arc-consistency (MAC) [7, 29]. In accordance with the general approach of the present book, one can try and design a method of adapting lookahead to benefit distributed search. This idea leads to the *Asynchronous Forward-Checking (AFC)* algorithm that will be introduced in Chapter 6. In AFC a single search process induces a distributed and asynchronous forward-checking procedure that is performed by all agents. This generates a different kind of concurrency and turns out to be very efficient (see Chapter 6).

An important component of centralized search, both on CSPs and in other fields, has to do with heuristic selection of steps. In CSP this takes the form of ordering the variables for assignment and ordering values within domains of variables [14]. Following our approach, one can try and order agents in DISCSP search. When the DISCSP search algorithm assigns variables sequentially, the ordering of agents can be easily achieved and performance is indeed greatly improved [11, 44]. When the algorithm uses asynchronous assignments, as in ABT, ordering dynamically is much more difficult and a correct and elegant distributed algorithm was only published quite recently [71, 74]. The interesting part about ordering heuristics is that they improve dramatically the performance of most search algorithms, both centralized and distributed. As a result, some simple beliefs about concurrency of search have been shattered when ordering heuristics were used. For example, synchronous backtracking (SBT) was believed to be much slower than asynchronous backtracking (ABT) (cf. [61, 63]). Brito and Meseguer have shown that this is not true in the presence of heuristics [11].

A completely different approach to concurrency of distributed search is to run multiple search processes that scan the search space concurrently. This can in principle be done by splitting the search space during search and letting the agents participate in all search processes. The resulting algorithm is termed *Concurrent Backtraking (ConcBT)* [69]. The splitting of the search space can be done dynamically, to balance the load of computation among all agents. When search processes cooperate by backjumping across different processes, the algorithm performs dynamic backtracking (e.g., ConcDB) and is the best performing DISCSP algorithm to date [74]. It is described in Chapter 7.

In analogy to centralized search, algorithms can be designed so that they do not guarantee completeness. In other words, when the algorithm fails to find a solution it does not guarantee that a solution does not exist. The reason for designing such algorithms is that they can be fast on large and hard problems [63, 66]. The common approach to incomplete search is to design search steps that perform local computaions. This fits very well the nature of distributed computation. Agents exchange messages with their neighbors, achieving agreement on their assignment in a local neighborhood, such that some objective function is minimized. For a DISCSP, the objective function can be the number of constraints violations (e.g., conflicts). In order to achieve locally consistent assignments, in a stable distributed process, it is necessary to *synchronize* each step of the algorithm across all neighborhoods in the problem. This makes distributed stochastic search algorithms behave similarly to centralized local search algorithms [61] and puts them outside the scope of this book.

The next section presents an intuitive description of asynchronous backtracking. This description serves two goals. It introduces the classically most important search algorithm for DISCSPs in an intuitive way, describing its run on a simple problem. In addition, it gives the reader a first feeling of the step-by-step run of a distributed search algorithm. A detailed description of ABT, with its pseudo-code and a correctness proof will be given in Chapter 5.

4.2 Introducing Asynchronous Backtracking

Asynchronous backtracking (ABT) uses a complete order among all agents. Agents receive messages informing them about assignments of agents that are ahead of them in the total order (i.e. **ok?** messages). After performing an assignment, each agent sends **ok?** messages to agents that are ordered after it [9, 61, 64]. In ABT, agents always have their variables assigned. Initially, variables are assigned without waiting for messages informing about assignments of other (constraining) agents. When messages informing of assignments of other agents that conflict with the current assignment of the receiving agent arrive, the receiving agent performs one of two actions. Either it finds an alternative assignment that is consistent with the received message or it sends back a *Nogood* message. The *Nogood* message informs the receiving agent that its assignment has to be changed. Having sent back this *Nogood* (backtracking) message, the agent than assumes that the culprit assignment will be changed and proceeds to assign its variables accordingly. This is the way in which all agents running ABT keep being assigned at all times (cf. [9, 61]).

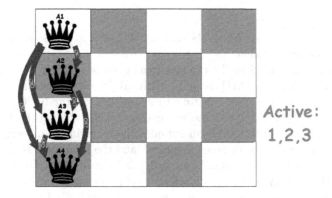

Fig. 4.1. First cycle of ABT for 4-queens

In order to gain some intuitive understanding of ABT, consider its run on a simple problem. We will describe here the first two steps or cycles of ABT on the problem. This will give the reader some flavor of the behavior of ABT (or any other distributed and asynchronous search algorithm). In Chapter 5

Nogood message: $A_1=1 \wedge A_2=1 \Rightarrow A_3 \neq 1$

Fig. 4.2. Second cycle of ABT for 4-queens

the example will be run to its end and references to the code of ABT will make it easier to follow.

Figures 4.1, 4.2 describe the first two cycles of running ABT. Dividing the asynchtonous run of ABT is quite artificial. This will become clearer in our description of concurrent run-time measures in Chapter 10. The two states in figures 4.1, 4.2 describe the first two cycles of ABT, solving the 4-queens problem. Each cycle of computation includes the receiving of messages, computations triggered by the received messages, and the sending of messages [61, 63]. The four agents A_1, A_2, A_3, A_4 are ordered from top to bottom.

In the first cycle all agents select a value for their variable (i.e., position their queen). For no better reason we assume that all of them position their queens at the first square of their row. Agents 1, 2, 3 each send **ok?** messages to the agents ordered after it. Agent A_1 sends three messages, to all agents ordered after it. Agent A_2 sends two messages and agent A_3 sends a single message. Agent A_4 does not have any agent after it, so it sends no messages informing of its position. All agents are active in this first cycle of the algorithm's run.

In the second cycle agents A_1, A_2, A_3 recieve the **ok?** messages sent to them and proceed to assign consistent values to their variables. Agent A_3 assigns the value 3 that is consistent with the assignments of A_1 and A_2 that it received. Agent A_4 has no consistent value with the assignments of A_1, A_2, A_3. It sends a *Nogood* containing these three assignments to A_3 and removes the assignment of A_3 from its *Agent_View*. Then, it assigns the value 2 that is consistent with the assignments that it recieved from A_1, A_2 (having erased the assignment of A_3, assuming it will be replaced because of the NOGOOD message). The active agents in this cycle are A_2, A_3, A_4. Agent A_2 acts according to its information about A_1's position and moves to square 3, sending two **ok?** messages to inform its successors about its value. As can be seen in Figure 4.2, Agent A_3 has moved to square 4, after receiving the **ok?** messages of agents A_1 and A_2. Note that agent A_3 thinks of the positions of these two agents as being in square 1 of their respective rows. This is a manifestation of concurrency which causes each agent to act at all times in a form that is based only on its *Agent_ View*. The *Agent_View* of agent A_3 includes the **ok?** messages it received. We will leave for now the run of ABT on the 4-queens example and will return to its complete description in Chapter 5.

5

Asynchronous Backtracking (ABT)

The *asynchronous backtracking* algorithm (*ABT*) first presented by Yokoo [18] was constructed to remove the drawbacks of *synchronous backtracking* (*SBT*) by allowing agents to perform assignments asynchronously. In all the presentations of ABT, the algorithm is presented for DISCSPs in which each agent holds exactly one variable. This avoids the problem of reconciling the total order of the agents, which is assumed by ABT, with the order of the variables. When agents hold multiple variables, these are two distinct orders that the algorithm has to address. Each agent assigns its variable and communicates the assignment it made to the relevant agents.

The ABT algorithm in its standard form assumes that a total order of priorities is defined among agents. In Chapter 9 a new and innovative version of the ABT algorithm will be presented, in which agents can change their order dynamically during search [74]. However, in order to both make the understanding of ABT simpler and follow its history, it will be presented here in the form in which it was used for most of the last decade [9, 63]. Each binary constraint is known to both of the constrained agents and is checked in the algorithm by the agent with the lower priority among the two. A link in the constraint network is *directed* from the agent with the higher priority to the agent with the lower priority among the two constrained agents.

Agents instantiate their variables concurrently and send their assigned values to the agents that are connected to them by outgoing links. All agents wait for and respond to messages. After each update of its assignment, an agent sends through all outgoing links its new assignment. An agent which receives an assignment (from the higher-priority agent of the link) tries to find an assignment for its variable which does not violate a constraint with the assignment it received.

ok? messages are messages carrying an assignment of an agent. When an agent A_i receives an **ok?** message from agent A_j, it places the received assignment in a data structure called *Agent_View*, which holds the last assignment A_i received from higher-priority neighbors such as A_j. Next, A_i checks if its current assignment is still consistent with its *Agent_View*. If it is consistent,

A_i does nothing. If not, then A_i searches its domain for a new consistent value. If it finds one, it assigns its variable and sends **ok?** messages to all lower-priority agents linked to it. Otherwise, A_i backtracks.

The *backtrack* operation is executed by sending a NOGOOD message that contains an inconsistent partial assignment. NOGOODs are sent to the agent with the lowest priority among the agents whose assignments are included in the inconsistent tuple in the NOGOOD. Agent A_i that sends a NOGOOD message to agent A_j assumes that A_j will change its assignment. Therefore, A_i removes from its *Agent_View* the assignment of A_j and makes an attempt to find an assignment for its variable that is consistent with the updated *Agent_View*.

The issue of how to resolve the inconsistent partial assignment (NOGOOD) which will be sent in the backtrack message evolved through the different versions of ABT. A shorter NOGOOD would mean backjumping further up the search tree, but finding such a short NOGOOD can be wasteful in computational time. In the early versions of ABT ([18, 64]), Yokoo proposes to send the full *Agent_View* as a NOGOOD. The full *Agent_View* is in many cases not a minimal NOGOOD. In other words, it might contain assignments that, if removed, the remaining partial assignment still eliminates all values in the agent's domain. The reason that sending the whole *Agent_View* back is correct (but unsatisfactory) can be explained by the following example.

Consider an agent A_6 which holds an inconsistent *AgentView* with the assignments of agents A_1, A_2, A_3, A_4, and A_5. If we assume that A_6 is only constrained by the current assignments of A_1 and A_3, sending a NOGOOD message to A_5 which contains all the assignments in the *Agent_View* seems to be a waste. After sending the NOGOOD to A_5, A_6 will remove its assignment from the *Agent_View* and make another attempt to assign its variable which will be followed by an additional NOGOOD sent to A_4 and the removal of A_4's assignment from the *Agent_View*. These attempts will continue until a minimal subset is sent as a NOGOOD. In this example, it is the NOGOOD sent to A_3. The assignment with the lower priority in the minimal inconsistent subset is removed from the *Agent_View* and a consistent assignment can now be found. In this example the computation ended by sending a NOGOOD to the culprit agent, which would have been the outcome that would have been achieved if the agent would have computed a minimal subset.

Let us turn now to the code of ABT in its simplest form. Algorithm 5.1 presents Yokoo's code that assumes sending complete *Agent_Views* as NO-GOODs. It can be rougfly divided into two parts - moving forward and moving back. Note that due to ABT's asynchronous nature, the moves forward or backward are performed at the same time. There is no synchronization among actions taken by agents. Assignments and revoking of assignments are performed concurrently. When an assignment is performed by an agent, it sends an **ok?** message and upon receiving it the receiving agent performs lines 1-2 of the code in Algorithm 5.1. The function *Check_Agent_View*

Algorithm 5.1: ABT algorithm (Complete *Agent_Views* as Nogoods)

- **when received** (**ok?**, (x_j, d_j)) **do**
  1. add (x_j, d_j) to *Agent_View*;
  2. **check_agent_view**;**end_do**;

- **when received** (**Nogood**, x_j, *nogood*) **do**
  1. add Nogood to Nogood list;
  2. **when** *Nogood* contains an agent x_k that is not its neighbor **do**
  3.   request x_k to add x_i as a neighbor,
  4.   and add (x_k, d_k) to *Agent_View*; **end_do**;
  5.   *old_value* ← *current_value*; **check_agent_view**;
  6.   **when** *old_value* = *current_value* **do**
  7.   send (**ok?**, $(x_i, current\_value)$) to x_j ; **end_ do**; **end_do**;

  procedure **check_agent_view**
  1. **when** *Agent_View* and *current_value* are not consistent **do**
  2.   **if** no value in D_i is consistent with *Agent_View*
  3.   **then backtrack**;
  4.   **else** select $d \in D_i$ where *Agent_View* and d are consistent;
  5.   *current_value* ← d;
  6.   send (**ok?**,(x_i, d)) to *low_priority_neighbors*; **end_if**; **end_do**;

  procedure **backtrack**
  1. *nogood* ← *inconsistent_subset*;
  2. **when** *nogood* is an empty set **do**
  3.   broadcast to other agents that there is no solution;
  4.   terminate this algorithm; **end_do**;
  5. select (x_j, d_j) where x_i has the lowest priority in Nogood;
  6. send (**Nogood**, x_i, *nogood*) to x_j;
  7. remove (x_j, d_j) from *Agent_View*; **end_do**;
  8. **check_agent_view**

---

which is called attempts to assign a value that is consistent with the agent's *Agent_View*. If it fails, it calls **backtrack**.

Moving backward (e.g., replacing assignments) can be trigered by receiving a NOGOOD. An agent A_i that receives a NOGOOD adds it to its list of constraints. Since the NOGOOD can include assignments of some agent A_j, which A_i was not previously constrained with, A_i after adding A_j's assignment to its *Agent_View*, sends a message to A_j asking it to add A_i to its list of outgoing links (line 3 of the relevant function in Algorithm 5.1) [61, 63]. A_j after adding the link, will send an **ok?** message to A_i each time it reassigns its variable. After storing the NOGOOD, A_i checks if its assignment is still consistent. If it is, a message is sent to the agent the NOGOOD was received from. This re-sending of the assignment is crucial since, as mentioned above, the agent sending a NOGOOD assumes the receiver of the NOGOOD, replaces its assignment. Therefore it needs to know that the assignment stayed. If the old assignment that was forbidden by the NOGOOD is inconsistent, A_i tries to find a new assignment similarly to the case when an **ok?** message is received.

The ABT algorithm ends successfully when the agents are all idle (i.e., their assignment is consistent with their *Agent_View*) and no message that will change any agent's *Agent_View* (e.g., an **ok?** message) or add to the constraints of agents (e.g., a NOGOOD message) is traveling around in the system between agents. In such a case the assignments the agents hold are the solution to the DISCSP. The algorithm fails if some agent creates an *empty* NOGOOD.

In Algorithm 5.1 every NOGOOD is stored by the receiving agent. Since the number of inconsistent subsets can be exponential, constraints lists with exponential size will be created, and a search through such lists requires exponential computation time in the worst case. In [63], Yokoo proposes that agents keep only NOGOODs consistent with their *Agent_View*, and claims that preserving this property reduces the number of NOGOODs to the size of the variables domain. However, the maximal number of minimal Nogoods which are consistent with the *Agent_View* (i.e., Nogoods which do not include other Nogoods), is the number of subsets of the *Agent_View* which do not contain one another. This number is exponential in the size of the *Agent_View*. In order to hold a number of NOGOODs not larger than the size of the domain a NOGOOD must be stored only if it is consistent with the agent's *Agent_View* and with its current assignment [8]. Since storing such a NOGOOD causes a change of the current assignment, only one NOGOOD can be stored for each value removed from the domain. Consequently, the number of NOGOODs stored at any single agent is not larger than the size of the domain. This approach to asynchronous backtracking is the best version of ABT, which will be presented in detail in Section 5.2. First, we will follow the run of ABT on the 4-queens problem to its end.

5.1 A Complete 4-Queens Example

Continuing the example of Chapter 4, we will commence from the third cycle, that follows immediately the state desribed in Figure 4.2. The third cycle is desribed in Figure 5.1. In the third cycle only agent A_3 is active. After receiving the assignment of agent A_2, it sends back a NOGOOD message to agent A_2. It then erases the assignment of agent A_2 from its *Agent_View* and validates that its current assignment (the value 4) is consistent with the assignment of agent A_1. Agents A_1 and A_2 continue to be idle, having received no messages that were sent in cycle 2. The same is true for agent A_4. Agent A_3 also receives the NOGOOD sent by A_4 in cycle 2, but ignores it since it

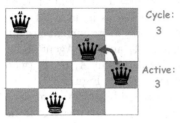

Nogood message: $A_1=1 \Rightarrow A_2 \neq 3$

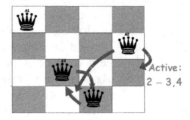

Nogood message: $A_1=1 \wedge A_2=4 \Rightarrow A_3 \neq 4$

Fig. 5.1. Cycle 3 of ABT for 4-Q   **Fig. 5.2.** Cycles 4-5 of ABT 4-Q

includes an invalid assignment of A_2 (i.e., $< 2, 1 >$ and not the currently correct $< 2, 4 >$).

Cycles 4 and 5 are depicted in Figure 5.2, so that the positions of the four queens are at their state after both cycles. In cycle 4 A_2 moves to square 4 because of the NoGood message it received. Its former value was ruled out and the new value is the next valid one. It informs its successors A_3 and A_4 of its new position/value by sending two **ok?** messages. In cycle 5 agent A_3 receives agent A_2's new position and selects the only value that is compatible with the positions of its two predecessors, square 2. It sends a message to its successor informing it about this new value. Agent A_4 is now left with no valid value to assign and sends a NoGood message to A_3 that includes all its conflicts. The NoGood message appears at the bottom of Figure 5.2. Note that the NoGood message is no longer valid. Agent A_4, however, assumes that A_3 will change its position and moves to its only valid position (with A_3's anticipated move) - square 3.

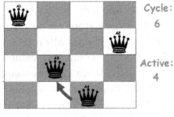

Nogood message: $A_1=1 \wedge A_2=4 \Rightarrow A_3 \neq 2$

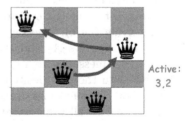

Nogood messages: $A1=1 \Rightarrow A2 \neq 4, \Rightarrow A_1 \neq 1$

Fig. 5.3. Cycle 6 of ABT for 4-Q   **Fig. 5.4.** Cycles 7-8 of ABT 4-Q

Consider now cycle 6. Agent A_4 receives the new assignment of agent A_3 and sends it a NOGOOD message. Having erased the assignment of A_3 after sending the NOGOOD message, it then decides to stay at its current assignment (the value 3), since it is compatible with agents A_1 and A_2. Agent A_3 is idle in cycle 6, since it receives no messages from either agent A_1 or A_2 (who are idle too). So, A_4 is the only active agent at cycle 6 (see Figure 5.3).

Cycles 7 and 8 involve a series of NOGOOD sending. Both are depicted in Figure 5.4. First agent A_3, after receiving the NOGOOD message from A_4, finds that it has no valid values left and sends a NOGOOD to A_2. Next, in cycle 8, agent A_2 also discovers that its domain of values is exhausted and sends a NOGOOD message to its successor A_1. Both of the sending agents erase the value of their successors (to whom the NOGOOD message was sent) from their *Agent_Views* and therefore remain in their positions which are now conflict free.

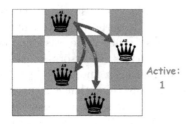

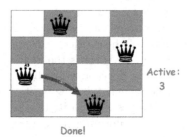

Fig. 5.5. Cycle 9 of ABT for 4-Q   **Fig. 5.6.** Cycle 10 (last) of ABT 4-Q

Cycle 9 involves only agent A_1, which receives the NOGOOD message from A_2 and moves to its next value - square 2. Next, it sends **ok?** messages to its three successors. The last cycle to establish the solution is cycle 10. Agent A_3, upon receiving the **ok?** message of A_1 moves to a consistent value - square 1 of its row. Agents A_2 and A_4 check their *Agent_Views* after receiving the same **ok?** messages from agent A_1 and find that their current values are consistent with the new position of A_1. Agent A_3 sends an **ok?** message to its successor A_4, informing of its move, but A_4 finds no reason to move. It is consistent with all value assignments of all of its predecessors. After cycle 10 all agents remain idle, having no constraint violations with assignments on their *Agent_Views* [63]. This is a final state of the ABT algorithm when it finds a solution.

The pseudo-code of Algorithm 5.1 is quite difficult to prove correct and its implementation is actually a very slow version of ABT, due to the need to save all NOGOODs in order to maintain correctness. In the following section a more modern version of the ABT algorithm will be presented, following Bessiere et al. [9]. Based on its clearly defined parts, such as keeping a polynomial number of NOGOODs, its correctness is proven formally [9].

5.2 The ABT Algorithm - Polynomial Storage

This section follows closely the presentation of [9]. Identical names will be used for all data structures and all procedures. In fact, the pseudo-code is copied by permission from [9] and is presented in Algorithm 5.2. As in the classical version of ABT (Algorithm 5.1), a total order of priorities among agents is assumed. Agents hold a data structure called *myAgentView* which contains the most recent assignments received from agents with higher priority. The algorithm starts by each agent assigning its variable, and sending the assignment to neighboring agents with lower priority in procedure **CheckAgentView()** in Algorithm 5.2). Algorithm 5.2 uses two data structures that hold, for each agent, two lists. $\Gamma^+(Self)$ holds all agents constrained by the current agent $(Self)$ that are *after it in the global order*. $\Gamma^-(Self)$ holds all agents constraining the current agent that are *before it* in the global order. $Self$ is used to denote the current agent that is running the algorithm [9].

When an agent receives a message containing an assignment (an **ok?** message [61]), it updates its *myAgentView* with the received assignment by calling procedure **ProcessInfo()**. It calls procedure **CheckAgentView()**, which checks whether its assignment is still consistent or it needs to be replaced (first procedure in Algorithm 5.2). If no consistent value can be found, the **Backtrack()** procedure is called. The procedure **UpdateAgentView()** ensures the polynomial space in memory for storing NOGOODs by *erasing all NOGOODs that are not consistent with the updated myAgentView*. This is the most important difference of Algorithm 5.2 from the original Yokoo version (cf. Algorithm 5.1 [63]).

An elegant way of maintaining such a limited *myNogoodStore* is by keeping NOGOODs as *explanations* for removed values from the agent's domain. Whenever a value is removed from a domain, the reason can be either a conflict with some assigned higher priority agent, or a NOGOOD received from a lower-priority agent. The former reason reflects a known constraint between the two agents. In such a case the NOGOOD (explanation) is of length one. The second potential reason for eliminating a value is the receiving of a (valid) NOGOOD. This can create an explanation that is longer than a single term (e.g., more than a single assignment on the LHS of the NOGOOD). All of this mechanism was introduced by Ginsberg for the *Dynamic Backtracking (DBT)* algorithm in [23]. In fact, the initial version of the polynomial storage version of ABT was proposed in 2001 by Bessiere et. al under the title *Distributed Dynamic Backtracking (DisDB)* [8].

When the **Backtrack()** procedure is called, the NOGOOD to be sent back is constructed by the procedure **solve(***myNogoodStore***)**, which resolves all

---

Algorithm 5.2: The ABT algorithm with polynomial space (from [9])

---

procedure ABT()
  $myValue \leftarrow$ empty; $end \leftarrow$ false; compute Γ^+, Γ^-;
  CheckAgentView();
  while ($\neg end$) **do**
    $msg \leftarrow$ getMsg();
    switch($msg.type$)
      ok?   : ProcessInfo(msg);
      ngd   : ResolveConflict(msg);
      adl   : SetLink(msg);
      stp   : $end \leftarrow$ true;

procedure CheckAgentView(msg)
  if $\neg$consistent($myValue, myAgentView$) **then**
    $myValue \leftarrow$ ChooseValue();
    if ($myValue$) **then for each** $child \in \Gamma^+(self)$ **do** sendMsg:ok?($child, myValue$);
    else Backtrack();

procedure ProcessInfo(msg)
  UpdateAgentView($msg.Assig$);
  CheckAgentView();

procedure ResolveConflict(msg)
  if Coherent($msg.Nogood, \Gamma^-(self) \cup \{self\}$) **then**
    CheckAddLink(msg);
    add($msg.Nogood, myNogoodStore$); $myValue \leftarrow$ empty;
    CheckAgentView();
  else if Coherent($msg.Nogood, self$) **then** SendMsg:ok?($msg.sender, myValue$);

procedure Backtrack()
  $newNogood \leftarrow$ solve($myNogoodStore$);
  if ($newNogood =$ empty) **then**
    $end \leftarrow$ true; sendMsg:**stp**($system$);
  else
    sendMsg:**ngd**($newNogood$);
    UpdateAgentView(rhs($newNogood$) $\leftarrow$ unknown);
    CheckAgentView();

function ChooseValue()
  for each $v \in D(self)$ not eliminated by $myNogoodStore$ **do**
    if consistent($v, myAgentView[\Gamma^-(self)]$) **then return** ($v$);
    else add($x_j = val_j \Rightarrow self \neq v, myNogoodStore$); /*$v$ is inconsistent with x_j's value */
  return (empty);

procedure UpdateAgentView($newAssig$)
  add($newAssig, myAgentView$);
  for each $ng \in myNogoodStore$ **do**
    if $\neg$Coherent(lhs(ng), $myAgentView$) **then** remove($ng, myNogoodStore$);

function Coherent($nogood, agents$)
  for each $var \in nogood \cup agents$ **do**
    if $nogood[var] \neq myAgentView[var]$ **then return** false;
  return true;

procedure SetLink(msg)
  add($msg.sender, \Gamma^+(self)$);
  sendMsg:ok?($msg.sender, myValue$);

procedure CheckAddLink(msg)
  for each ($var \in$ lhs($msg.Nogood$))
    if ($var \notin \Gamma^-(self)$) **then**
      sendMsg:**adl**($var, self$);
      add($var, \Gamma^-(self)$); UpdateAgentView($var \leftarrow varValue$);

NOGOODS of the agent's store and produces the resolvant. The explanation of the value that was eiminated by this NOGOOD is erased (line 6 of procedure **Backtrack()** in Algorithm 5.2) and the resolvant NOGOOD is sent to the lowest-priority agent whose assignment is included in the NOGOOD [9]. After the eliminating explanation (i.e., culprit) assignment is removed from *myAgentView* the agent makes another attempt to assign its variable by calling the procedure **UpdateAgentView()** (procedure **backtrack** lines 5-9).

Agents that receive a NOGOOD check its relevance against the content of their *myAgentView* by calling procedure **ResolveConflict()**. If the NO-GOOD is relevant the agent stores it, and tries to find a consistent assignment. If the agent receiving the NOGOOD keeps its assignment, it informs the NO-GOOD sender by re-sending it an **ok?** message with its assignment. In order to demonstrate the fine points of Algorithm 5.2 let us follow the detailed example of resolving NOGOODS step by step, from the original paper of Bessiere et al. [8] that proposed this algorithm.

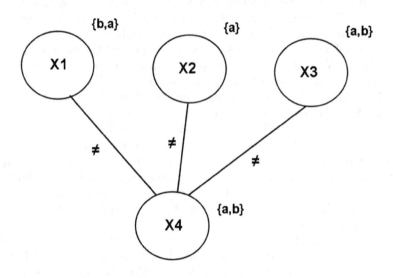

Fig. 5.7. An example DisCSP

Consider the example problem in Figure 5.7. The problem consists of four variables $X_1, \ldots, X_4$, each with its domain of values. Constraints are depicted by lines connecting the constrained pairs of variables and all constraints are constraints of inequality. Let us follow in detail the step by step run of the

ABT algorithm in its improved form, keeping a polynomial number of No-GOODS (Algorithm 5.2). The steps are quite arbitrary as the algorithm runs asynchronously. The main emphasis is on the resolving of NOGOODS and especially on discarding invalid NOGOODS. The scheme of the run is depicted in the form of a table in Figure 5.8, which is taken from [8]. Each row of the table in Figure 5.8 describes a further step (or cycle) of the run of ABT on the problem in Figure 5.7. Each column describes the state of one of the agents during the steps of running the algorithm. A state consists of the *myAgentView* of the agent, with assignments of all agents that are predecessors, the *myNogoodStore*, and the current assignment of the agent. Agents are ordered from left to right, in lexicographical order.

In the first step or round of the agents running the ABT algorithm, each assigns its variable the first value in its domain. Each sends an **Info()** message to its successor, informing them of its assignment. For all three first agents there is a single successor - X_4. This is depicted in the first row of the table in Figure 5.8, where the **Info()** messages appear at the sending agent's description. Note that the *myAgentViews* of all agents, which appear as a vertical column on the left of each cell of the table, include only the assignment of the agent itself. This being the first step, no message has yet been accepted.

Continuing the description of the run as a step-by-step scenario, we move to the second cycle, when messages are received and computations take place. Agent X_4 computes two NOGOODS that rule out both of its values after receiving all **Info()** messages. These are $(X_1 = b \Rightarrow X_4 \neq b)$ and $(X_2 = a \Rightarrow X_4 \neq a)$. Resolving the two NOGOODS that emptied its domain, X_4 generates the NOGOOD $(X_1 = b \Rightarrow X_2 \neq a)$ and sends it in a **back()** message to X_2. Let us continue carefully now. Following the sending of the **back()** message, X_4 erases the assignment of X_2 from its *myAgentView*. However, its value a is now ruled out by the NOGOOD (explanation) $(X_3 = a \Rightarrow X_4 \neq a)$. An empty domain triggers again a resolution of all NOGOODS to generate another **back()** message, this time to X_3, containing the NOGOOD $(X_1 = b \Rightarrow X_3 \neq a)$. Now X_4 is left with an assignable value and it assigns the value a.

The third cycle of computations is shown in the third row of Figure 5.8. Agent X_2 resolves the NOGOOD it received, since it has no value left in its domain. As a result it sends back to X_1 a **back()** message containing the NOGOOD $(\Rightarrow X_1 \neq b)$. Following that, X_2 erases the assignment of X_1 from its *myAgentView* and assigns the value a (the only one in its domain). Next, it sends an **Info()** to its only successor X_4.

In the same third cycle agent X_3 receives the **Back()** message and adds to its *myAgentView* the assignment $X_1 = a$. Then it changes its assignment to b and sends an **Info()** message to X_4. Finally, let us squeeze into the third cycle of computation also the receiving of the **Back()** message by X_1. In response to this message X_1 keeps it, erases the value b from its domain and assigns the remaining value a. This assignment is sent in an **Info()** message to X_4.

In the fourth step of the distributed computation agent X_4 receives the two **Info()** messages sent to it in the third cycle by agents X_1 and X_3. These

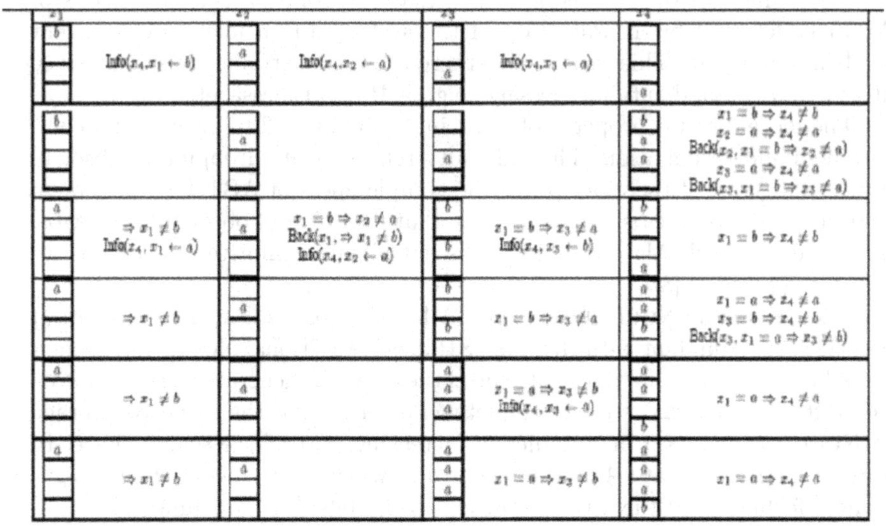

Fig. 5.8. A detailed run of ABT on the example

rule out its two values (each by a different agent) and it resolves them into a new **Back()** message that contains the NOGOOD ($X_1 = a \Rightarrow X_3 \neq b$) (fourth row of Figure 5.8). Note that all agents keep their relevant NOGOODs and the relevant assignments of predecessor agents.

In the fifth step (one before last row of Figure 5.8) agent X_3 receives the **Back()** messages, changes the assignment of X_1 in its *myAgentView* to a, changes its own assignment to b, and sends an **Info()** message to X_4. This ends the computation. Agent X_4 receives this message and updates its *myAgentView* accordingly. It retains its assignment because there is no conflict with any of the three assignments of the other agents. The DISCSP network remains idle and this is the final step of finding a solution.

5.3 Correctness of ABT

Let us start by noting that ABT in its form of Algorithm 5.2 uses polynomial storage space for its NOGOODs. This is immediately clear from the fact that NOGOODs are kept as explanations to erased values in the domains of agents that received these NOGOODs. For n agents and k values in the largest domain the total storage space is bound by $n \times k$. Note that a maximum of a single NOGOOD is kept for each value and obsolete NOGOODs are erased.

The soundness of ABT is also immediate. A solution (in all versions of ABT) is detected by an idle state of the system. In an idle state no agent sends any message. This means that there are no constraint violations, since any violation would entail a message [e.g., a **Back()** message].

The more difficult property of ABT in Algorithm 5.2 to prove, is its completeness and termination. This difficulty relates to its dropping of obsolete NOGOODS. We will therefore prove the completeness of ABT for the version that keeps all NOGOODS and then show that dropping of obsolete NOGOODS, in accordance with Algorithm 5.2, does not violate completeness. In this we follow the proof of [8].

Assume that all NOGOODS are kept. All NOGOODS resulting from an **Info()** message are redundant with the DISCSP itself. Additional NOGOODS are generated by resolution and due to its correctness cannot generate the empty NO-GOOD if a solution exists (i.e., completeness). Moreover, the extensive storage of NOGOODS prunes a monotonically increasing part of the search space. In a finite time some state A will be reached in which every inconsistent assignment is forbidden. If there is no solution to the DISCSP, an empty NOGOOD will be generated and the algorithm will terminate.

If a solution exists one may prevent an agent from taking a consistent value, by keeping an obsolete NOGOOD (because all are kept). To see why this is impossible consider two cases for such an obsolete NOGOOD. Assume that agent X_i stores the obsolete NOGOOD that is made obsolete by a change in the state of agent X_j. If $X_j \in \Gamma^-$, an **Info()** message is on its way and will enable the needed assignment of X_i. Otherwise, agent X_i will be left with no values (because its only value that participates in a solution is forbidden by the obsolete NOGOOD) and will eventually send a **Back()** message and erase the obsolete NOGOOD. In both cases completeness is ensured.   □

We have shown that the ABT algorithm is sound, complete, and terminates when it keeps all NOGOODS. This is actually the original version pf ABT that was proposed by Yokoo [64] and is presented in Algorithm 5.1. What we need to show now is that these properties of ABT remain true in the presence of erasing obsolete NOGOODS. It is important to remember that obsolete NOGOODS are erased when either an **Info()** or a **Back()** message is received, in which some assignment of an agent that is of higher priority is no longer valid.

The proof by induction starts with the first agent in the ordering of the DISCSP (say, X_1). Clearly, X_1 receives no **Info()** messages and all **Back()** messages it receives have an empty left side. As a result, agent X_1 can never make any of its NOGOODS obsolete. But this means that X_1 can never go into an infinite loop - erasing a NOGOOD and later storing it.

Assume now that the first $k - 1$ agents in the ordering are not trapped in an infinite loop because of discarding of obsolete NOGOODS. Consider the next agent in the ordering - X_k. If it goes into an infinite loop, that means that it keeps sending NOGOOD messages to some of the first $k - 1$ agents and keeps discarding them infinitely. But, since the first $k-1$ agents do not loop infinitely, this is impossible. Either they will stop sending messages and X_k will not be in an infinite loop, or they will generate an empty NOGOOD which stops all agents eventually. This completes the proof that ABT in its polynomial storage version that discards all obsolete NOGOODs (Algorithm 5.2) is complete and terminated. Soundness was proven immediately for all versions of ABT.   □

5.4 Improving Performance of ABT

The main potential problem for the performance of ABT arises directly from its most important virtue - its asynchronicity. As a true asynchronous algorithm it responds to every message it receives by the apropriate actions. Imagine that for some reason in message delivery by the system agent A_i receives **ok?** messages from two agents A_j and A_k that are both of higher priority than A_i. Assume that the first message to arrive at A_i is from A_j, but that $A_k \prec A_j$. This of course has nothing to do with the time these messages were sent, since the system is asynchronous. After agent A_i deals with updating, checking, and adjusting its *Agent_View* and consequently its assignment with the information contained in the message from A_j, an **ok?** messages arrives (asynchronously) from agent A_k. This message in fact caused A_j to change its assignment and send to A_i another message that may be on its way. Imagine that the combination of the assignments of A_j and A_k causes A_i to send a NOGOOD message to A_j. Now to complete the example imagine that the above two messages are first in the queue of A_i's mailbox and after them has already arrived a message from A_j, informing A_i that it has already changed its assignment, say, because it conflicts with A_k's assignment. Clearly, when A_i's NOGOOD messages finally arrives at A_j it will not do anything except for sending A_i an additional **ok?** message to make sure it adds its assignment back to its *Agent_View* (having erased it for the NOGOOD sending).

Yokoo noticed this problem early on and proposed to improve the performance of ABT by having agents read all messages they receive before performing computation [63]. A formal protocol for such an algorithm was not published. The idea is not to reassign the variable until all the messages in the agent's mailbox are read and the status it keeps of all other agents' assignments (i.e., its *Agent_View*) is updated. This technique was actually found to improve the performance of ABT on the harder instances of randomly generated DISCSPs by a factor of 4 [68]. However, this property makes the efficiency of ABT dependent on the contents of the agent's mailbox in each step, i.e., on potential message delays (see Chapter 12 and Chapter 13).

If messages do not arrive instantaneously, the inconsistency between the *Agent_View* and the system's state tends to grow. Furthermore, if messages do not arrive at the same time, the agents are more likely to respond to a single message, which tends to deteriorate the algorithm's performance. On systems with random delay which simulate real-world systems, the improvement that results from reading all incoming messages in each cycle is washed out completely. This was a major experimental result of [4, 19], but did not have a clear explanation there. The mechanism is more clearly understood in [72, 73].

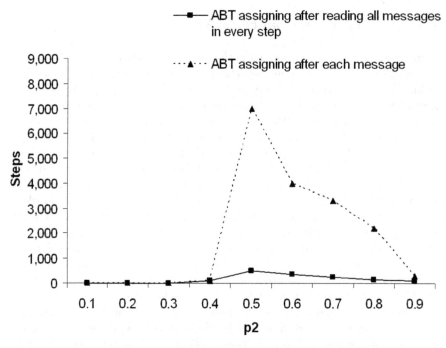

Fig. 5.9. Non-concurrent computation steps of ABT - reading complete mailboxes

The improvement to the performance of ABT by reading complete mailboxes, as presented in Figure 5.9, is quite impressive. The resulting version of ABT, which reads complete mailboxes at each step and that keeps a polynomial number of NOGOODs, is the best version. It is used routinely in all experimental studies that compare performance of DISCSP algorithms, in particular in all empirical results throughout the present book. As will be seen in Chapter 13, it slows down very strongly in the presence of delayed messages.

According to Yokoo, ABT eliminates the main drawback of Synchronous Backtrack (SBT) by allowing agents to assign their variables concurrently. During all stages of the algorithm's run, agents assign values to their variables, consistent with the current view that the agent holds on other agents' states. This property of ABT enhances the degree of concurrency of the algorithm but raises a major drawback. The *Agent_Views* may not be relevant. This can happen for two reasons:

1. Assignments of other agents may have changed and the notifying message has not been received yet.
2. The partial assignment held in the *Agent_View* may contain conflicting assignments and therefore it is not a partial solution.

As a result of the above phenomena, during the run of the ABT algorithm agents may waste computational effort, checking their assignments against irrelevant assignments of other agents. This is in turn followed by sending inconsistent assignments in messages that may create more inconsistent computation at other agents. This state of affairs is in contrast to the main motivation for the ABT algorithm: the wish to benefit from concurrency by having each agent maintain its own view of the current search state (its own *Agent_View*) and perform its computation based on that state. A major motivation for using an asynchronous algorithm is that no waiting or synchronization is needed. Agents are free to progress in the search at their own rate, hopefully maximizing parallelism while still assuring that the algorithm is both complete and sound. The tradeoff, it seems, comes at the expense of algorithmic difficulty.

Let us consider once again the main features of ABT. It performs a backtracking search process of all agents, *asynchronously*. This in turn means that agents perform both computations and assignments concurrently, as part of the same search process. The difficulty of concurrency of assignments in a backtracking search process arises intuitively from the fact that agents need to take into account the possibility that other agents see different search states. For example, an agent can report that some combination of assignments is a NOGOOD, and report this NOGOOD to another agent. The receiving agent, at the time of receiving, may find that this combination of assignments does not exist in its view of the search state. This agent is unable to know whether this is because its agent view is not yet updated (but may be updated soon), or that it is the sending agent's view that is obsolete. This was the deep reason for the keeping of all NOGOODs by the original version of the algorithm [63]. The great advantage of the formulation of Algorithm 5.2 is that it determines easily that such a NOGOOD does not need to be kept, while the correctness of the algorithm is kept intact [8, 9]. Therefore, it turned out that it is important to invest efforts in researching other forms of concurrency for DisCSP search algorithms. Either concurrent computation and *no concurrent assignments* by agents, as is done in the *Asynchronous Forward-Checking* algorithm in Chapter 6. Or concurrent search processes, in the *Concurrent Dynamic Backtracking* algorithm in Chapter 7.

6

Asynchronous Forward-Checking

Asynchronous Forward-Checking (AFC) is a family of distributed search algorithms on DisCSPs that utilizes concurrency differently than ABT. To avoid the problems that arise when agents process concurrent assignments by other agents, it maintains *a single and a synchronous set of assignments among all agents* at all times. Its concurrency of computation arises from processing forward-checking (FC) asynchronously (as it name clearly shows) [44]. In the AFC algorithm, the state of the search process is represented by a data structure called the *Current Partial Assignment (CPA)*. The CPA starts empty at some initializing agent that records its assignments on it and sends it to the next agent. Each receiving agent adds its assignment to the CPA, if a consistent assignment can be found. Otherwise, it backtracks by sending the same CPA to a former agent to revise its assignment on the CPA.

Each agent that performs an assignment on the CPA sends forward a copy of the updated CPA, requesting all agents to perform forward-checking. This is the mechanism for concurrently computing forward-checking. Agents that receive copies of assignments filter their domains and in case of a dead-end send back a *Not_OK* message. The concurrency of the AFC algorithm is achieved by the fact that forward-checking is performed concurrently by all agents. The protocol of the AFC algorithm enables agents to process forward-checking (FC) messages concurrently and yet block the assignment process at the agent that violates consistency with future variables. On hard instances of randomly generated DisCSPs with different message delays, AFC outperforms ABT by a large factor [44] (see Chapter 11).

An interesting improvement to AFC can be made. In addition to concurrency of checking forward, a concurrency of backtracking was introduced by [48]. When a backtrack is initiated by a *Not_OK* message, it is sent directly to the culprit agent. This triggers an additional search process, starting at the backtracking agent. An intuitive way to understand this improvement to AFC is to say that it adds concurrent backtracking processes to its asynchronous forward-checking. All the generated concurrent search processes, save one, are unsolvable (i.e., contain a NOGOOD that generated the backtrack message).

Consequently, the improved AFC algorithm terminates all of these search processes as soon as their unsolvability is validated (within a small number of steps).

The AFC algorithm combines the advantage of assigning values consistent with all former assignments and of propagating the assignments forward asynchronously. Assignments in AFC are performed by one agent at a time. The assigning agent keeps the partial assignment consistent. Each such assignment is checked by multiple agents concurrently. Although forward-checking is performed asynchronously, at most one backtrack operation is generated for a failure in a future variable.

Agents assign their variables only when they hold the current partial assignment (CPA). The CPA is a unique message that is passed between agents, and carries the partial assignment that agents attempt to extend into a complete solution by assigning their variables on it. In that sense one can think of the CPA as a unique token.

Forward-checking is performed as follows. Every agent that sends the CPA forward sends copies of the CPA, in messages we term *FC_CPA*, to all agents whose assignments are not yet on the CPA (except for the agent the CPA itself is sent to). Agents that receive *FC_CPA*s update their variables domains, removing all values that conflict with assignments on the *FC_CPA*. Asynchronous forward-checking enables agents an early detection of inconsistent partial assignments and initiates backtracks as early as possible. An agent that generates an empty domain as a result of a forward-checking operation, initiates a backtrack procedure by sending *Not_OK* messages which carry the inconsistent partial assignment which caused the empty domain.

A *Not_OK* message is sent to all agents with unassigned variables on the (inconsistent) *CPA*. An agent that receives the *CPA* and is holding a *Not_OK* message, sends the *CPA* back in a backtrack message. The uniqueness of the *CPA* ensures that only a single backtrack is initialized, even for multiple *Not_OK* messages. In other words, when multiple agents reject a given assignment by sending *Not_OK* messages, *only one agent that received any of those messages will eventually backtrack*. The first agent that will receive a *CPA* and is holding a relevant *Not_OK* message. The *Not_OK* message becomes obsolete when the partial assignment it carries is no longer a subset of the *CPA*. (Other options for initializing backtrack operations were suggested by [48]; see Section 6.3.)

The AFC algorithm is run on each of the agents in the DisCSP and uses the following objects and messages:

- *CPA (current partial assignment)*: a message that carries the currently valid (and consistent) partial assignment. A CPA is composed of triplets of the form $< A, X, V >$ where A is the agent that owns variable X and V is the value that was assigned to X by A. Each CPA contains a counter that is updated by each agent that assigns its variables on the CPA. This counter is used as a time stamp by the agents in the AFC algorithm and is termed the step-counter (SC). The partial assignment in a CPA is maintained in the order the assignments were made by the agents.

- *FC_CPA*: a message that is an exact copy of a CPA. Every agent that assigns its variables on a CPA, creates an exact copy in the form of an *FC_CPA* (with the same SC) and sends it forward to all unassigned agents.

- *Not_OK*: agents update their domains whenever they receive *FC_CPA* messages. When an agent encounters an empty domain, during this process, it sends a *Not_OK* message. The *Not_OK* message carries *the shortest inconsistent subset of assignments* from the *FC_CPA* and informs other agents that this partial assignment is inconsistent with the sending agent's domain.

- *AgentView*: each agent holds a list of assignments which are its updated view of the current assignment state of all other agents. The *AgentView* contains a consistency flag *AgentView.consistent*, that represents whether the partial assignment it holds is consistent. The *AgentView* contains a step-counter (SC) which holds the value of the highest SC received by the agent.

- *Backtrack*: An inconsistent CPA (i.e., a NOGOOD) sent to the agent with the most recent conflicting assignment.

6.1 *AFC* - Algorithm Description

The main function of the algorithm **AFC** is presented in Algorithm 6.1 and performs two tasks. If it is run by the initializing agent (IA), it initiates the search by generating a CPA (with SC = 0), and then calling function **assign_CPA** (line 2-4). All agents performing the main function wait for messages, and call the functions dealing with the relevant type of message received. The two functions dealing with receiving the CPA and assigning variables on it are also presented in Algorithm 6.1.

Function **receive_CPA** is called when the CPA is received either in a forward move or in a backtrack message. After storing the CPA, the agent checks its *AgentView* status. If it is not consistent and it is a subset of the received CPA, this means that a backtrack of the CPA has to be performed. If the inconsistent *AgentView* is not a subset of the received CPA, the CPA is stored as the updated *AgentView* and it is marked consistent. This reflects the fact that the received CPA has revised assignments that caused the original inconsistency. The rest of the function calls **assign_CPA**, to extend the current partial assignment. If the CPA is a backtrack, the last assignment is removed first (lines 8, 9). Otherwise, the *AgentView* is updated to the received CPA and its consistency with current domains is checked and updated. The assignment of variables of the agent currently holding the CPA is performed by the function **assign_CPA**.

Algorithm 6.1: AFC algorithm - receive and assign CPA

AFC:
1. done ← false
2. **if**(IA)
3.   CPA ← generate_CPA
4.   assign_CPA
5. **while**(**not** done)
6.   msg ← receive_msg
7.   **switch** msg.type
8.   stop: done ← true
9.   FC_CPA: forward_check
10.   Not_OK: process_Not_OK
11.   CPA: receive_CPA
12.   backtrack_CPA: receive_CPA

receive_ CPA:
1. CPA ← msg_CPA
2. **if**(**not** AgentView.consistent)
3.   **if**(contains(CPA, AgentView))
4.   backtrack
5.   **else**
6.   AgentView.consistent ← true
7. **if**(AgentView.consistent)
8.   **if**(msg.type = backtrack_CPA)
9.   remove_last_assignment
10.   assign_CPA
11.   **else**
12.   **if**(update_AgentView(CPA))
13.   assign_CPA
14.   **else**
15.   backtrack

assign_ CPA:
1. CPA ← *add_local_assignments*
2. **if**(is_assigned(CPA))
3.   **if**(is_full(CPA))
4.   report_solution
5.   stop
6.   **else**
7.   CPA.SC++
8.   send(CPA,next)
9.   send(FC_CPA,other_unassigned_agents)
10. **else**
11.   AgentView ← *shortest_inconsistent_partial_assignment*
12.   backtrack

Function **assign_ CPA** tries to find an assignment for the agent's local variables which is consistent with local constraints and does not conflict with previous assignments on the CPA. If the agent succeeds it sends forward the CPA or reports a solution, when the CPA includes all agents assignments (lines 2-5). If the agent fails to find a consistent assignment, it calls function **backtrack** after updating its *AgentView* with the inconsistent partial assignment, that was just discovered (lines 11-12). Whenever an agent sends forward a CPA (line 8), it sends a copy of it in a *FC_CPA* message to every other agent whose assignments are not yet on the CPA (line 9).

The rest of the AFC algorithm deals with backward-moving CPAs and with propagation of the current assignment. It is presented in Algorithm 6.2.

Function **backtrack** is called when the agent is holding the CPA in one of two cases. Either the agent cannot find a consistent assignment for its variables, or its *AgentView* is inconsistent and is found to be relevant with the received CPA. In case the agent is the IA the search ends unsuccessfully (lines 1-3). Other agents performing a backtrack operation copy to the CPA the shortest inconsistent partial assignment from their *AgentView* (line 6), and send it back to the agent which is the owner of the last variable in that partial assignment. The *AgentView* of the sending agent retains the NOGOOD that was sent back.

The next two functions in algorithm Algorithm 6.2 implement the asynchronous forward-checking mechanism. Two types of messages can be received by an agent, *FC_CPA* and *Not_OK* (lines 9, 10 of the main function in Algorithm 6.1).

Function **forward_ check** is called when an agent receives a *FC_CPA* message. Since an *FC_CPA* message is relevant only if the message is an update of partial assignments received in previous messages, the SC value is checked to test the message relevance (line 1). Older SCs represent partial assignments that have already been checked within the partial assignment of the current (larger) SC of the receiving agent. When the *AgentView* is inconsistent, the agent checks whether its *AgentView* is still relevant. If not, the *AgentView* becomes consistent (lines 2-4). In the case of a consistent *AgentView*, the agent updates its *AgentView* and current-domains by calling the function **update_ AgentView**. If this causes an empty domain, the agent sends *Not_OK* messages to all agents which are unassigned in the inconsistent partial assignment found and stored in the *AgentView* (lines 6-7).

Function **process_ Not_ OK** checks the relevance of the received inconsistent partial assignment, with the *AgentView*. If the *Not_OK* message is relevant, it replaces the *AgentView* by the content of the *Not_OK* message (lines 2-3).

Function **update_ AgentView**(*partial_assignment*) is called in the case of a CPA moving forward is received or a relevant *FC_CPA*. It sets the *AgentView* and current domains to be consistent with the received partial assignment. In the case of an empty domain, **update_ AgentView** returns

---

Algorithm 6.2: AFC algorithm - backtracking and forward-checking

---

backtrack:
1. if(IA)
2.   send(stop, all_other_agents)
3.   done ← true
4. **else**
5.   AgentView.consistent ← false
5.   backTo ← last(AgentView)
6.   CPA ← AgentView
7.   send(backtrack_CPA, backTo)

forward_check:
1. if(msg.SC > AgentView.SC)
2.   if(**not** AgentView.consistent)
3.   if(**not** contains(FC_CPA, AgentView))
4.   AgentView.consistent ← true
5.   if(AgentView.consistent)
6.   if (**not**(update_AgentView(FC_CPA)))
7.   send(Not_OK, unassigned_agents(AgentView))

process_Not_OK:
1. if(contains(AgentView, Not_OK))
2.   AgentView ← Not_OK
3.   AgentView.consistent ← false
4. **else if**(not-contains(Not_OK,AgentView))
5.   if(msg.SC > AgentView.SC)
6.   AgentView ← Not_OK
7.   AgentView.consistent ← false

update_AgentView(partial_assignment):
1. adjust_AgentView(partial_assignment)
2. if(empty_domain)
3.   AgentView ← *shortest_inconsistent_partial_assignment*
4.   **return** $false$
5. **return** $true$

---

false and sets the *AgentView* to hold the shortest inconsistent partial assignment.

Function **adjust_AgentView**(*partial_assignment*) changes the content of the *AgentView* to that of the received partial assignment. It also updates the current domains of the variables to be consistent with the *AgentView's* new content.

The protocol of the AFC algorithm is designed so that *only one backtrack operation* is triggered by any number of Not_OK messages. This can be seen from the pseudo-code of the algorithm, in Algorithm 6.1 and Algorithm 6.2 as follows:

- If a single agent discovers an empty domain, all Not_OK messages carry the same inconsistent partial assignment (NOGOOD) and each agent that receives such a Not_OK message has a consistent $AgentView$. In this case the CPA will finally reach an agent that holds an inconsistent $AgentView$, which is a subset of the set of assignments on the CPA. This CPA, at that step, will be sent back as a backtrack message.
- If two agents discover an empty domain as a result of receiving an identical FC_CPA and create Not_OK messages with identical inconsistent partial assignments. Other agents will receive two copies of the same Not_OK message. The second Not_OK message will be ignored since the NOGOOD it carries is the same as the one the receiving agent already holds. The rest of the processing will be the same as in the single empty domain case above.
- The general case is when two different agents send Not_OK messages that include two different inconsistent partial assignments. If one message is included in the other (i.e., a shorter NOGOOD), then the order of their arrival is irrelevant. If the shortest one arrives first, the long one is ignored. If the longer one arrives first the shorter one will replace it. If the two Not_OK messages include a different assignment to a common agent, then the receiving agent uses the SC on the messages to determine the more recent one and ignores the other.

At least one of the agents that must receive and process the CPA holds the NOGOOD (the creator of the NOGOOD itself). This ensures that the backtrack operation will take place.

6.2 Correctness of AFC

A central fact that can be established immediately is that agents send forward only consistent partial assignments. This fact can be seen in lines 1, 2 and 8 of procedure **assign_ CPA**. This implies that agents process, in procedures **receive_ CPA** and **assign_ CPA**, only consistent CPAs. Since the processing of CPAs in these procedures is the only means for extending partial assignments, the following lemma holds:

Lemma 6.2.1 *AFC extends only consistent partial assignments. The partial assignments are received via a CPA and are extended and sent forward by the receiving agent.*

The correctness of AFC includes soundness and completeness. The soundness of AFC follows immediately from the above lemma. The only lines of the algorithm that report a solution are lines 3, 4 of procedure **assign_ CPA**. A solution is reported when a CPA includes a complete and consistent assignment.

In order to prove the completeness and termination of AFC, one needs to make a few changes to function **assign_ CPA**, in order to avoid stopping after finding the first solution. Assume therefore that, instead of stopping after the first solution is found (line 5 of **assign_ CPA**), the agent simply records the solution, removes its assignment and recalls function **assign_ CPA**. The second needed change is to make the procedure of assigning values to variables concrete. This enables to prove the exhaustiveness of the assignments produced by AFC and to show termination. Assume that the function **add_ local_ assignments**, in line 1 of **assign_ CPA** scans all values of a variable in some predefined order, until it finds a consistent assignment for the agent's variable. For the rest of the completeness proof it is assumed with no loss of generality that each agent holds exactly one variable.

Backtrack steps of AFC remove a single value from the domain of the agent that receives the backtrack message. This is easy to see in lines 8-10 of function **receive_ CPA** in Algorithm 6.1. The only way that a value removed by a backtrack step from agent A_i can be reassigned is after the CPA is sent further back to some agent A_j ($j < i$) and returns. Since there are a finite number of values in all agents domains, the following lemma is established.

Lemma 6.2.2 *AFC performs a finite number of backtrack steps.*

The termination of AFC follows immediately. Any infinite loop of steps of AFC must include an infinite number of backtrack steps and this contradicts Lemma 6.2.2.

AFC can in principle avoid sending forward consistent partial assignments through the mechanism of Not_OK messages. An agent that fails to find a value that is consistent with a received FC_CPA message sends a Not_OK message. This message may stop a recipient from trying to extend a valid and consistent assignment on a CPA. However, every Not_OK message is generated by a failure of the function **update_ AgentView** (lines 6, 7 of function **forward_ check** in Algorithm 6.2). The failure corresponds to a CPA that has no consistent value in the agent that generates the Not_OK message. Thus, the rejected CPA (i.e. its partial assignment) cannot be part of a solution of the DisCSP. This observation is stated by the next lemma.

Lemma 6.2.3 *Consistent CPAs that are not sent forward for extension because of a Not_OK message, cannot be extended to a solution (i.e., they are* NOGOODs*).*

If AFC can be shown to process every consistent partial assignment (for a given order of agents/variables), this would establish the completeness of the algorithm. Completeness follows from this fact in analogy to the completeness proof for centralized backtracking in [31]. By Lemma 6.2.3, it is enough to prove completeness for the case where there are no Not_OK messages.

Assume by contradiction that there is a solution $S = (< A_1, V_1 >, < A_2, V_2 >, \ldots, < A_n, V_n >)$ that is not found by AFC. This means that some partial assignment of S is not sent forward by some agent. Let the longest partial assignment of S that is not sent forward be $S' = (< A_1, V_1 >, < A_2, V_2 >, \ldots, < A_k, V_k >)$ where $k < n$. S' is consistent, being a subset of S. There is at least one such partial assignment $(< A_1, V_1 >)$, performed by the first agent, because of its exhaustive scan of values. But, by lines 2, 8, 9 of function **assign_ CPA**, agent A_k sends the partial assignment S' to the next agent because it is consistent. This contradicts the assumption of maximality of S'. This completes the correctness proof of algorithm AFC, soundness, termination, and completeness.

6.3 Improved Backtrack Method for AFC

In [48], an elegant method for initializing the backtrack operation in AFC was proposed. Instead of sending Not_OK messages to all unassigned agents in the inconsistent partial assignment, the agent whose domain emptied and triggered a backtrack operation, sends a *Backtrack* message to the last agent assigned in the inconsistent partial assignment (e.g., a NOGOOD). All other agents receive a NOGOOD message which indicates that the former CPA is inconsistent. The receiver of the NOGOOD generates a new CPA and continues the search. The old CPA is detected as obsolete and discarded using the following method for time-stamping CPAs:

- The time stamp is an array of counters, a single counter for each agent.
- An agent increments its counter when it performs an assignment.
- When two CPAs are compared, the more up-to-date is the one whose time-stamp is larger lexicographically (i.e., the first different counter is larger).

Using this method agents which receive a Not_OK method that reveals the inconsistency of the former CPA and then receive the CPA itself simply terminate the old CPA. The only CPA which will not be terminated is the most updated according to the lexicographic time-stamp. The improvement in performance of AFC with this method is presented in detail in the Chapter 11. It turns out to be not very important, compared to the impact of ordering heuristics on AFC [44] (see Chapter 8).

Concurrent Dynamic Backtracking

A different way of achieving concurrency for search on DISCSPs, both from asynchronous backtracking and from asynchronous forward-checking, is to run multiple search processes concurrently. *Concurrent search* performs multiple concurrent backtrack search processes asynchronously on disjoint parts of the DISCSP search space. Each search space includes all variables and therefore involves all agents [25, 67, 70, 75]. One approach to concurrent search was proposed by Hamadi and Bessiere in the *interleaved parallel search algorithm* (IDIBT) [25]. IDIBT runs multiple processes of asynchronous backtracking and its multiplicity is fixed at the start of its run [24, 25]. The performance of IDIBT was found to deteriorate for more than two contexts (i.e., more than two concurrent ABT processes) [25].

Concurrent search is a family of algorithms which perform multiple concurrent backtrack search processes asynchronously on disjoint parts of the DISCSP search space. Each agent holds a set of data structures, one for each search process. These data structures, which we term *Search Processes* (SPs), include all the relevant data for the state of the agent on each of the search processes. Agents in concurrent search algorithms pass their assignments to other agents on a special type of message - a Current Partial Assignment (CPA). Each CPA represents a single search process, and holds the agents' current assignments in the corresponding search process. An agent that receives a CPA tries to assign its local variables with values that are not conflicting with the assignments already on the CPA, using only the current domains in the SP that is related to the received CPA. The uniqueness of the CPA for every search space ensures that assignments are not done concurrently (and conflictingly) in a single sub-search-space [69, 75].

An agent can generate a set of SPs and corresponding CPAs that split the search space of a single SP whose CPA has passed through that agent, by splitting the domain of one of its variables. Agents can perform splits independently and keep the resulting data structures (*SPs*) privately. All other agents need not be aware of the split; they process all CPAs in exactly the same manner (see Section 7.2 and Figures 7.8 and 7.9). CPAs are created either by the Initializing Agent (IA) at the beginning of the algorithm run, or dynamically by any agent that splits an active search space during the algorithm run. A simple heuristic of counting the number of times agents pass a given CPA (without finding a solution) is used to determine the need for resplitting of the search space traversed by that CPA. This generates a mechanism of load balancing, creating more search processes on heavily backtracked search spaces.

Figure 7.1 presents an example of a DisCSP, searched concurrently by two search processes represented by two CPAs - CPA_1 and CPA_2. Each of the four agents A_1 to A_4 holds two search processes (SPs). The domains of all four agents are the same - $\{1..4\}$. The current domains of the SPs are shown in Figure 7.1. The domains on the left represent the state after three assignments to CPA_1. The domains on the right-hand side of Figure 7.1 represent the state after the second assignment to CPA_2.

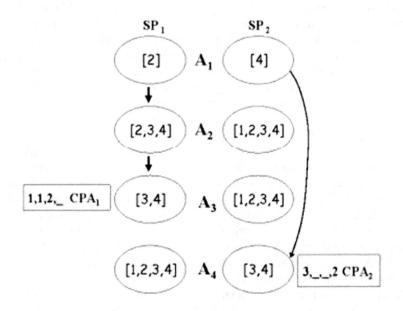

Fig. 7.1. Simple *Concurrent Search* with two CPAs

Agent A_1 has assigned the value 1 on CPA_1 and the value 3 on CPA_2. The values that are left in each of its domains are 2 in SP_1 and 4 in SP_2. Agent A_3 has assigned the value 2 to CPA_1, having failed to assign the value 1. This leaves its current domain, for SP_1, with the values [3,4]. The two CPAs are traversing non intersecting sub-search-spaces in which CPA_1 is exploring all tuples beginning with 1 or 2 for agent A_1, and CPA_2 all tuples beginning with 3 or 4. CPA_1 is depicted on the LHS of Figure 7.1 and CPA_2 is on the RHS. CPA_1 moves among the agents in the order $A_1 \rightarrow A_2 \rightarrow A_3$. CPA_2 moves in the order $A_1 \rightarrow A_4 \rightarrow ...$

A backtrack operation is performed by an agent which fails to find a consistent assignment with the partial assignment on the CPA that it is currently holding. A backtrack operation sends a CPA backwards, requesting the receiving agent to revise its assignment on the CPA. Agents that have performed dynamic splitting have to collect all of the returning CPAs of the relevant SP before declaring that a sub-search-space does not contain a solution. In this case all consistent values of the split domain have been sent forward on some CPA and failed, which means the agent must perform a backtrack operation.

The search ends unsuccessfully when all CPAs return for backtrack to the IA and the domain of the first variable of each CPA is empty. In this case all the search processes are stopped. The search ends successfully if *one CPA contains a complete assignment*, a value for every variable in the DISCSP.

There is no synchronization between the assignments performed in different SPs and the splitting of different CPAs. Due to the random choice of the next agent and the dynamic asynchronous splitting of search spaces, the steps of agents in different search process are interleaved in a non predefined order. This makes concurrent search algorithms asynchronous [37]. The concurrent backtracking (*ConcBT*) algorithm runs multiple backtrack search processes asynchronously. Search processes are initiated and stopped dynamically and this dynamicity was found to enhance the performance of both the original *ConcBT* [69] and the improved Concurrent Dynamic Backtracking (*ConcDB*) [75] algorithms to outperform all other DISCSP search algorithms.

The best version of concurrent search is concurrent dynamic backtracking (ConcDB), which performs dynamic backtracking [23] on each of its concurrent sub-search spaces [75] (see Section 7.3). Since search processes are dynamically generated by *ConcDB*, the performance of backjumping in one search space can indicate that other search spaces are unsolvable. This feature, combined with the random ordering of agents in each search process, enables early termination of search processes discovered by ConcDB to be unsolvable.

7.1 4-Queens with Concurrent Search

To see the difference of concurrent search from asynchronous backtracking, let us take the 4-queens example and run *ConcBT* on it (Figures 7.2 and 7.3). Three concurrent search prosses (SPs) are started by agent A_1. The three SPs are represented by a triangle, a diamond, and a circle. In the first cycle of computation, agent A_1 splits its domain into three parts and assigns values to the three SPs. These are values 1, 2, and 3. The three CPAs are sent forward to different agents. SP_1 (triangle) is sent to agent A_2, SP_2 (diamond) is sent to agent A_3, and SP_3 (circle) is sent to agent A_4. Each agent keeps a separate data structure for each SP and computes its assignments, upon receiving a CPA, separately. In the second cycle of computation, agents A_2, A_3, A_4 compute concurrently, each assigning a value to its variable on the CPA it is holding. Each assignment is consistent with all former assignments on the CPA. Agent A_2, for example, assigns the value 3 to CPA_1. Having performed their assignments, all agents send the CPAs to unassigned agents. A_2 sends CPA_1 to agent A_3, agent A_3 sends CPA_2 to agent A_4, and agent A_4 sends CPA_3 to agent A_2.

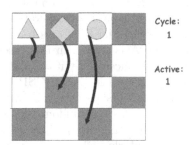

Fig. 7.2. First cycle of $ConcBT$ on 4-queens

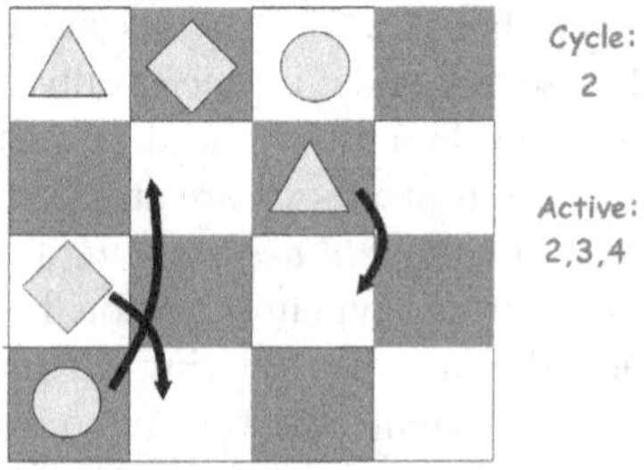

Fig. 7.3. Second cycle of $ConcBT$ on 4-queens

In cycle 3 again agents A_2, A_3, A_4 are active. Agent A_4 performs a compatible assignment on CPA_2 and sends it further. It sends it to the only unassigned agent of CPA_2 (diamond), agent A_2. Agent A_2 cannot find a compatible assignment to its variable on CPA_3 (circle). As a result, it sends CPA_3 in a backtrack step to agent A_4. Similarly, agent A_3 cannot assign its variable CPA_1 (triangle) and sends CPA_1 in a backtrack message to its predecessor, agent A_2. Cycle 3 is shown in Figure 7.4.

It is easy to follow the next steps of computation. Agents A_2 and A_4 adjust their positions (values) in cycle 4, to be compatible with the backtrack messages they received. In cycle 5 agent A_2 receives two messages. One is from agent A_4 that sent it CPA_3 (circle), having revised its assignment from value 1 to value 2. The other message contains CPA_2 (diamond) with agent A_4's assignment. For clarity of presentation agent A_2 performs the assignments on these two CPAs in two separate cycles of computation. In cycle 5 it assigns CPA_3 with the value 1. CPA_3 is then sent to the only unassigned agent on it - A_3 (the arrow in Figure 7.5). In cycle 6 it assigns CPA_2 with the value 4, thus completing a solution. It is important to note that at the same cycle agent A_3 completes another solution concurrently; that of CPA_3 (circle), as can be seen in Figure 7.6.

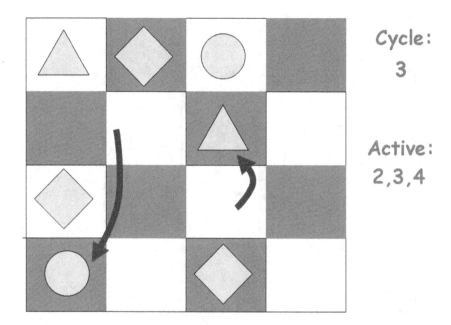

Fig. 7.4. Cycle 3 of *ConcBT* on 4-queens

7.2 The *ConcBT* Algorithm

Concurrent backtracking (*ConcBT*) is the common part to several concurrent search algorithms. Its best extension, the *Concurrent Dynamic Backtracking (ConcDB)* algorithm, will be described in detail in Section 7.3. The main data structure that is used and passed between the agents in concurrent search is a *current partial assignment (CPA)*. A CPA contains an ordered list of triplets $< A_i, X_j, val >$, where A_i is the agent that owns the variable X_j and val is a value, from the domain of X_j, assigned to X_j. This list of triplets starts empty, with the agent that initializes the search process, and includes more assignments as it is passed among the agents. Each agent adds to a CPA that passes through it, a set of assignments to its local variables that is consistent with all former assignments on the CPA. If successful, it passes the CPA to the next agent. If not, it *backtracks*, by sending the CPA to the agent from which it was received.

Every agent that receives a CPA for the first time creates a local data structure which we call a *search process (SP)*. This is true also for the initializing agent (IA), for each created CPA. The SP holds all data on current domains for the variables of the agent, such as the remaining and removed values during the path of the CPA.

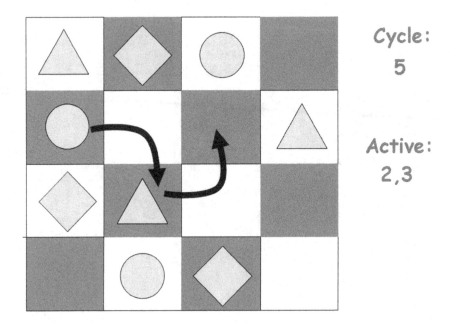

Fig. 7.5. Cycle 5 of *ConcBT* on 4-queens

The structure of the ID of a CPA and its corresponding SP is a pair $< A, j >$, where A is the ID of the agent that created the CPA and j is the number of CPAs this agent created so far. This enables all agents to create CPAs with a unique ID. When a split is performed during search, the generated CPA has a unique ID and carries the ID of the CPA from which it was split.

Although any agent can split its domain, the current version of the algorithm splits search spaces as high as possible in the search tree. This generates split sub-search-spaces that are as large as possible and a larger number of agents participate in the divided search procedure. When agents have no further opportunity to split an SP because of lack of values in their current domain, split messages are transferred down the search tree to agents lower in the current order of the search (see Algorithm 7.2, procedure **per-form_split**, lines 2, 8 and 9). Note that different concurrent search processes are ordered differently. Therefore, the splitting of the search space occurs at different agents in different concurrent SPs.

Splitting the search space on some variable divides the values in the domain of this variable into several groups. Each subdomain defines a unique sub-search-space and a unique CPA traverses this search space. Dynamic splitting

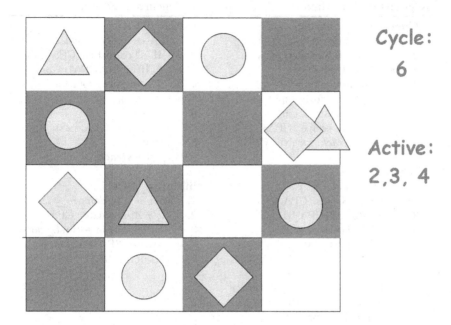

Fig. 7.6. Cycle 6 of *ConcBT* on 4-queens

is triggered by the number of assignment steps performed on a CPA, without returning back to its initiator. This is an intuitive meaning of thrashing and can be based on a simple threshold for the number of unsuccessful assignments - *steps_limit*.

The following terminology is used in the description of all concurrent search algorithms:

- *CPA_generator*: every CPA carries the *ID* of the agent that created it.
- *origin_SP*: an agent that performs a dynamic split holds in each of the new SPs the ID of the SP it was split from (i.e., of *origin_SP*). An analogous definition holds for *origin_CPA*. The *origin_SP* of an SP that was not created in a dynamic split operation is its own ID.
- *split_set*: the set of SP IDs, that are stored in an *origin_SP*. Every *origin_SP* holds in its *split_set* the IDs of all the SPs for which it is their *origin* (i.e., all SPs which were split from it by the agent holding it). For every active SP, the only *split_set* relevant is the *split_set* of its *origin_SP*.
- *steps_limit*: the number of steps (from one agent to the next) that will trigger a split, if the CPA does not find a solution or does not return to its generator.

Algorithm 7.1: Main and Assign parts of Concurrent Search

Concurrent_Search:
1. done ← false
2. **if**(IA) **then** initialize_SPs
3. **while**(**not** done)
4.   **switch** msg.type
5.   *split*: perform_split
6.   *stop*: done ← true
7.   *CPA*: receive_CPA
8.   *backtrack*: receive_CPA

receive_CPA:
1. CPA ← *msg.CPA*
2. **if**(first_received(CPA.ID))
3.   create_SP(CPA.ID)
4. **if**(CPA.generator = ID)
5.   CPA.steps ← 0
6. **else**
7.   CPA.steps ++
8.   **if**(CPA.steps = *steps_limit*)
9.   splitter ← *select_assigned_agent*
10.   *CPA_steps* ← 0
11.   send(*split_msg splitter*)
12. **if**(msg.type = *backtrack*)
13.   remove_last_assignment
14. *assign_CPA*

assign_CPA:
1. CPA ← assign_local
2. **if**(is_consistent(CPA))
3.   **if**(is_full(CPA))
4.   *report_solution*
5.   stop
6.   **else**
7.   send(CPA, next_agent)
8. **else**
9.   *backtrack*

initialize_SPs:
1. **for** i ← 1 to *domain_size*
2.   *CPA* ← create_CPA(i)
3.   SP[i].domain ← first_var[value_i]
4.   create_SP(CPA.ID)
5.   *assign_CPA*

1

The messages exchanged by agents in concurrent search are the following:

- **CPA** - the message carrying a *Current Partial Assignment*.
- **backtrack_msg** - a CPA sent in a backtrack operation.
- **stop** - a message indicating the end of the search.
- **split** - a message that is sent in order to trigger a split operation. Contains the ID of the SP to be split.

Algorithm 7.1 and Algorithm 7.2 present the functions which are performed in any type of concurrent search algorithm. The main function of the algorithm and functions that perform assignments on the CPA when it moves forward are presented in Algorithm 7.3.

- The main function **Concurrent_Search** is run by all agents. If it is run by the *initializing agent (IA)*, it initializes the search by creating multiple SPs, assigning each SP with one of the first variable's values. After initialization, it loops forever, waiting for messages to arrive.
- **receive_CPA** first checks if the agent holds an SP with the ID of the *current_CPA* and, if not, creates a new SP. If the CPA is received by its

---

Algorithm 7.2: Backtrack and Split procedures for concurrent search

---

backtrack:
1. delete(CPA.ID from *origin_SP.split_set*)
2. **if**(*origin_SP.split_set* is_empty)
3.   **if**(IA)
4.   CPA ← no_solution
5.   **if**(no_active_CPAs)
6.   report_no_solution
7.   stop
8.   **else**
9.   send(*backtrack, last_assignee*)
10. **else**
11.   *mark_fail*(CPA)

perform_split:
1. **if(not_backtracked(***CPA***))**
2.   var ← *select_split_var*
3.   **if**(var ≠ null)
4.   create_split_SP(var)
5.   create_split_CPA(SP.ID)
6.   add(CPA.ID to *origin_SP.split_set*)
7.   *assign_CPA*
8.   **else**
9.   send(*split, next_agent*)

stop:
1. send(*stop, all_other_agents*)
2. done ← true

---

generator, it changes the value of the steps counter (*CPA_steps*) to zero. This prevents unnecessary splitting. Otherwise, it checks whether the CPA has reached the *steps_limit* and a split must be initialized (lines 7-9). The splitting agent, which we term *splitter*, is selected to be any one of the assigned agents (line 9). A specific heuristic for splitting is to send the split message to the *CPA_generator* (as defined above the *CPA_generator* is the first part of any *CPA_ID*). This is equivalent to splitting the search tree as high as possible. Before assigning the CPA a check is made of whether the CPA was received in a *backtrack_msg*. If so, the previous assignment of the agent, which is the last assignment made on the CPA, is removed before *assign_CPA* is called (lines 12-13).

• **assign_CPA** tries to find an assignment for the local variables of the agent which is consistent with the assignments on the CPA. If it succeeds, the agent sends the CPA to the selected *next_agent* (line 7). If not, it calls the *backtrack* method (line 9).

The rest of the functions of concurrent search are presented in Algorithm 7.2.

- The **backtrack** method is called when a consistent assignment cannot be found in a SP. Since a split might have been performed by the current agent, a check is made of whether all the CPAs in the *split_set* of the *origin_CPA* of the backtracking CPA have also failed (line 2). If not, then only the current CPA is marked (line 11) and no further action need take place. When all split CPAs have returned unsuccessfully, the search space of the SP is unsolvable and a backtrack operation is initialized.

  In the case of an IA, the SP and the corresponding *origin_CPA* are marked as a failure (lines 3-4). If all other CPAs are marked as failures, the search is ended unsuccessfully (line 6). If the current agent is not the IA, a backtrack message is sent to the agent whose assignment is the latest of the assignments included in the inconsistent CPA (line 9).

- The **perform_split** method tries to find in the SP specified in the *split_message*, a variable with a non-empty *current_domain*. It first checks that the CPA to be split has not been sent back already, in a backtrack message (line 1). If it does not find a variable for splitting, it sends a **split_message** to *next_agent* (lines 8-9). If it finds a variable to split, it creates a new SP and CPA, and calls *assign_CPA* to initialize the new search (lines 3-5). The ID of the generated CPA is added to the split set of the divided SPs *origin_SP* (line 6).

Figure 7.7 extends the example presented in Figure 7.1. For each SP (except for the ones holding the corresponding CPA), the content of the *origin* and the *split-set* are displayed. The *origin* of all SPs except for the SPs of agent A_1 are their own IDs since they were not created in a dynamic split operation. Their *split-set* includes only their own ID, since they are not yet an origin of any SP created by a dynamic split operation. In this example the SP $< 1, 2 >$ held by agents A_2 and A_3 will only be created when they will first receive the corresponding CPA. The *origin* of SP $< 1, 2 >$ is the SP it was split from, which is $< 1, 1 >$. The split set of SP $< 1, 2 >$ is empty since the relevant *split-set* is only its *origin_SP*'s *split-set*. The *split-set* of SP $< 1, 1 >$, includes its own ID and the ID of the SP that was split from it, which is $< 1, 2 >$

7.2.1 A splitting of search space example

To visualize the main feature of concurrent search, the dynamic splitting of search spaces, consider the constraint network that is described in Figure 7.8 (taken from [75]). All three agents own one variable each, and the initial domains of all variables contain four values $\{1..4\}$. The constraints connecting the three agents are: $X_1 < X_2$, $X_1 > X_3$, and $X_2 < X_3$. The initial state

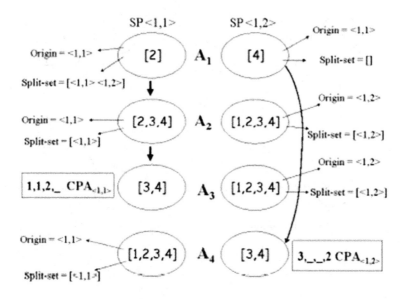

Fig. 7.7. Concurrent search with two CPAs - contents of data structures

of the network is described on the LHS of Figure 7.8. In order to keep the example small, no initial split is performed, only dynamic splitting. The value of *steps_limit* in this example is 4. The first five steps of the algorithm run produce the state that is depicted on the RHS of Figure 7.8. The circled values in the current domains of agents X_1 and X_2 are the assigned values on the CPA. The current domain of X_2 had only two values left, [3, 4]. X_3 is now holding the CPA and has no assignment that is consistent with it.

The run of the algorithm during these five steps is as follows:

1. X_1 assigns its variable the value 1, and sends to X_2 a CPA with a step counter $CPA\_steps = 1$.
2. X_2 assigns its variable the value 2, and sends the CPA with both assignments, and with $CPA\_steps = 2$, to X_3.
3. X_3 cannot find any assignment consistent with the assignments on the CPA. It passes the CPA back to X_2 to reassign its variable, with $CPA\_steps = 3$.
4. X_2 reassigns its variable with the value 3, and sends the CPA again to X_3 after raising the step counter to 4.
5. X_3 receives the CPA with X_2's new assignment.

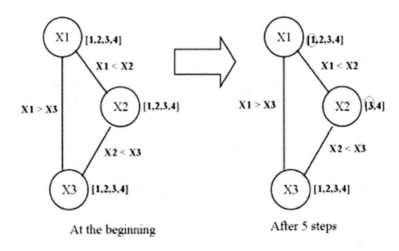

Fig. 7.8. Initial state and the state after the CPA travels five steps without returning to its initializing agent

In the current step of the algorithm, agent X_3 receives a CPA which has reached the *step_limit*. It has to generate a split operation. Before trying to find an assignment for its variable, X_3 sends a split message to X_1 which is the CPAs generator and changes the value of the *CPA_steps* counter to 0. Next, it sends the CPA to X_2 in a backtrack message. The algorithm run proceeds as follows:

- When X_1 receives the split message it performs the following operations:
  - Creates a new (empty domain) SP data structure.
  - Deletes values 3 and 4 from its original domain and inserts them into the domain of the new split SP.
  - Creates a new CPA and assigns it 3 (a value from the new domain).
  - Sends the new CPA to a randomly selected agent.
- Other agents that receive the new CPA create new SPs with a copy of their initial domain.

The resulting split search spaces are depicted in Figure 7.9. Circled values represent those that are currently assigned on the corresponding CPA_1 or CPA_2. After the split, two CPAs are passed among the agents. The two CPAs perform search on two non intersecting search-spaces. In the original SP *after the split*, X_1 can assign only values 1 or 2 (see LHS of Figure 7.9).

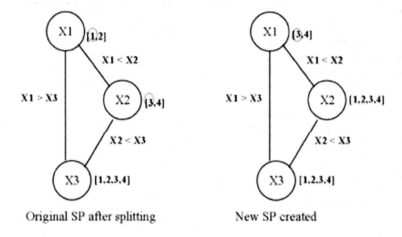

Fig. 7.9. Non-intersecting search spaces - two different CPAs

The search on the original SP is continued from the same state it was in before the split. Agents X_2 and X_3 continue the search using their current domains to assign the original CPA. Therefore, the current domain of X_2 (on SP_1) does not contain values 1 and 2 which were eliminated in earlier steps. In the newly generated search space, X_1 has the values $[3, 4]$ in its domain. Agent X_1 assigns 3 to its variable and the other agents that receive CPA_2 check the new assignment against their full domains (RHS of Figure 7.9).

7.3 Concurrent Dynamic Backtracking

The method of backjumping that is used in the $ConcDB$ algorithm is based on *Dynamic Backtracking* [23]. Each agent that removes a value from its current domain stores the partial assignment that caused the removal of the value. This stored partial assignment is called an *eliminating explanation* by [23]. When the current domain of an agent empties, the agent constructs a back-track message from the union of all assignments in its stored removal explanations. The union of all removal explanations is an inconsistent partial assignment, or a NOGOOD [23, 61]. The backtrack message is sent to the agent which is the owner of the most recently assigned variable in the inconsistent partial assignment.

Algorithm 7.3: Main methods for *ConcDB*

ConcDB:
1. done ← false
2. **if**(IA) **then** *initialize_SPs*
3. **while**(**not** done)
4.   **switch** msg.type
5.   *split*: perform_split
6.   *stop*: done ← true
7.   *CPA*: receive_CPA
8.   *backtrack*: receive_CPA
9.   *unsolvable*: mark_unsolvable(msg.SP)

receive_CPA:
1. CPA ← *msg.CPA*
2. **if**(unsolvable SP)
3.   terminate CPA
4. **else**
5.   **if**(first_received(CPA_ID))
6.   create_SP(CPA_ID)
7.   **if**(*CPA_generator* = ID)
8.   CPA_steps ← 0
9.   **else**
10.   CPA.steps ++
11.   **if**(*CPA_steps* = *steps_limit*)
12.   *splitter* ← *CPA_generator*
13.   send(*split_msg, splitter*)
14.   **if**(msg.type = *backtrack*)
15.   check_SPs(CPA.inconsistent_assignment)
16.   last_sent_CPA.*remove_last_assignment*
17.   *CPA* ← *last_sent_CPA*
18.   **if**(*sp*.split_ahead)
19.   send(unsolvable, *sp*.next_agent)
20.   *sp*.rename_SP
21. *assign_CPA*

In concurrent dynamic backtracking, a short NOGOOD can rule out multiple sub-search-spaces, all of which contain no solution and are thus unsolvable. In order to terminate the corresponding search processes, an agent that receives a backtrack message performs the following procedure:

- Detect the SP to which the received (backtrack) CPA either belongs or was split from.
- Check if the CPA corresponding to the detected SP was split down its path.
- If it was:

Algorithm 7.4: Dynamic backtracking of *ConcDB*

---

backtrack:
1. delete(current_CPA from *origin_split_set*)
2. **if**(*origin_split_set* is_empty)
3.   **if**(IA)
4.   CPA ← no_solution
5.   **if**(no_active_CPAs)
6.   report_no_solution
7.   stop
8.   **else**
9.   *backtrack_msg* ←
         inconsistent_assignment
10.   send(*backtrack_msg*,
         lowest_priority_assignee)
11. **else**
12. *mark_fail(current_CPA)*

mark_unsolvable(SP)
1. mark SP unsolvable
2. send(unsolvable, SP.next_agent)
3. **for each** split_SP in SP.origin.split_set
4.   mark split_SP unsolvable
5.   send(unsolvable, split_SP.next_agent)

check_SPs(inconsistent_assignment)
1. **for each** *sp* in {*SPs* \ *current_SP*}
2.   **if**(*sp*.contains(inconsistent_assignment))
3.   send(unsolvable, *sp*.next_agent)
4.   last_sent_CPA.*remove_last_assignment*
5.   *CPA* ← last_sent_CPA
6.   *sp*.rename_SP
7.   *assign_CPA*

- Send an *unsolvable* message to the *next_agent* of the related SP, thus generating a series of messages along the former path of the CPA.
- choose a new unique ID for the CPA received and its related SP.
- continue the search using the SP and CPA with the new ID.
• Check if there are other SPs which contain the inconsistent partial assignment received (by calling function **check_SPs**), send corresponding *unsolvable* messages and resume the search on them with new generated CPAs.

The change of ID makes the resumed search process independent of the process of terminating unsolvable search spaces. If the agents would have resumed the search using the ID of the original SP or of the received CPA, a race condition would arise since there is no synchronization between the process of terminating unsolvable search procedures to that of the resumed valid search procedure. In such a case, an agent that received an *unsolvable message* might have marked an active search space as unsolvable.

The *unsolvable* message used by the *ConcDB* algorithm, is a message not used in general concurrent search (e.g., *ConcBT*). It indicates an unsolvable sub-search-space. An agent that receives an *unsolvable* message performs the following operations for the unsolvable SP and each of the SPs split from it:

- mark the SP as unsolvable.
- send an *unsolvable* message which carries the ID of the SP to the agent to whom the related CPA was last sent.

Algorithm 7.3 and Algorithm 7.4 present the methods **ConcDB**, **receive_ CPA**, and **backtrack**, that were changed from the general description of concurrent search in Algorithm 7.1 and Algorithm 7.2. Algorithm 7.4 contains also two additional methods needed for adding Dynamic Backtracking to concurrent search.

In method *receive_CPA* a check is made in lines 2, 3 whether the SP related to the received CPA is marked unsolvable. In such a case the CPA is not assigned and the related SP is terminated. If the *split_limit* is reached the *split* message is sent to the generator of the CPA to create the split as high as possible in the search tree (lines 11-13). This is a specific heuristic for *select_assigned_agent* of the general *receive_CPA* in Algorithm 7.1 (line 9). For a backtracking CPA (lines 14-20) a check is made whether there are other SPs which can be declared unsolvable. This can happen when the head (or prefix) of their partial assignment (their *common head, CH*) contains the received inconsistent partial assignment. Procedure **check_ SPs** for every such SP found, initiates the termination of the search process on the unsolvable sub-search-space and resumes the search with a newly generated CPA. Next, a check is made of whether the SP was split by agents who received the CPA after this agent (line 18) (this fact can be recorded on the CPA when its holder initiates the split). If so, the termination of the unsolvable SP is initiated by sending an *unsolvable* message. A new ID is assigned to the received CPA and to its related SP (line 20).

The inconsistent partial assignment received in the *backtrack* message may rule out more than one active search process. The check performed by the function **check_ SPs** triggers the termination of these inconsistent search processes. For each of the terminated SPs a new CPA is created and the search process is resumed after the culprit assignment is revised.

In method **backtrack**, the agent inserts the culprit inconsistent partial assignment into the backtrack message (line 9) before sending it back in line 10. This is the only difference from the standard backtrack method in Algorithm 7.2.

As described above, method **mark_ unsolvable** is part of the mechanism for terminating SPs on unsolvable search spaces. The agent marks the SP related to the message received, and any SP split from it, as unsolvable and sends unsolvable messages to the agents to whom the corresponding CPAs were sent.

7.4 Correctness of Concurrent Search

To prove the correctness of a search algorithm for DISCSPs one needs to prove that it is sound, complete, and that it terminates. A central fact that can be established immediately is that agents send forward only consistent partial assignments. This fact can be seen at lines 1, 2 and 7 of procedure **assign_CPA** in Algorithm 7.1. This implies that agents process, in procedure **assign_CPA**, only consistent CPAs. Since the processing of CPAs in this procedure is the only means for extending partial assignments, the following lemma holds:

Lemma 7.4.1 Concurrent search *extends only consistent partial assignments. The partial assignments are received via a* CPA, *extended and sent forward by the receiving agent.*

The following theorem derives immediately from Lemma 7.4.1.

Theorem 7.4.2 Concurrent search *is sound.*

The only lines of the algorithm that report a solution are lines 3, 4 of procedure **assign_CPA**. These lines follow a consistent extension of the partial assignment on a received CPA. It follows that a solution is reported *iff* a CPA includes a complete and consistent assignment.   □

To prove completeness for concurrent search, one needs first to eliminate the stopping condition for the first solution (lines 3-5 of function **assign_CPA** in Algorithm 7.1). Another important point is the exact manner in which domains of values of variables are scanned for the next consistent assignment. Values for assignment are selected only in line 1 of the function **assign_CPA**. For the completeness proof one naturally assumes that the function *assign_local*, that is run by every agent, scans all values of the current domain exactly once. This is equivalent to the common assumption in all exhaustive backtracking algorithms that all values are tried until a consistent assignment is found (cf. [31]).

With the above assumptions, the completeness of concurrent search is established in three steps. First, for the case of a single CPA. Then, for several CPAs generated by the IA. Finally, for dynamic generation of CPAs during search. The following lemma establishes the completeness of the *1-CPA* case.

Lemma 7.4.3 *Concurrent search sends forward in a* CPA **every** *consistent partial assignment.*

To prove Lemma 7.4.3, one proceeds in analogy to the proof of completeness for centralized backtrack by Kondrak and van Beek [31]. With no loss of generality assume that every agent holds one variable. Assume that there is some consistent assignment $(X_1, X_2, \ldots X_k)$ of length k that is not received by any agent. Take the highest $j < k$, such that assignment $(X_1, X_2, \ldots X_{j-1})$ is sent forward (by agent $j - 1$) on a CPA that is received by agent j, there is at least one, sent by the initializing agent. Agent j, has a consistent assignment $(X_1, X_2, \ldots X_j)$ that extends $(X_1, X_2, \ldots X_{j-1})$, being a subtuple of $(X_1, X_2, \ldots X_k)$. When agent j extends the received CPA, it succeeds in a consistent partial assignment $(X_1, X_2, \ldots X_j)$ and sends it forward. This can be seen clearly in lines 1, 2, 7 of function *assign_ CPA* in Algorithm 7.1. This contradicts the above assumption on the maximality of the assignment $(X_1, X_2, \ldots X_{j-1})$ that is sent forward.   □

To complete the correctness proof one also needs to show that concurrent search terminates. The messages of concurrent search carry CPAs and move either forward or backward. The number of backward moves is finite, since each backward move deletes a value from the domain of the receiving agent (lines 10-11 of function *receive_ CPA* in Algorithm 7.1). To prove termination one needs to show that there can only be a finite number of forward moves (i.e., carrying CPAs). Every agent keeps its current domain in the SP structure and scans its values exactly once for every different partial assignment received on a CPA. Every move forward carries a consistent partial assignment (by Lemma 7.4.3). There is a finite number of different consistent partial assignments, hence a finite number of forward moves in concurrent search. Theorem 7.4.4 follows immediately.

Theorem 7.4.4 *The 1-CPA version of concurrent search is complete and terminates.*

Having shown the correctness of concurrent search for a single CPA, one needs to show correctness for the more general case of multiple CPAs generated at the algorithm start.

Theorem 7.4.5 *A version of concurrent search which includes a single split into* **k** *search processes at the beginning of the search is complete and terminates.*

Consider a CPA, C_i, that corresponds to a partial domain of one variable of the initializing agent and is passed through the network of all agents. Each agent A_j it passes through generates a data structure SP_i with all domains of its local variables (lines 2, 3 of procedure *receive_ CPA*). The only difference between the data structures corresponding to C_i and those that are generated for a 1-CPA version of concurrent search is in the structure SP_i of the initializing agent. In every other agent, the data structure SP_i and the code it runs are exactly equal to those run for concurrent search with one CPA. For agents different than the IA, the search procedure of C_i scans exactly the same subspace that is scanned for the 1-CPA version of concurrent search. Consequently, the search procedure corresponding to C_i is correct.

The union of all domain values of the selected variable for a split (in the IA) is exactly equal to the original domain of values of that variable. As shown above, the search sub-trees spanned by all agents that are not the IA, are equal to those spanned for the 1-CPA algorithm. Each of those equal search subspaces is scanned completely and correctly and all these scans terminate and are performed for every value of the variable of the IA that was selected for the split operation. Consequently, the union of the sub-trees that corresponds to each of the CPAs is exactly equal to the search tree that is spanned by the one-CPA version of concurrent search.   □

The final step in the correctness proof of concurrent search is to show that a dynamic split operation does not interfere with the correctness of the algorithm.

Theorem 7.4.6 Concurrent Search *with dynamic splitting is complete and terminates.*

Consider agent A_i which is not the initializing agent, that receives a *split_msg* and runs the procedure ***perform_ split***. It sends forward one or more consistent CPAs that represent non intersecting sub-search-spaces. The completeness and termination of the search on each of these sub-search-spaces follows from the completeness of the search initialized by any CPA of an initializing agent. Agent A_i will declare *no solution* by sending a backtrack message, only after all of its split-SPs failed (lines 1, 2 of procedure ***backtrack***). In other words, backtracking from multiple CPAs preserves completeness at the splitting agent. The condition to receive failure messages for all values for which a CPA was generated ensures that backtrack corresponds exactly to the case where there is no solution in the scanned search space. The sum of the number of tuples explored in the split search space is equal to the number of tuples in the original search space and therefore the algorithm termination is not affected by the split.   □

For the completeness of $ConcDB$ one needs to show also that the additional mechanism for terminating unsolvable search processes on unsolvable sub-search-spaces does not terminate a search process which explores a sub-search-space that includes a solution. To do so we continue as follows. In every sub-search-space, all tuples of assignments share the head (or prefix) of the assignment. Thus for every sub-search-space we define:

Definition 7.1. *A common head (CH) is the maximal prefix of assignments which is included in all partial assignments in a sub-search-space.*

Lemma 7.4.7 *A sub-search-space whose CH includes an inconsistent subset of assignments does not include a solution to the DisCSP.*

The proof of Lemma 7.4.7 derives from the method of constructing an inconsistent assignment in dynamic backtracking [23]. A partial assignment is declared inconsistent only if it causes an empty domain in one of the variables. This implies that this partial assignment cannot be part of a solution. From definition 7.1 we derive that if a CH includes an inconsistent partial assignment, it must be included in all the assignments in its related sub-search-space, which means that none of these assignments is a solution to the DisCSP. □

Theorem 7.4.8 *ConcDB does not terminate search-processes which lead to a solution.*

ConcDB terminates a search process by sending forward unsolvable messages (line 19 in function **receive_ CPA**, line 5 in function *mark_unsolvable*, line 3 in function **check_ SPs**). Only SPs that have a CH that is an extension of the CH that was found inconsistent are marked unsolvable. The search on these SPs is terminated when the agent receives the CPA corresponding to the unsolvable SP (lines 2, 3 of function **assign_ CPA**). Lemma 7.4.7 implies the proof for Theorem 7.4.8. It is immediately clear from Theorem 7.4.8 that all partial assignments that lead to a solution will be extended, which implies the completeness of *ConcDB*.   □

8

Distributed Ordering Heuristics

Ordering heuristics, for both variables and values, play an important role in centralized CSP search [14]. Orders of variables can be either static or dynamic. If variables are ordered before the start of the run of the search algorithm and the order is not changed during the run of the algorithm, it is called *static*. Such a heuristic does not take into consideration changes in the relations among variables that occur during search. A typical example of a static ordering heuristic is to use the features of the constraints graph. A popular example is to select variables with a high degree to be higher in the order [15]. A higher degree means that the variable is constrained by a larger number of variables. A common search heuristic is to try earlier branches on the search tree that have a higher chance to fail. Variables that are constrained by a larger number of other variables seem more likely to fail, so they are selected to be higher in the static order that is based on the constraint graph. This general approach, of trying earlier variables that have a higher chance to fail, is called the *fail-first* principle (cf. [16]). It is considered to lead to a more effective pruning since it potentially prunes (fails) nodes earlier.

Since the early 1990s researchers in standard (centralized) CSPs have found that *dynamic ordering heuristics* are far more successful than static heuristics. The standard use of dynamic ordering is to select the *next variable* to be assigned. The idea is that during search many parameters of the variables change dynamically. If search takes the form of assigning values to variables one after the other, a natural place to insert the ordering heuristics is to pause for computation immediately after the assignment of some variable. Based on the results of the computation, the next variable to be assigned is selected. A very simple and very successful general heuristic is to select the variable with the smallest domain size among the unassigned variables. A small domain size seems intuitively to represent a faster way to fail (smaller number of trial assignments), so it conforms with the above principle of *Fail First (FF)*. In fact, the FF principle is nowadays used synonymously with selecting the smallest domain.

The use of ordering heuristics in distributed search is a much more complex problem. The best known algorithm - asynchronous backtracking (ABT) - uses static ordering of agents, simply by the agents' IDs [64]. As we have seen, the static order of agents is essential for the proof of correctness of ABT (see Chapter 5).

There are two main points that need consideration for ordering a distributed search algorithm:

- Agents in a DISCSP do not know the parameters of other agents during search and therefore miss information that is needed in order to make ordering decisions.
- When the search algorithm is asynchronous the meaning of ordering of assignments is not clear. Would a heuristic change anything? What should be the rational?

The first point raises the need to accumulate knowledge about the state of other agents during search. As we will show in the sections below, this can be addressed by either additional computation or by additional information that is sent by messages. The second point raises a very complex issue. When the DISCSP search algorithm is either completely synchronous or performs assignments sequentially, the intuitive meaning of ordering is still analogous to that of centralized CSPs. A consistent partial assignment exists and a *next_agent* has to be selected for assignment. This selection process, though distributed, is similar to the centralized process. As we will see in the following two sections, the main difference from standard CSPs is the means of processing the distributed information about states of agents. The heuristics themselves are very similar to standard ones (e.g., Min-Domain).

For asynchronous backtracking, the situation is completely different. The ABT algorithm uses strictly static ordering, that is essential for its correctness proof [9]. A pioneering attempt to introduce dynamic ordering into asynchronous backtracking, was proposed by Yokoo as early as 1995. The idea was to implement a specific ordering, in which a failing (e.g., backtracking) agent was always moved to be first in the global order [61, 62]. The algorithm was called Asynchronous Weak-commitment (AWC) search in its original paper, but is very similar to ABT. However, AWC needs exponential storage space in order to store all potential NOGOODS (cf. [61]). In 2005 a generalized version of ABT was published, enabling a general dynamic order for agents [71, 73]. This version of asynchronous backtracking, that includes dynamic ordering - ABT_DO, includes a special time-stamping mechanism that enables agents to change their order and retain the correctness of asynchronous backtracking. The issue of asynchrous ordering heuristics is presented in detail in Chapter 9, including both the ABT_DO algorithm and several innovative asynchronous heuristics.

8.1 Ordering heuristics for Synchronous Backjumping

In centralized CSPs, dynamic variable ordering is known to be an effective heuristic for gaining efficiency [16]. A recent study has shown that the same is true for algorithms which perform synchronous (sequential) search on distributed CSPs [11]. In fact, the essence of the study by Brito and Meseguer in [11] is to show that simple distributed synchronous backjumping outperforms ABT on randomly generated DisCSPs. This strong result demonstrates that an ordering heuristic can transform the performance of a synchronous search algorithm into the class of an asynchronous algorithm that performs its assignments and computations concurrently. Moreover, a synchronous (sequential assignments) algorihm may even improve on the concurrent algorithm's performance [11].

The different ordering heuristics can be divided into two groups, heuristics which can be performed without additional overhead in messages and heuristics that need this overhead.

8.1.1 Heuristics with no additional messages

The heuristics which do not need additional messages are either heuristics which can be performed in any synchronous backtracking algorithm or heuristics for which the additional information needed can be carried by the messages which are sent as part of the algorithm. The following examples all fall into one of these characteristics.

- Random: an agent which successfully assigned its variables on the CPA chooses randomly the next agent to send the CPA to, among all unassigned agents.
- Estimation of minimum domain size for unassigned variables by each agent maintaining an upper and a lower bound on the domain size of unassigned variables that are ordered after it [11].

Brito and Meseguer propose a method for maintaining lower and upper bounds on the domain sizes of agents by assigning agents [11]. It is assumed that agents hold all the constraints they are involved in and know the initial size of the domains of other agents. In order to choose the next agent to send the CPA, the agents maintain two bounds for the size of the domain of each unassigned agent. Each agent that performs an assignment updates these bounds according to the number of conflicts its new assignment has with each of the unassigned agents. The lower bound of agent A_j is calculated by the following formula:

$$l\_bound_j \leftarrow max(l\_bound_J, conflicts\_num(< A\_i, v_i >, A_j))$$

The lower bound is the maximum between the former lower bound and the number of conflicts the new assignment has. The upper bound of agent

A_j is calculated as follow:

$$u\_bound_j \leftarrow min(|D_j|, u\_bound_j + conflicts\_num(< A\_i, v_i >, A_j))$$

The upper bound is the minimum between the size of the initial domain and the sum of the former upper bound and the number of conflicts. After all bounds are updated, if there exists an unassigned agent whose lower bound is the size of its domain or is higher than any other upper bound of any unassigned agent, the CPA is sent to it. Otherwise, it is sent to the agent with the highest upper bound among all unassigned agents.

8.1.2 Heuristics with additional network overhead

Using additional messages which are not sent by the standard search algorithm, one can in principle send the *actual current domain size*. When the synchronous algorithm performs chronological backtracking, agents are able to record their actual domain size on the CPA. This cannot be done exactly if the algorithm uses backjumping. These two options of recording the actual domain size and using it for ordering heuristics were compared by Brito and Meseguer [11]. They report that dynamically ordered sequential backtracking outperformed backjumping, apparently because of the superior heuristic computation [11]. The drastically improved performance of distributed search algorithms that perform assignments sequentially is surprising and will be presented among the many empirical comparisons of DisCSP algorithms in Chapter 11. Our next step is to present below heuristic ordering methods for concurrent search algorithms. First, for the sequentially assigning Asynchronous Forward-Checking algorithm, which is close to synchronous algorithms. Finally, for asynchronous backtracking (in Chapter 9), where the algorithm itself needs to be changed in order to accomodate dynamic ordering and maintain correctness.

8.2 Ordering heuristics for *AFC*

Since the assignments in the *AFC* algorithm are performed sequentially by agents, as in the different versions of *synchronous backtracking* or *synchronous backjumping*, after each successful assignment an agent can choose a different agent to send the CPA to. The asynchronous forward-checking mechanism enables heuristics which are not possible in simple synchronous algorithms.

An ordering heuristic for *AFC* that needs no additional messages is the *Nogood-triggered* heuristic, which is inspired by *dynamic backtracking* [23]. The idea is to move forward the agent which initialized the backtrack operation. In *AFC*, in order to implement this idea an agent which receives a *Not_OK* message stores the ID of the agent it was received from. When the CPA is sent backwards the sending agent records the ID of the sender of the *Not_OK* message which triggered this backtrack operation on the CPA. The agent that receives the backtrack message, after replacing its assignment, sends the CPA to the triggering agent.

A heuristic for variable and value ordering was presented in [48] for the direct backtracking version of *AFC*. Each agent holds a counter for each of the values in its domain and for each of the other agents. The counters are incremented as a result of a backtrack operation. When an agent encounters an empty domain it decreases the counter of the culprit agent to which it backtracks. The agent that receives the backtrack message increments the counter of the sending agent. The sender of the backtrack message also checks, for each value removed from its domain, which agent's assignment was the first to conflict with it. The counter of each of these agents is incremented and a message is sent to them which indicates a possible conflict between the sending agent and the current value of the receiving agent. An agent that receives such a possible conflict message increases the counter of the sending agent and the counter of its current value. When agents assign their variables they choose the value with the lowest counter in their domain. When an agent successfully assigns its variable, it chooses the agent with the highest counter among the unassigned agents to send the CPA to. All of the above heuristics will be compared empirically to both synchronous search and asynchronous backtracking in Chapter 11. The improvement in performance induced by ordering heuristics is very large.

In order to enable sound empirical evaluation of DISCSP algorithms, one needs to define asynchronous performance measures for concurrent algorithms. Such measures took a long time to appear on the stage of distributed constraints research [45] and were established and accepted by the DISCSP and DISCOP community after DCR-04 [17]. Asynchronous measures of performance for distributed search will be described in Chapter 10. In Chapter 11, the empirical comparisons of the performance of many algorithms and their dynamically ordered versions will be presented.

Asynchronous Ordering Heuristics

The case of asynchronous ordering is quite complex. Assignments of agents are performed concurrently and asynchronously, so the selection of a next agent to be assigned is not clear. The order of agentshere is expected to have some impact, depending on the algorithm. However, unlike centralized or synchronous search it is not clear how the order changes the traversal of the search tree. Intuitively, a given order selects a subset of paths on the search tree - those that have the nodes in a similar enough order. Since nodes perform their computations asynchronously, two ordered agents $A_i < A_j$ can have their assignments performed in any order. The order just dictates that, when the assignments of these two agents are part of a NoGOOD, only agent A_j can backtrack to A_i and not vice versa.

An attempt to order the agents dynamically during the run of an asynchronous search algorithm was performed quite early. In 1995 Yokoo proposed an asynchronous search algorithm, similar to ABT, that does not use a static order of agents. This first attempt at asynchronous ordering is described in the following section. It uses a specific ordering, moving an agent that performs a backtrack (e.g., sends a NoGOOD) to the top place in the order.

9.1 Specific Asynchronous Heuristics

As mentioned before, the first attempt to introduce dynamic ordering into asynchronous backtracking was performed by Yokoo in 1995 (cf. [62, 63]). The idea was to take ABT and make a small change, so that some reordering would be done during search. The *Asynchronous Weak Commitment (AWC)* algorithm implements a specific ordering heuristic. Order can be changed only after a backtrack operation and only the agent sending the NoGOOD changes its position. The only change of position is for the NoGOOD sending agent to move to the first position and it must do so. This is a specific ordering heuristic, of moving all the way to the first position and it is performed everytime that a NoGOOD message is sent. The code needed for *AWC*, in

addition to standard ABT that sends complete *Agent_View*s as NOGOODs
(Algorithm 5.1), is presented in Algorithm 9.1.

Algorithm 9.1: Additional code for the AWC algorithm

- procedure **check_agent_view**
  1. **when** *Agent_View* and *current_value* are not consistent **do**
  2.   **if** no value in D_i is consistent with *Agent_View*
  3.   **then backtrack**;
  4.   **else** select $d \in D_i$ where *Agent_View* and d are consistent **and**
  5. d minimizes the number of constraint violations
              with lower priority agents ;
  6.   *current_value* $\leftarrow d$;
  7.   send (**ok?**,(x_i, d), *current_priority*) to *neighbors*;
  8.   **end_if; end_do;**

- procedure **backtrack**
  1. *nogood* $\leftarrow$ *inconsistent_subset*;
  2. **when** *nogood* is an empty set **do**
  3.   broadcast to other agents that there is no solution;
  4.   terminate; **end_do**;
  5. **when** *nogood* is a new NOGOOD **do**
  6.   send *nogood* to the agents in the *nogood*
  7.   *current_priority* $\leftarrow 1 + p_{max}$
              # p_{max} is the maximal priority value over all neighbours
  8.   select $d \in D_i$ where *Agent_View* and d are consistent **and**
  9. d minimizes the number of constraint violations
              with lower priority agents;
  10.   *current_value* $\leftarrow d$;
  11.   send (**ok?**,(x_i, d), *current_priority*) to *neighbors*;

As can be seen in Algorithm 9.1, another major heuristic for *ordering
values* is employed in AWC. Whenever a value is selected for assignment,
either in the **check_agent_view** procedure or during backtrack, the value
selected minimizes conflicts with *lower priority agents*. This is a very special
change from standard ABT, since in any version of ABT agents do not know
the value of lower-priority agents. The reason for this possiblity in AWC is
that **ok?** messages are *sent to all neighnoring agents* (line 7 in procedure
check_agent_view in Algorithm 9.1).

The interesting point about the AWC algorithm is that it can be easily
proven correct even with its reordering procedure. To see why it is correct, all
one needs is to observe that the correctness arguments for the ABT version
with complete *Agent_View*s as NOGOODs applies to AWC as well. Consider
the proof of correctness for ABT with complete *Agent_View*s as NOGOODs
in Section 5.3. Soundness applies immediately because an idle state means

that there are no constraint violation in any form of asynchronous backtracking. However, for completeness one needs to keep all the NOGOODs that are generated. This is because keeping all NOGOODs guarantees termination. Due to the changes in order all NOGOODs may be relevant and must be kept. This causes the worst drawback of the AWC algorithm, its need for exponential storage in the worst case for storing all NOGOODs.

9.2 Dynamically ordered ABT

The asynchronous backtracking algorithm, was presented in Chapter 5 in a form follwing [9, 61]. In ABT agents hold an assignment for their variables at all times, which is consistent with their view of the state of the system (i.e., the assignments of their neighboring agents). When the agent cannot find an assignment which is consistent with the assignments of higher-priority neighboring agents, it changes its view by sending a NOGOOD to an agent with a conflicting assignment and eliminating this conflicting assignment from its current view. Then it makes another attempt to assign its variable (see Chapter 5).

The dynamically ordered asynchronous backtracking (ABT_DO) algorithm that will be presented below is a simple algorithm for dynamic ordering in asynchronous backtracking. The ABT_DO algorithm uses polynomial space, as does standard ABT. In ABT_DO the agents of the DISCSP choose orders dynamically and asynchronously. Agents in ABT_DO perform according to the current, most up-to-date order they hold. Each agent can change the order of all agents with lower priority. An agent can propose an order change each time it replaces its assignment. Each order is time-stamped according to the assignments of agents. The method of time-stamping for defining the most updated order is the same that was used in [48] (and described in Section 6.3) for choosing the most up-to-date partial assignment. A simple array of counters represents the priority of a proposed order, according to the global search tree.

Each agent in ABT_DO holds a *Current_order* which is an ordered list of pairs. Every pair includes the ID of one of the agents and a counter. Each agent can propose a new order for agents that ha ave lower priority each time it replaces its assignment. This makes the sending of an ordering proposal message always coincide with an **ok?** message. An agent A_i can propose an order according to the following rules:

1. Agents with higher priority than A_i, and A_i itself, do not change priorities in the new order.
2. Agents with lower priority than A_i, in the current order, can change their priorities in the new order *but not to a higher priority than A_i itself.* (This rule enables a more flexible order than in the centralized case.)

The counters attached to each agent ID in the *order* list form a time stamp. Initially, all time-stamp counters are set to zero and all agents start with the same *Current_Order*. Each agent A_i that proposes a new order, changes the order of the pairs in its own ordered list and updates the counters as follows:

1. The counters of agents with higher priority than A_i, according to the *Current_order*, are not changed.
2. The counter of A_i is incremented by one.
3. The counters of agents with lower priority than A_i in the *Current_order* are set to zero.

Consider an example in which agent A_2 holds the following *Current_order*: $(1,4)(2,3)(3,1)(4,0)(5,1)$. There are five agents $A_1 \ldots A_5$ and they are ordered according to their IDs from left to right. After replacing its assignment it changes the order to: $(1,4)(2,4)(4,0)(5,0)(3,0)$.

In the new order, agent A_1 which had higher priority than A_2 in the previous order keeps its place and the value of its counter does not change. A_2 also keeps its place and the value of its counter is incremented by one. The rest of the agents, which had lower priority than A_2 in the previous order, change places and are still located lower than A_2. The new order for these agents is A_4, A_5, A_3 and their counters are set to zero.

In ABT, agents send **ok?** messages to their neighbors whenever they perform an assignment. In *ABT_DO*, an agent can choose to change its *Current_order* after changing its assignment. If that is the case, besides sending **ok?** messages an agent sends **order** messages to all lower-priority agents. The **order** message includes the agent's new *Current_order*.

For simplicity of presentation we assume that agents send **order** messages to all lower-priority agents. In the more realistic form of the algorithm, agents send **order** messages only to their lower-priority *neighbors*. Both versions are proven correct in Section 9.3.

An agent which receives an **order** message must determine if the received order is more up-to-date than its own *Current_order*. It decides by comparing the time stamps lexicographically. Since orders are changed according to the above rules, every two orders must have a common prefix of the agents IDs since the agent that performs the change does not change its own position and the positions of higher priority agents. In the above example the common prefix includes agents A_1 and A_2. Since the agent proposing the new order increases its own counter, when two different orders are compared, at least one of the time-stamp counters in the common prefix is different between the two orders. The more up-to-date order is the one for which the first different counter in the common prefix is larger. In the example above, any agent which will receive the new order will know it is more up-to-date than the previous order since the first pair is identical, but the counter of the second pair is larger.

When an agent A_i receives an order which is more up-to-date than its *Current_order*, it replaces its *Current_order* by the received order. The new order might change the location of the receiving agent with respect to other agents (in the new *Current_order*). In other words, one of the agents that had higher priority than A_i according to the old order, now has a lower priority than A_i or vice versa. Therefore, A_i rechecks the consistency of its current assignment and the validity of its stored NOGOODs according to the new order. If the current assignment is inconsistent according to the new order, the agent makes a new attempt to assign its variable. In *ABT_DO* agents send **ok?** messages to all constraining agents (i.e., their neighbors in the constraints graph). Although agents might hold in their *Agent_views* assignments of agents with lower priorities, according to their *Current_order*, they eliminate values from their domain *only if they violate constraints with higher priority agents*.

A NOGOOD message is always checked according to the *Current_order* of the receiving agent. If the receiving agent is not the lowest priority agent in the NOGOOD according to its *Current_order*, it sends the NOGOOD to the lowest priority agent and sends an **ok?** message to the sender of the NOGOOD. This is a similar operation to that performed in standard ABT for any unaccepted (inconsistent) NOGOOD.

Algorithm 9.2 and Algorithm 9.3 present the code of asynchronous back-tracking with dynamic ordering (*ABT_DO*). When an **ok?** message is received (first procedure in Algorithm 9.2), the agent updates the *Agent_view* and removes inconsistent NOGOODs. Then it calls **check_agent_view** to make sure its assignment is still consistent.

A new order received in an order message is accepted only if it is more up to date than the *Current_order* (second procedure of Algorithm 9.2). If so, the received order is stored and **check_agent_view** is called to make sure the current assignment is consistent with the higher priority assignments in the *Agent_view*.

When a NOGOOD is received (third procedure in Algorithm 9.2) the agent first checks if it is the lowest priority agent in the received NOGOOD according to the *Current_order*. If not, it sends the NOGOOD to the lowest priority agent and an **ok?** message to the NOGOOD sender (lines 1-3). If the receiving agent is the lowest priority agent it performs the same operations as in the standard ABT algorithm (lines 4-12).

Procedure **backtrack** (Algorithm 9.3) is the same as in standard *ABT*. The NOGOOD is resolved and the result is sent to the lowest priority agent in the NOGOOD, according to the *Current_order*.

Procedure **check_agent_view** (Algorithm 9.3) is very similar to the same procedure in standard ABT but the difference is important (lines 5-9). If the current assignment is not consistent and must be replaced and a new consistent assignment is found, the agent chooses a new order, according to the algorithms rules and the heuristic used, as its *Current_order* (line 7) and updates the corresponding time stamp. Next, **ok?** messages are sent to all neighboring agents. The new order and its time-stamp counters are sent to all lower priority agents.

Algorithm 9.2: The ABT_DO algorithm (first part)

---

when received (ok?, (x_j, d_j)**):**
1. add (x_j, d_j) to *agent_view*;
2. remove inconsistent *nogoods*;
3. **check_agent_view**;

when received (order, *received_order***):**
1. **if** (*received_order* is more updated than *Current_order*)
2.   *Current_order* ← *received_order*;
3.   remove inconsistent nogoods;
4.   **check_agent_view**;

when received (nogood, x_j, *nogood***)**
1. **if** (*nogood* contains an agent x_k with lower priority than x_i)
2.   send (**nogood,** $(x_i, nogood)$) to x_k;
3.   send (**ok?,** $(x_i, current\_value)$ to x_j;
4. **else**
5.   **if** (*nogood* consistent with $\{Agent\_view \cup current\_assignment\}$)
6.   store *nogood*;
7.   **if** (*nogood* contains an agent x_k that is not its neighbor)
8.   request x_k to add x_i as a neighbor;
9.   add (x_k, d_k) to *agent_view*;
10.   **check_agent_view**;
11.   **else**
12.   send (**ok?,** $(x_i, current\_value)$) to x_j;

9.3 Correctness of *ABT_DO*

In order to prove the correctness of the *ABT_DO* algorithm we first establish two facts by proving the following lemmas:

Lemma 9.3.1 *The highest priority agent in the initial order remains the highest priority agent in all proposed orders.*

The proof for Lemma 9.3.1 is immediate from the two rules of reordering. Since no agent can propose a new order which changes the priority of higher priority agents and its own priority, no agent including the first can move the highest priority agent to a lower position. □

Lemma 9.3.2 *When the highest priority agent proposes a new order, it is more up to date than all previous orders.*

This proof is again immediate. In all previous orders the time-stamp counter of the first agent is smaller than the counter of the time-stamp counter of the first agent in the new proposed order. □

Algorithm 9.3: Two additional procedures of the ABT_DO algorithm

---

procedure **check_agent_view**
1. **if**(*current_assignment* is not consistent with all
        higher priority assignments in *agent_view*)
2.   **if**(no value in D_i is consistent with all higher priority
          assignments in *agent_view*)
3.   **backtrack**;
4.   **else**
5.   select $d \in D_i$ where *agent_view* and d are consistent;
6.   *current_value* $\leftarrow d$;
7.   *Current_order* $\leftarrow$ **choose_new_order**
8.   send (**ok?**,(x_i, d)) to *neighbors*;
9.   send (**order**,*Current_order*) to *lower priority agents*;

procedure **backtrack**
1. *nogood* $\leftarrow$ **resolve_inconsistent_subset**;
2. **if** (*nogood* is empty)
3.   broadcast to other agents that there is no solution;
4.   **stop**;
5. select (x_j, d_j) where x_j has the lowest priority in nogood;
6. send (**nogood**, x_i, *nogood*) to x_j;
7. remove (x_j, d_j) from *agent_view*;
8. remove all *Nogoods* containing (x_j, d_j);
9. **check_agent_view**;

To prove correctness of a search algorithm for DisCSPs one needs to prove that it is sound, complete, and that it terminates. *ABT_DO*, like ABT, reports a solution when all agents are idle and no messages are sent. Its soundness follows from the soundness of ABT (see for example [9]). One point needs mentioning. Since no messages are traveling in the system in the idle state, all overriding messages have arrived at their destinations. This means that for every pair of constraining agents an agreement about their pairwise order has been achieved. One of each pair of constraining agents checks their constraint and no messages mean no violations, as in the proof for ABT [9].

Theorem 9.1. *ABT_DO is complete and it terminates.*

To prove the completeness and termination of *ABT_DO* we use induction on the number of agents (i.e., number of variables) in the DisCSP. For a single-agent DisCSP the order is static therefore the completeness and termination of ABT implies the same for *ABT_DO*. Assume *ABT_DO* is complete and terminates for every DisCSP with k agents, where $k < n$. Consider a DisCSP with n agents. According to Lemma 9.3.1 the agent with the highest priority in the initial order will not change its place. The highest priority agent assigns its variable for the first time and sends it along with its order proposal to other agents.

The remaining DISCSP has $n - 1$ agents and its initial order is that proposed by the first agent (all other orders are discarded according to Lemma 9.3.2). By the induction assumption the remaining DISCSP is complete and terminates. If a solution to the induced DISCSP is found, this means that the lower priority $n - 1$ agents are idle and so is the first (highest priority) agent since none of the others sends it any message. If a solution is not found, by the $n - 1$ lower priority agents, either an empty NOGOOD was found by one of the agents and the whole search is terminated, or a single assignment NOGOOD will be sent to the highest priority agent which will cause it to replace its assignment. The new assignment of the first agent and the new order proposed will induce a new DISCSP of size $n - 1$. The search on this new DISCSP of size $n - 1$ is also complete and terminates according to the induction assumption. The number of induced $DisCSPs$, created by the assignments of the highest priority agent is bound by the size of its domain. Therefore, the algorithm will terminate in a finite time. The ABT_DO algorithm is complete since a solution to the DISCSP must include one of the highest priority agent value assignments, which means that one of the induced $DisCSPs$ includes a solution iff the original DISCSP includes a solution. This completes the correctness proof of ABT_DO □

If the network model, or privacy restrictions, enable agents to communicate only with their neighbors in the constraint network, some small changes are needed in order to maintain correctness. First, agents must be allowed to change only the order of lower priority *neighbors*. This means that the method **choose_new_order**, called in line 7 of procedure **check_agent_view**, changes the order by switching between the position of lower priority neighbors and leaving other lower priority agents at their current position. Second, whenever an updated order message is received, an agent informs its neighbors of its new *Current_order*.

In order to prove that the above two changes do not affect the correctness of the algorithm we first establish the correctness of Lemmas 9.3.1 and 9.3.2 under these changes. Lemma 9.3.1 is not affected by the change since the rules for changing agents positions have become more strict, and still do not allow to change the position of higher priority agents. Lemma 9.3.2 holds because the time-stamp mechanism which promises its correctness has not changed. These lemmas are the basis for the correctness of the induction which proves the algorithm is complete and terminates. However, we still need to prove that the algorithm is sound. One of the assumptions that our soundness proof depended on was that an idle state of the system would mean that every constrained pair of agents agrees on the order between them. This claim might not hold since the most up-to-date order is not sent to all agents. The following lemma proves this claim is still true after the changes in the algorithm:

Lemma 9.3.3 *When the system reaches an idle state, every pair of constrained agents hold the same order.*

According to the changes described above, whenever one of the constrained agents receives an updated order message, it informs its neighbors. Therefore, all agents which have constraints with it will be notified and hold the updated order. If two agents are not informed with the most up-to-date order, this would mean that *both of them* are not lower priority neighbors of the reordering agent and as a result their current position in the order stays the same. Lemma 9.3.3 implies that the algorithm is sound for versions of *ABT_DO* that are restricted to send messages only between pairs of constraining agents.□

9.4 A new class of asynchronous heuristics

The results presented in [72] have shown that the performance of *ABT_DO* is highly dependent on the selected heuristic. The classic *Min-Domain* heuristic was implemented by including the current domain size of agents in the messages they send. Surprisingly, this heuristic which in centralized algorithms and in distributed algorithms using a sequential assignment protocol produces a large improvement over static order, was found not to be efficient for Asynchronous Backtracking. A heuristic which achieved a significant improvement was inspired by *dynamic backtracking* [2, 23] in which the agent which sends a NOGOOD is advanced in the new order to be immediately after the agent to whom the NOGOOD was sent. The explanation for the success of this heuristic is that it does not cause the removal of relevant NOGOODs as do other heuristics [72]. All of these results are presented in some detail in section 11.2.2.

The present section investigates further the relation between the success of this heuristic and the min-domain heuristic which was found to be successful for sequential assignments (synchronous) algorithms on DISCSPs [11, 44]. It turns out that the effect of NOGOOD loss as a result of reordering is probably the cause of the failure of the *min domain* heuristic. Removal of NOGOODs cause the return of values to the agents' domains. This harms the accuracy of the information that agents hold on the domain size of other agents. On the other hand, the *Nogood-triggered* heuristic of [71] does not loose valid information and moves agents with a potential of having a small domain to a higher position.

In order to maximize the *min-domain* property, a more flexible heuristic can be used, which belongs to a completely new class of asynchronous ordering heuristics. The new class of dynamic ordering heuristics violates the restrictions on the ordering of agents in [72]. The idea is to employ changes of order that move agents to a higher position, replacing agents that were ahead of them including the first agent. This new type of heuristics is termed *Retroactive ordering* and is based on a slightly modified version of the *ABT_DO* algorithm.

The main idea behind the new class of heuristics is that moving the NO-GOOD sender as high as possible in the priority order is successful only if the domain size of agents is taken into consideration. In other words, in the combined *min-domain* scheme agents are moved to a higher position only if their current domain size is smaller than the current domain of agents they are moved in front of. Moving an agent before the agents which are included in the NOGOOD actually *enlarges* its domain. The best heuristic found experimentally in Section 11.2.2 is that agents which generate a NOGOOD are placed in the new order between the last and the second last agents in the generated NOGOOD. This heuristic is the asynchronous form of the Min-Domain heuristic. Results on both random DISCSPs and on *structuredDisCSPs* show that the proposed heuristic improves the best results to date [72] by a large factor.

To understand the possible reasons for the failure of the *min-domain* heuristic and the success of the *Nogood-triggered* heuristic when used in asynchronous backtracking [71, 72], consider the example in Figure 9.1. The agents are ordered by their indices. Each agent has a single variable and three values, a, b and c, in its domain. The eliminated values are crossed and each points to its eliminating explanation (i.e. the assignment which caused its removal). The circled values represent the current assignments. In this example, agent A_5 has exhausted its domain and must create a NOGOOD. The NOGOOD it generates includes the assignments of A_1 and A_2 therefore the NOGOOD is sent to A_2. According to the rules of the *ABT_DO* algorithm agent A_2 can reorder agents A_3, A_4 and A_5. Now, if it will reorder them according to their current domain sizes then A_3 and A_4 will switch places. But, since both of the values eliminated from the domain of A_4 are in conflict with the assignment of A_3 then after they change places, these values will be returned to the domain of A_4 and its domain size will be larger than the domain of A_3.

In contrast, if A_2 reorders according to the *Nogood-triggered* heuristic then the only agent to change places is A_5 which is moved to be after A_2 and before A_3. Now, after A_2 replaces its assignment we get the situation in Figure 9.2. We can see that an agent with a small domain was moved forward while the others kept their domain sizes and places.

The example demonstrates why the min-domain heuristic fails when used in asynchronous backtracking. In asynchronous backtracking, all agents hold an assignment throughout the search. Conflicts with these assignments affect the size of domains of other agents. For each value which is removed from an agent's domain an explanation NOGOOD is stored. When an agent is moved in front of an agent whose assignment is included in one of its NOGOODs, this NOGOOD must be eliminated and the corresponding value is returned to the domain. Thus, in contrast to sequential ordering algorithms, in asynchronous backtracking the resulting domain sizes after reordering cannot be anticipated by the ordering agent. The example demonstrates how this phenomena does not affect the *Nogood-triggered* heuristic.

Following the example one can see that the Nogood-triggered heuristic is successful because in many cases it moves an agent with a small domain

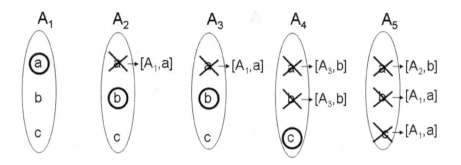

Fig. 9.1. Heuristics example - state before backtrack

to a higher position. Only values whose NOGOOD explanation includes the assignment of the culprit agent are returned to the moving agent's domain. In fact, the agent can be moved up past the culprit, and as long as it does not pass the second last assignment in the NOGOOD its domain size will stay the same. In Figure 9.2, Agent A_5 is moved right after agent A_2. Its domain size is one, since the NOGOODs of its other two values are valid. If A_5 is moved before A_2 its domain size will stay the same as both eliminating NOGOODs include only the assignment of A_1. However, if A_5 will be moved in front of A_1 then all its values will return to its domain. This possibility of moving an agent with a small domain beyond the culprit agent to a higher position is the basic motivation for retroactive ordering.

In contrast to the rules of *ABT_DO* (Section 9.2), the new type of ordering can change the order of agents with higher priority than the agent which replaces its assignment. A *retroactive* heuristic would enable moving the NO-GOOD sender to a higher position than the NOGOOD receiver [77]. In order to preserve the correctness of the algorithm, agents must be allowed to store NOGOODs. In order to generate a general scheme for retroactive heuristics,

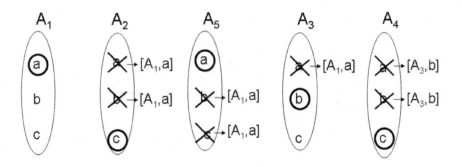

Fig. 9.2. After reordering and using the NG-triggered heuristic

one can define a global space limit for the storage of NOGOODS. The specific realization is to limit the storage of NOGOODS that are smaller or equal to some predefined size k.

The proposed ordering heuristic is triggered by the sending of a NOGOOD. The reordering operation can be generated by either the NOGOOD generator or by the NOGOOD receiver (but not by both). In contrast to [71, 72] (Section 9.2), we choose the NOGOOD sender to be the one to reorder. The only agent which can loose a relevant NOGOOD as a result of the reordering is the NOGOOD sender (the only one moving to a higher position). Therefore, since it is aware of its own state and the others do not loose information, the NOGOOD sender is the best candidate for selecting the new order.
The new order is selected according to the following rules:

1. The NOGOOD generator can be moved to any position in the new order.
2. If the Nogood generator is moved to a position which is *before the second last in the Nogood* (the one before the culprit) all the agents included in the NOGOOD must hold the NOGOOD until the search is terminated.

3. Agents with lower priority than the NOGOOD receiver can change order but not move in front of it (as in standard *ABT_DO*).

According to the above rules, agents which detect a dead end are moved to a higher position in the priority order. If the length of the created NOGOOD is larger than k, they can be moved up to the place that is right after the agent which is the last to be included in the NOGOOD according to the current order and is not the culprit (i.e. second last in the NOGOOD).

If the length of the created NOGOOD is smaller or equal to k, the sending agent can be moved to a position before all the participants in the NOGOOD and the NOGOOD is sent and saved by all of them. In the extreme case where k is equal to the number of agents in the DISCSP (i.e. $k = n$), the NOGOOD sender can always move to be first in the priority order and the resulting algorithm is a generalization of AWC [61]. Note that the specific heuristic that *always moves the* NOGOOD *sender to the first position* is the fixed heuristic of the AWC algorithm (see Section 9.1) [77].

Algorithm 9.4 and Algorithm 9.5 present the code of *Retroactive ABT_DO*. The difference from standard *ABT_DO* (Algorithm 9.2 and Algorithm 9.3) in the code performed when a NOGOOD is received (Algorithm 9.4) derives from the different possible types of NOGOODs. A NOGOOD smaller or equal to k is actually a constraint that will be stored by the agent until the search is terminated. In the case of NOGOODs which are longer than k, the algorithm treats them as in standard *ABT_DO* i.e. accepts them only if the receiver is the lowest priority agent in the NOGOOD and the NOGOOD is consistent with the *Agent_view* and *current_assignment* of the receiver. In any case of acceptance of a NOGOOD, the agent searches for a new assignment only if it happens to be the lowest priority agent in the NOGOOD. As stated above, only the NOGOOD generator is allowed to change order.

Procedure **backtrack** (Algorithm 9.5) is changed mainly in the code related to the retroactive heuristic version of *ABT_DO*. When an agent creates a NOGOOD it determines whether it is larger than k or not. If it is larger, a single NOGOOD is sent to the lowest priority agent in the NOGOOD in the same way as in *ABT_DO*. Consequently, the agent selects a new order in which it puts itself not higher than the second lowest priority agent in the NOGOOD. When the NOGOOD is smaller or equal to k, if it is the first time this NOGOOD is generated, the NOGOOD is sent to all the agents included in the NOGOOD and the agent moves itself to an unlimited position in the new order. In this case the function **choose_new_order** is called with no limitations. In both cases, order messages are sent to all the lower priority agents in the new order. The assignment of the lowest priority agent in the NOGOOD is removed from the *Agent_view*, the relevant NOGOODs are removed and the agent attempts to re-assign its variable by calling **check_agent_view**.

Procedure **check_agent_view** (Algorithm 9.4) is slightly changed from that of Algorithm 9.3 [72] since the change of order in the new scheme is performed by the NOGOOD sender and not by its receiver.

Algorithm 9.4: The retroactive ABT_DO algorithm (*main*)

---

when received (ok?, (x_j, d_j)) do:
1. add (x_j, d_j) to *agent_view*;
2. remove inconsistent *nogoods*;
3. **check_agent_view**;

when received (order, *received_order*) do:
1. **if** (*received_order* is more updated than *Current_order*)
2.   *Current_order* ← *received_order*;
3.   remove inconsistent nogoods;
4.   **check_agent_view**;

when received (nogood, x_j, *nogood*)
1. *old_value* ← *current_value*
2. **if** (*nogood* contains an agent x_k
        with lower priority than x_i and *nogood*.size $> K$)
3.   send (**nogood**, $(x_i, nogood)$) to x_k;
4. **else**
5.   **if** (*nogood* consistent with {*Agent_view*∪
          current_assignment} or *nogood*.size $\leq K$)
6.   store *nogood*;
7.   **if** (*nogood* contains an agent x_k that is not its neighbor)
8.   request x_k to add x_i as a neighbor;
9.   add (x_k, d_k) to *agent_view*;
10   **if**(x_i is with lowest priority in *nogood*)
11.   **check_agent_view**;
12. **if**(*old_value* $=$ *current_value*)
13.   send (**ok?**, $(x_i, current\_value)$) to x_j;

9.5 Correctness of Retroactive *ABT_DO*

In order to prove the correctness of *Retroactive ABT_DO* we assume the correctness of the standard *ABT_DO* algorithm (see proof in Section 9.3 and prove that the changes made for retroactive heuristics do not damage its correctness. We first prove the case for no NOGOOD storage ($k = 0$):

Theorem 9.2. Retroactive ABT_DO *is correct when $k = 0$.*

There are two differences between standard *ABT_DO* and *Retroactive ABT_DO* with $k = 0$. First, order is changed whenever a NOGOOD is sent and not when an assignment is replaced. This change does not make a difference in the correctness since when a NOGOOD is sent there are two possible outcomes. Either the NOGOOD receiver replaces its assignment, which makes it effectively the same as in standard *ABT_DO*, or the NOGOOD is rejected. A rejected NOGOOD can only be caused by a change of assignment either of the receiving agent or of an agent with higher priority. In all of these cases, the

---

Algorithm 9.5: The retroactive ABT_DO algorithm (*secondpart*)

---

procedure **backtrack**
1. $nogood \leftarrow$ **resolve_inconsistent_subset**;
2.   **if** ($nogood$ is empty)
3.   broadcast to other agents that there is no solution;
4.   **stop**;
5.   select (x_j, d_j) where x_j has the lowest priority in $nogood$;
6.   **if**($nogood.size > K$)
7. $Current\_order \leftarrow$ **choose_new_order**()
             where x_l has the second lowest priority in $nogood$;
8.   send (**nogood**, x_i, $nogood$) to x_j;
9.   **else if**($is\_new(nogood)$)
10. $new\_position \leftarrow unlimited$
11.   send (**nogood**, x_i, $nogood$) to all agents in $nogood$;
12.   store sent nogood;
13. $Current\_order \leftarrow$ **choose_new_order**(x_l)
14. send (**order**,$Current\_order$) to *lower priority agents*;
15. remove (x_j, d_j) from $agent\_view$;
16. remove all $nogoods$ containing (x_j, d_j);
17. **check_agent_view**;

procedure **check_agent_view**
1.   **if**($current\_assignment$ is not consistent with all
             higher priority assignments in $Agent\_view$)
2.   **if**(no value in D_i is consistent with all higher priority
                 assignments in $Agent\_view$)
3.   **backtrack**;
4.   **else**
5.   select $d \in D_i$ where $Agent\_view$ and d are consistent;
6. $current\_value \leftarrow d$;
7.   send (**ok?**,(x_i, d)) to $neighbors$;

---

most relevant order is determined lexicographically. Ties which could not have been generated in standard *ABT_DO*, are broken using the agents indexes.

The second change in the code for $k = 0$ is that in *Retroactive ABT_DO* a NOGOOD sender can move to a position in front of the agent that receives the NOGOOD. Since the NOGOOD sender is the only agent moving to a higher position, it is the only one that can lose a NOGOOD as a result. However, the NOGOOD sender removes all NOGOODs containing the assignment of the No-GOOD receiver and it does not pass any other agent contained in the NOGOOD. Thus, no information is actually lost by this change. Moreover, the number of times two agents can move in front of one another without a higher priority agent changing its assignment is bounded by their domain sizes.   □

Theorem 9.3. *RetroactiveABT_DO is correct when $n \geq k > 0$.*

In order to prove that *RetroactiveABT_DO* is correct for the case that $n \geq k > 0$ we need to show that infinite loops cannot occur. In the case of NOGOODs which are smaller or equal to k the case is very simple. All agents involved in the NOGOOD continue to hold it, therefore the same assignment can never be produced again. The number of these Nogoods with a limited length is finite. In finite time the algorithm reaches a state in which no permanent NOGOODs are added. In this state, agents do not move in front of the second last in the NOGOODs generated and the previous proof holds.   □

Performance measures for distributed search

Standard CSP algorithms are routinely measured by the number of constraints checks they perform while searching for a solution [52, 56]. In contrast to run time, this measure is implementation independent and is considered a good performance measure [16, 56]. The main idea is that search algorithms for a solution to a CSP traverse the search tree by constructing a solution through a sequence of assignments. At each assignment the algorithm checks for the validity of the current partial solution by accessing the constraints matrix and checking the proposed new assignment against either existing assignments or future unassigned variables (e.g., backtracking with or without lookahead [31]). The performance measure of counting constraints checks (CCs) is univerally accepted for standard CSP algorithms. It is desirable to have a similar implementation-independent measure for distributed CSPs. However, the first years of research have yielded only simple synchronous measures, like the number of *rounds* of the simulator running the distributed algorithm (cf. [61]). As was clear in our small running examples of algorithms like *ABT* or *ConcBT* in Sections 5.1, 7.1, the division of a distributed run into steps (e.g., rounds or cycles) is quite ad hoc. The present chapter will present a framework for measuring the concurrent performance of all distributed search algorithms. For DisCSPs the measure will use the concept of *nonconcurrent constraints checks*, as presented below.

Distributed search algorithms on distributed constraints satisfaction problems (DisCSPs) are executed by a set of agents, where the sequence of computations of one agent depends in general on the intermediate results of other agents, as can be seen in Chapter 5, Chapter 6, and Chapter 7. The intermediate results of computations of agents are distributed by exchanging messages between the agents. Usually, messages about assignments trigger the checking of constraints against received assignments by the receiving agent. If the check fails, the sending agent is requested to choose another assignment for its variables (see, for example, Chapter 5).

Distributed search algorithms on DisCSPs assume implicitly that all agents run the same algorithm, receiving messages about assignments of other agents and sending messages with their own assignments to other agents. As we have seen, the majority of DisCSP algorithms are asynchronous and let all agents perform computations (and report about their resulting assignments) in a distributed manner. As a result, *part of the constraint checks of a distributed algorithm are performed concurrently*, and the fraction of this part (out of the total number of CCs) depends on the specific algorithm in question. The concurrency of a DisCSP search algorithm transforms the performance measurement of such algorithms into a nontrivial task.

Measurement of the computational efforts of an algorithm is mostly motivated by the need to estimate the time that will pass between the starting time of the algorithm and the time it returns with a satisfying solution. Standard measures of constraints processing algorithms (cf. [52, 56]) count the total number of constraints checks (CCs) that were executed. The number of CCs performed is generally accepted as a machine (and implementation) independent measure, because it counts the main computing operation of all backtracking algorithms (cf. [31]). It is also the generally accepted measure for the investigation of phase transitions in problem difficulty, for example (cf. [33, 36, 65]). However, the simple counting of CCs is insufficient for DisCSPs for two main reasons:

1. It does not take into account the time intervals in which agents run concurrently and the time intervals in which agents wait for other agents to finish their computations.
2. No account is taken of the time needed for an agent to send or receive a message, nor of the time for the message to be delivered.

The waiting periods were probably the trigger for the first discussion in the literature of how one can measure and compare the computational efforts of DisCSP algorithms. Yokoo [62, 63] proposes to divide the time that the algorithm consumes into *rounds*, where at the start of each round at least one agent has the necessary information to carry on its computation. The division of distributed computation into strict rounds is a simplification of the dependency between computations of different agents. An example in Section 10.3 demonstrates that this simplification generates an estimation of the nonconcurrent search efforts that is not tight enough.

We will consider here a more general method of measurement, present it in the form of a clear and general model, and present an algorithm for computing the measure. The proposed methods rely explicitly on the dependency among computations of agents and it is expected to generate a tighter (better) performance measure for DisCSP algorithms. In the following sections the measurement problem is presented by analyzing a series of simple examples of DisCSPs.

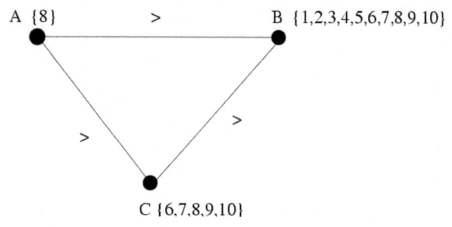

A {8}   >   B {1,2,3,4,5,6,7,8,9,10}

C {6,7,8,9,10}

Fig. 10.1. A simple DisCSP

10.1 A Simple Example with Naive Methods

Consider the network in Figure 10.1 and assume agents run a search algorithm that orders the agents lexicographically $< A, B, C >$. Assume the simplest algorithm - each agent waits for the agents preceding it to assign their variable before it assigns its own variable. Upon receiving a message with former agent assignments, the agent attempts to assign values to its own variable, rejecting values that are inconsistent with former agents. Assume that agents scan their domain of values from left to right and after each assignment trial perform constraints checks against former assignments of other agents. During the run of this search algorithm, agents perform the following series of actions:

1. Agent A assigns the value 8 to its variable and sends messages with this value to B and C.
2. Agent B receives a message from A with $A's$ assignment. It traverses the values in its domain from left to right, checking each assignment against the constraint with A. After performing nine constraints checks, B assigns the value 9 to its variable and sends a message with this value to agent C.
3. Agent C gets a message from A with value 8 (with no loss of generality we assume that it receives this message almost simultaneously with B) and after four constraint checks assigns the value 9 to its variable. Afterwards it receives a message from agent B with the value 9 and after one additional constraint check assigns the value 10 to its variable.
4. The first solution is found.

A simple time plot of this series of operations is presented in Figure 10.2. Here the sequences of constraints checks (as a measurement unit for the search computations) that each of the three agents performs during the above sequence is plotted as a horizontal segment.

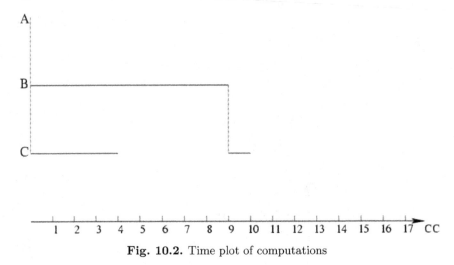

Fig. 10.2. Time plot of computations

One can measure the search effort of this algorithm by summing all constraints checks of all agents. This naive measurement method will result in 14 constraints checks. Another naive option is to take the maximal number of constraints checks performed by any of these three agents (assuming they all work concurrently); the result will be a total of nine constraints checks.

A close inspection of the time plot of the computation segments of the agents in Figure 10.2 enables the following insight into this specific example. In the current algorithm, agent B performs nine constraints checks. This computation triggers the last computation sequence of agent C. In our example, agent C can perform its first four constraints checks concurrently with agent B. A reasonable estimation for the total computation time of this algorithm (expressed in units of constraints checks), is the sum of nine of agent B plus the final one of agent C, producing a result of 10 nonconcurrent constraints checks altogether. In this simple example, none of the above naive measurement methods (i.e., the sum of all CCs of all agents, or the maximum of all CCs of all agents) can deliver this tight estimate.

10.2 Dividing concurrent search into rounds

Asynchronous search algorithms on DisCSPs can be viewed as a loop that each agent is running: the agent receives a message, computes assignments based on these messages, and then sends one or more messages, if needed. If one adds an assumption that all messages are delivered instantly and in the order they were sent, then the concurrent computation can be divided into *rounds*. This is the model that was proposed by Yokoo [62, 63]. This model was used for our simple demonstrating examples for DisCSP algorithms in Chapter 5 and in Chapter 6. This division enables one to measure the computing efforts of the search algorithm as a sum of the concurrent constraints checks that are performed in each round. A natural measure of the concurrent constraints checks in each round is the *maximum over all the agents* for that round.

The constraints checks performed by each agent in each round *depend on the assignments of a subset of the agents during the former round*. Dividing the computation of a distributed search algorithm for DisCSP into a series of rounds is somewhat of a simplification. Any sequence of constraints checks of agent may depend on the assignments of different agents in many ways.

If we apply the rounds model of Yokoo to our simple example in Figure 10.1 and Figure 10.2 we can see that in the first round only agent A can perform its assignment. This round has zero constraints checks. In the second round both agents B and C perform computations based on the message received from agent A. Both agents search for an assignment that is consistent with the assignment of agent A. In this, second round, agents B and C perform nine and four constraints checks, respectively. Both of these computations are done concurrently and therefore we take the maximum of nine CCs as the computational cost of this round.

The third round of computations involves only agent C, which has to find a consistent assignment to the new assignment of agent B. This needs only one constraint check, so the cost of this round is 1.

The total number of *nonconcurrent constraints checks* (NCCCs) is the sum of all NCCCs of all rounds of the computation, producing in our example the final result of $0 + 9 + 1 = 10$ nonconcurrent constraints checks. Note, that this result is identical to our intuitive calculation in the former subsection.

The general idea behind the model of computing nonconcurrent constraints checks in *rounds* is a notion of *dependency*. When we say that an event b **depends on an event** a, we mean that **event** b **cannot start before** a **finishes.** *Dependency* relations define parts of the computation of agents that cannot be performed in parallel. For example, the search for an assignment of agent C (in Figure 10.1) that is consistent with the assignment of agent B must be performed *sequentially* to that of agent B. It is easy to see that computing the search efforts by simply summing the CCs of all agents assumes **total dependency** of computations of all different agents. The other extreme approach, which take the maximum number of CCs performed by all agents (over the whole search process), assumes **total independence** of all agents. The model of *rounds* assumes that the dependent events are complete rounds. We now turn to a more complex example of search over a DisCSP to demonstrate that a refinement of the dependent events is needed.

10.3 A More Complex Example for Computing NCCCs

Assume that the agents of the DISCSP in Figure 10.3 are ordered by $<$ $A, D, B, E, C >$ and run the same algorithm as in the previous example. The sequence of computations for this example will be as follows:

1. Agent A assigns the value 0 to its variable and sends messages with this assignment to B and D.
2. Agent B gets the message from A and after 11 CCs assigns the value 0 to its variable. Then it sends a message with this value to agent C.
3. Agent D gets the message from agent A and after six CCs it assigns the value 0 to its variable. Next, it sends a message with this assignment to agent E.
4. Agent C gets a message from agent B and after two CCs assigns the value 0 to its variable.
5. Agent E gets a message from agent D and after four CCs assigns the value 0 to its variable.

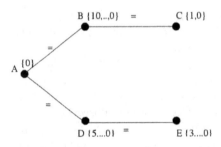

Fig. 10.3. A more complex example

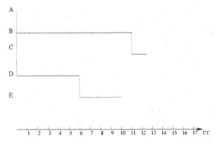

Fig. 10.4. Time plot of the more complex example, in CCs

The time plot of computations of all agents for this example is shown in Figure 10.4. Applying the rounds model of Yokoo, the computation is divided into three rounds:

1. *assignment of A:* the computation effort here is 0 CCs.
2. *assignment of B and D:* here the concurrent computation effort is 11 NCCCs
   $max(B, D) = max(6, 11) = 11$.
3. *assignment of C and E:* here four NCCCs are executed concurrently
   $max(C, E) = max(2, 4) = 4$.

The total computational effort according to the rounds model is, therefore, the sum of 0, 11, and 4, which amounts to 15 *nonconcurrent constraints checks* (NCCCs). However, in this example agents B and C act independently of agents D and E and vice versa. Inspecting the time plot in Figure 10.4, one can see two separate branches of computations.

One branch consists of agents A, B, C and the other of A, D, E. The first branch consumes 13 NCCCs and the second branch consumes 10. A good measure of the concurrent computation effort is the maximum of these two independent branches of computations. This more tight measurement results in 13 NCCCs.

This example demonstrates that the division of computations by agents in a distributed search algorithm into rigid rounds, is too simplistic. This chapter describes a more general dependency definition for distributed constraints processing algorithms and introduces an algorithm for computing the total number of nonconcurrent constraints checks (NCCCs). The NCCC-computing algorithm is proven to be a realization of the model definition.

10.4 A Model for Nonconcurrent Constraints Checks

The basic concept in our model is the *sequence of constraint checks* (SCC). An SCC is a set of constraint checks executed by a single agent, in one sequence, without sending or receiving any message during the execution of the sequence. Using the SCC object as a building block, one can assemble them together into a consistent model based on the **dependency** concept. The dependency between SCC objects is generated by the sending and receiving of messages among agents.

In the computing model for NCCCs, agent activities, while running a distributed search algorithm on a DisCSP, can be represented by two classes of objects:

- The set of messages sent and received by an agent
- The set of all *sequences of constraint checks* (SCCs)

Definition 10.1. An **event** of an agent A is either sending a message, receiving a message, or performing a single SCC.

Definition 10.2. An event x of agent A is **unary-dependent** on event y of the same agent if the event x occurs **after** event y and no event z of agent A exists, such that z is after x and y is after z.

Definition 10.3. Event x of agent A is **binary-dependent** on event y of agent B if the event y is the sending of some message M from B to A and x is the event of receiving the message M, by agent A.

Definition 10.4. Event x is **chain-dependent** or **dependent** on event y if one of the following three conditions holds:

- x is unary-dependent on y.
- x is binary-dependent on y.
- There is a sequence of events $x_1, ... x_k$, where $x_1 = y$ and $x_k = x$, such that for all $i = 2...k$, x_i is either unary-dependent or binary-dependent on x_{i-1}.

Definition 10.5. *For each SCC object* x *define a set of SCCs, the* **dependency set** $\Gamma^-(x) = \{y_1, y_2, \ldots, y_n\}$, *such that* x *is chain-dependent on any* $y_i \in \Gamma^-(x)$ *and* $\Gamma^-(x)$ *includes all SCC such that* x *is chain-depended on.*

Next, we define the cost of computing, for a single SCC and for sets of SCCs:

Definition 10.6. *The* **S_Cost** *of SCC* x *is the number of constraints checks that the agent performs during this SCC.*

The **cumulative cost (C_Cost)** of an SCC x is defined recursively to be the sum of costs of $\Gamma^-(x)$.

Definition 10.7. *If an SCC* x *is not chain-dependent on any other SCC then*

$$C\_Cost(x) = S\_Cost(x) \tag{10.1}$$

otherwise,

$$C\_Cost(x) = max_{y \,\in\, \Gamma^-(x)}(C\_Cost(y) + M\_Cost) + S\_Cost(x)) \tag{10.2}$$

The term M_Cost that appears in definition 10.7 is the cost of message transfer, in units of CCs. The *total number of nonconcurrent constraints checks (TCCC)* can be calculated recursively by using the cumulative costs of all SCCs. The TCCC, which represents the computing effort of a distributed search algorithm, is the maximal cumulative cost C_Cost over the set of all constraints checks sequences (*SCCset*). More formally:

Definition 10.8. *The total number of nonconcurrent constraints checks that a distributed algorithm performs during search is:*

$$TCCC = max_{x \in SCCset}(C\_Cost(x)) \tag{10.3}$$

To make the model clear, let us apply it to the scenario described in Figures 10.3 and 10.4. The events of the application of the algorithm are described in the form of a *dependencies graph*, defined on the set of events where (a, b) is an edge of this graph if the event b is either unary-dependent or binary-dependent on the event a. Each path in this graph is a *dependencies path*. The resulting graph is shown in Figure 10.5, where black circles represent SCCs and arrows connected dependent SCCs. Each message passing consists of two events: sending and receiving of the message, but for simplicity we show messages as atomic events. The SCC nodes of the dependencies graph in Figure 10.5 are labeled by triplets $< Node, S\_Cost, Dep\_Agent >$, where $Node$ is the ID of the agent, S_Cost is the cost (in CCs) of the SCC represented

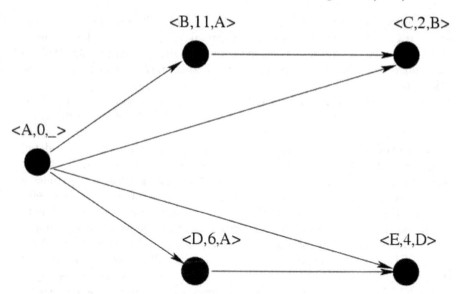

Fig. 10.5. Dependencies graph for the example in Figure 10.3. Black circles represent SCCs

by this node, and *Dep_Agent* is the name of the agent that sent the message that triggered this SCC.

The first event in this scenario is the zero-cost SCC performed by agent A. It is easy to see that the cumulative costs of SCCs performed by agents B, C,D,E are 11, 13, 6, 10, respectively, therefore the $TCCC$ is 13, which is equal to our intuitive estimation.

Note an important characteristic of the proposed model: event b depends on event a *iff* the computation of event a must finish *before* the computation of b starts. This partial temporal ordering of computations at different agents serves as the basis for a realistic model of distributed computation. Each dependency path includes a complete ordering of events and enables a simple calculation of the total computation effort along each path. This model bears a strong resemblance to time ordering, as proposed by Lamport in [32]. In the next section we design an algorithm to compute the nonconcurrent constraints checks (NCCCs) measure on a run of a DisCSP search algorithm. The algorithm uses the values of CC counters of agents to propagate the measure of concurrent constraints checks. It uses CC counter values in analogy to Lamport's concept of *logical clocks* [32].

10.5 The Cumulative Cost Algorithm (CCA)

Consider the dependencies graph in Figure 10.5. In order to calculate the total number of concurrent constraints checks (TCCC) that represents the computation effort of the algorithm in the example, all possible paths to the node with the final solution have to be followed. All edges in the dependencies graph in Figure 10.5 represent messages among agents. Each message triggers the computation that is represented by the cost of the SCC to which the edge is leading.

The recursive definition of Equation 10.2, for the cumulative cost, can be constructed on the fly during the computation of the DisCSP algorithm. To do that, each agent has to maintain a counter of CCs. The counter represents the agent view of the computation cost up to this point. This counter is updated at the end of each SCC computation. Messages include, in addition to the assignments of agents, the value of the counter of the sending agent. Since a distributed search algorithm is typically asynchronous, many agents receive messages that have different counter values written on them, corresponding to several paths that lead to a node of a given agent on the dependencies graph.

The basic scheme of the proposed algorithm for calculating the total cumulative cost is that each agent maintains a local counter of its view of the C_Cost. In the next section these counters will be shown to be equal to the C_Cost of the SCC node. We term these counters of the agents $AgentC\_Cost$. Each message that an agent sends includes the current value of the $AgentC\_Cost$ of the sending agent. We term the counter value on the message $SenderC\_Cost$. Upon receiving a message and before performing a sequence of constraints checks, the receiving agent updates its counter by comparing it to the $SenderC\_Cost$ that is written on the received message. After the agent performs the next SCC that this message triggered, the agent updates its $AgentC\_Cost$ counter to include the constraints checks it just performed in this SCC.

One way to understand the idea of the CCA algorithm is to think of it in terms of achieving a total ordering of events, where events are of three kinds - SCCs, sending messages, and receiving of messages. Our constraints checks counters behave exactly like Lamport's idealized (logical) clocks in [32]. They always increase in value for two events of the same agent. Following the algorithm for clock synchronization [32], the agents in the CCA algorithm send CC counter values that serve as time stamps. The result is a total ordering of events, as proven in [32], and therefore a total count of NCCCs (as defined in Section 10.4).

The target of the CCA algorithm is to return the computing cost of a given DisCSP algorithm. In order to incorporate CCA into a DisCSP algorithm one needs to perform the following steps:

- The first line of the agent's code initializes $AgentC\_Cost$ to 0.
- After every constraint check performed by an agent, the $AgentC\_Cost$ counter is increased by 1.
- All messages contain an additional field - $SenderC\_Cost$.
- When an agent sends a message, it sets $SenderC\_Cost$ on the message to the value of its $AgentC\_Cost$.

Algorithm 10.1: Cumulative Cost Algorithm (CCA)

Each agent initializes its $AgentC\_Cost$ counter to 0.
When an agent sends a message it includes in the message the value
of its $AgentC\_Cost$ counter
    After an agent performs any SCC it updates its $AgentC\_Cost$
        $AgentC\_Cost = AgentC\_Cost + S\_Cost$
    if(An agent receives a message with a counter $SenderC\_Cost$)
      if $(SenderC\_Cost + M\_Cost > AgentC\_Cost)$
      then $AgentC\_Cost = SenderC\_Cost + M\_Cost$
          # M_Cost is the message transfer cost
    if(a solution is found)
      then Return the maximal $AgentC\_Cost$ over all agents

- When an agent receives a message with a $SenderC\_Cost$ counter value
  plus transition cost larger than its own $AgentC\_Cost$ counter, it updates
  its $AgentC\_Cost$ counter to the value of the $SenderC\_Cost + M\_Cost$.

Let us trace the behavior of the CCA on the example in Figures 10.3
and 10.4. Initially the counter of agent A is 0. Agent B receives a message
from A with counter 0, after performing an SCC it updates its counter to 11.
Agent C receives a message from B with counter 11 and then updates it to
13 as the result of the execution of its SCC. In the same way, the counters
of agents D and E will eventually be updated to 6 and 10, respectively. The
maximal counter value is 13 and this value will be returned as the TCCC of
the computation. The result of applying the CCA is equal to the result of
application of our model. The CCA algprithm returns the number of nonconcurrent CCs (e.g., NCCCs) performed during the run of a distributed search
algorithm until it solves the DisCSP.

In the next section we prove this claim formally. The proof is given explicitly because counting NCCCs is computationally different than ordering
events in a distributed set of agents. Moreover, the CCA algorithm can include
in its cost calculation the cost of messages. In Chapter 12 the counting model
for NCCCs will be enhanced to deal with the simulation of message delays.

10.6 Realization of the Model by the CCA Algorithm

The goal of this section is to show that the inclusion of the CCA algorithm
in any distributed search algorithm for DisCSP will compute the TCCC as
defined by our model in Equation 10.3. This goal can be stated formally by
the following theorem:

Theorem 10.6.1 *Given that message transition cost* **M_Cost** *is zero for all messages, the CCA algorithm returns the total computing effort TCCC, as defined by Definition 10.8.*

A few lemmas are needed for the proof of this theorem. Let SV be the set of all the values of $AgentC\_Cost$ that was created during the run of the DISCSP algorithm that implements the CCA algorithm. Next, divide SV into equivalence classes by the use of the equality relation. Each value in the SV set is produced by one of the following two operations:

Update by message: an agent updates its old $AgentC\_Cost$ value by some larger $SenderC\_Cost$ value that it reads from a message.

SCC execution: the $AgentC\_Cost$ is updated *immediately after* the execution of an SCC sequence by adding the S_Cost to the current value of the $AgentC\_Cost$ counter.

The value created by the *Update by message* method is not new. In other words, at least one element of SV with the same value already exists in SV. This is because every message shows an existing $AgentC\_Cost$ of some agent. This observation is the essence of the first lemma.

Lemma 10.9. *In every equivalence class of SV there exists at least one element that was created by SCC execution of some agent.*

Let VT be the set of messages causing the $AgentC\_Cost$ value of some agent to be T. Let M be some message $\in VT$, passing from agent A to agent A'. This implies that the $AgentC\_Cost$ value of A just before sending M was T. This T value could be obtained in two ways: A got some message M' that set its $AgentC\_Cost$ value to T, or A performed some SCC.

In the first case, the message M' also belongs to VT. For the second case, observe an interesting fact: each message $\in VT$ is either binary-dependent on some other message that is also $\in VT$, or it is chain-dependent on some SCC which means that the $AgentC\_Cost$ value of the sending agent is T. Consider the graph of binary-dependencies induced by elements that are in VT. This graph is a collection of DAGs. Therefore, there are messages of VT that are independent of other messages of this set, and every message in VT is either independent or dependent on some independent message. But, by the fact observed above, every independent message in VT is dependent on some SCC causing the $AgentC\_Cost$ value of the agent performing it to be T. So, every message in VT is dependent on some such SCC. As can be seen from Figure 10.6, this implies that if an agent starts some SCC and its $AgentC\_Cost$ value is equal to $T > 0$ then this T value is the result of the finishing value of another agent just **after** some SCC. More formally:

Lemma 10.10. *If the AgentC_Cost value of agent A_1, just before execution of some SCC x is equal to T, and $T > 0$ then there exists at least one SCC y performed by some agent A_2 such that the AgentC_Cost value just after the execution of y is equal to T and that SCC x is chain-dependent on SCC y.*

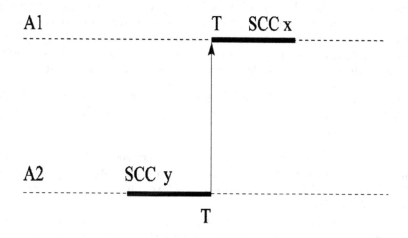

Fig. 10.6. Dependency between two SCCs

Clearly, x depends on the event causing the *AgentC_Cost* value to be T. This event is either the SCC y, or a message dependent on the SCC y, by the discussion above. In both of these cases the lemma holds. □

Dependency of events implies order in time. This means for our case that the path of dependencies in the dependencies graph is a growing series of values of CCs. More formally:

Lemma 10.11. *If SCC x_1 of agent A_1 depends on SCC x_2 of agent A_2 then the AgentC_Cost value of A_1 just before execution of x_1 is not less then the AgentC_Cost value of A_2 just after the execution of x_2.*

The proof is straightforward. If x_2 chain-depends on x_1, then there is some sequence of events E, where each event in the sequence E is either unary-dependent or binary-dependent on its predecessor. The first event in E is the execution of the SCC x_1 and the last event in E is the execution of x_2.

Let A_i be the agent initiating the i-th event in the sequence. Clearly, its *AgentC_Cost* counter value will not be less then the counter value of A_{i-1} after the occurrence of the *i-1-th* event. So, the counter of the agent initiating the last event in the sequence, **before the event** will not be less than the counter of the agent initiating the first event **after** its occurrence, by the transitivity of the $\leq$ relation □

Every path in the dependencies graph is a growing series of values of CCs, therefore the CCs value in each node is the largest value on this path up to this node. Many dependencies paths may lead to the same node, and the above conclusion is true for all of these paths. The immediate conclusion is that the CCs value at a mode is the maximal value over all the paths that leads to that node. The next lemma states the above conclusion in exact terms and shows that, if some $AgentC\_Cost$ value is created as the result of performing some SCC, then this value is the cumulative cost C_Cost of this SCC.

Lemma 10.12. *If a value of the counter $AgentC\_Cost = T$ of some agent A is produced as the result of execution of some SCC x then $T = C\_Cost(x)$ (as defined in Definition 10.7).*

Proof: Let us assume that there are no SCCs of zero cost and reformulate the lemma in the following way: if some agent A with current $AgentC\_Cost$ value of T' performs an SCC x then its $AgentC\_Cost$ value T after performing x is equal to $C\_Cost(x)$.

Because there is a finite number of possible values in SV for T', let us apply induction on these values in increasing order. If $T' = 0$ then clearly x does not depend on any other SCC because the dependency of x on any other SCC y contradicts Lemma 10.11. The counter value of A after performing x is equal to $S\_Cost(x)$, which is the same as $C\_Cost(x)$ for this case.

Otherwise, for $T' > 0$, assuming that the claim of the lemma holds for all $T' < Z$ $(Z \in SV)$, we will show it holds also for the case $T' = Z$. By Lemma 10.10 there is some SCC y performed by agent A', where x depends on y, and the value of A' after performing y is T'. Because the counter value of A' just before execution of y is less than T', $T' = C\_Cost(y)$ by the induction assumption. From $T = T' + S\_Cost(x)$ we derive that $T = C\_Cost(y) + S\_Cost(x)$.

To show that $T = C\_Cost(x)$ we have to show that, among all SCCs on which x is dependent, y is an SCC with the maximum cumulative cost. Assume that this is not true and there is some SCC z of agent A'' such that x depends on and $C\_Cost(z) > C\_Cost(y)$. Let T'' be the SCC z value of agent A'' after performing z. By Lemma 10.11 $T'' \leq T'$. Therefore, by the induction assumption $T'' = C\_Cost(z)$. Consequently $C\_Cost(z) \leq T'$ and $C\_Cost(z) \leq C\_Cost(y)$, which contradicts our assumption. Therefore $T = C\_Cost(x)$.   □

The proof of Theorem 10.6.1 is now immediate. By Lemma 10.12 all $AgentC\_Cost$ values produced by SCCs are the C_Costs of these SCCs. By Lemma 10.9 these values are representatives of SV. So, the set of all C_Costs is equal to the set of all SV. Consequently, their maximal element is also equal.   □

Corollary 10.13. *The claim of Theorem 10.6.1 holds also for messages which have non-zero costs (e.g., finite delays, see Chapter 12).*

Proof: To adapt the proof of Theorem 10.6.1 to non-zero cost messages, S_Costs may include the cost of the message received by the agent performing the SCC. In particular, for SCC x performed by agent A there may be two cases:

- The predecessor of x with maximal C_Cost is performed by the same agent. In this case the $S\_Cost(x)$ remains as is.
- The predecessor of x with maximal C_Cost is performed by another agent B. In this case, we add to $S\_Cost(x)$ the massage cost from B to A.

The above rule hides non-zero message costs within the cost of the consecutive SCC, and the cost of message sending itself remains zero. This way, both the model and the proof of Theorem 10.6.1 remain valid.   □

The model for the measurement of concurrent search effort on DisCSPs is based on Lamport's clock synchronization model. The model incorporates a dependencies graph among agents performing sequences of constraints checks and exchanging messages. The proposed model measures search effort by counting nonconcurrent constraints checks (NCCCs) on the dependencies graph. A simple algorithm for realizing the model within any distributed search algorithm, the cumulative cost algorithm (CCA), was defined and proven to realize the model. The implementation of the CCA within a DisCSP algorithm is very simple (see Algorithm 10.1).

The CCA algorithm can be implemented easily within a distributed algorithm, without any need for strong assumptions on the order of arriving messages and on instantaneous arrival of messages. In a realistic network of agents, where messages can arrive in any order and delay the distributed computation, the CCA is useful as it represents the actual computation.

By carrying counters within messages and updating counters by agents according to the most delayed message counter, the CCA will measure the real performance of the tested algorithm. It does not need any artificial division of the run of a DisCSP algorithm into rounds. The actual computation paths (sequences) among agents are measured and the costliest path is defined as the global cost (in NCCCs) of the computation. The NCCCs model has three main advantages:

- The definition of dependency among agents computations is realistic. Two events are dependent in the model if and only if there is a real dependencies path between these two events.
- The implementation of the model, in terms of the CCA, is very simple. It does not need any simplification assumptions on the sequentiality of a simulator, nor additional data structures. This advantage is important, because the implementation of a distributed algorithm in a sequential environment is a nontrivial task.
- The CCA can be easily implemented within a real distributed system, with concurrently running agents. Thus we compare a real, not simulated, computational effort.

In the extensive empirical study of all DisCSP search algorithms that is presented in Chapter 11 the run-time performance of all algorithms is measured in NCCCs. Additional measures of distributed computing will also be used in the empirical study, but NCCCs will be a central *asynchronous measure which is implementation independent and specifically suitable for constraints search algorithms.*

Experimental Evaluation of DɪsCSP Algorithms

The common approach to evaluating the performance of distributed algorithms is to compare two independent measures of performance: time, in the form of steps of computation [37, 61], and communication load, in the form of the total number of messages sent [37]. Comparing the number of nonconcurrent steps of computation of search algorithms on DɪsCSPs measures the time of run of the algorithms.

In order to take into account the effort an agent makes during its local assignment the computational effort can be measured by the number of constraints checks that agents perform. However, care must be taken to measure the *nonconcurrent* constraints checks, in other words, count computational effort of concurrently running agents *only once* during each concurrent running instance (see Chapter 10). Measuring the network load poses a much simpler problem. Network load is generally measured by counting the total number of messages sent during search [37].

Experiments with DɪsCSP search algorithms are standardly conducted on randomly generated networks of constraints. This is similar to the centralized CSP case [52, 56]. Random DɪsCSPs are characterized by n variables, k values in each domain, a constraints density of p_1, and tightness p_2 (commonly used in experimental evaluations of CSP algorithms, cf. [52, 56]). The density of the constraints satisfaction problem is defined to be the probability of a constraint among two variables. The *tightness* of constraints is the probability for a pair of values to violate the constraint, among a constrained pair of variables. All sets of experiments were conducted on networks with 10 to 20 agents (n=10-20) and 10 values for each variable ($k = 10$). To simplify algorithm implementation, all agents have a single variable. Typical values of the constraints density were used in different experiments and will be stated in each case. In many cases a density of $p_1 = 0.4$ was used to represent sparse constraint networks and a density of $p_1 = 0.7$ used for dense networks. The tightness value p_2 is varied in all experiments between 0.1 and 0.9 to cover all ranges of problem difficulty. This is aimed to test all algorithms near the phase transition region where some problem instances are very difficult to solve (see Section 2.3).

11.1 Comparing Different Algorithms

Chapter 5, Chapter 6, and Chapter 7 presented three different DISCSP search algorithms. In addition, the simplest distributed constraints search algorithm is synchronous backtracking (or synchronous backjumping), which was introduced in Chapter 4. As we already mentioned, SBJ was found empirically to outperform asynchronous backtracking when a good ordering heuristic is used [11].

We turn now to an extensive empirical evaluation of the main DISCSP search algorithms. First and foremost we will compare ABT to all other algorithms. Since ABT is the fully asynchronous search algorithm, that is expected to run completely concurrently, it is extremely interesting to compare its performance with competitor algorithms that perform only part of their potential computations concurrently. Consider first the *asynchronous forward-checking (AFC)* algorithm. As described in Chapter 6, it performs assignments sequentially. This is in contrast to ABT, in which agents perform assignments concurrently and asynchronously. This will be our first comparison (Section 11.1.1). The next comparison (in Section 11.1.2) will evaluate the performance of *ConcDB* and compare it to ABT. The *ConcDB* algorithm uses dynamic splitting of the search space to generate concurrent computation. However, its search processes all perform assignments sequentially (see Chapter 7). This makes the comparison in Section 11.1.2 of much interest.

In all of the empirical evaluations the ABT implementation used is the "best possible". It uses polynomial NOGOOD storage (e.g. Algorithm 5.2) and agents read complete mailboxes. This form of ABT is a bit more complex than the published pseudo-code versions in the literature. It needs code for discarding irrelevant messages and for ordering the messages when reading them from the agents' mailboxes.

The next step of empirical evaluation of the various algorithms is to measure their performance in the presence of ordering heuristics. The case of sequentially assigning algorithms, like *AFC*, is simple. Ordering heuristics are simple to devise and to implement. For asynchronous ordering heuristics the *ABT_DO* algorithm (Chapter 9) will be compared to standard ABT, for two different heuristics.

11.1.1 Asynchronous forward-checking vs. ABT

The performance of *AFC* is compared to asynchronous backtracking (ABT) as presented in Chapter 5. All NOGOODs are resolved and stored as explanations [9]. Based on Yokoo's suggestions [63] the agents read, in every step, all messages in their mailbox before performing computation.

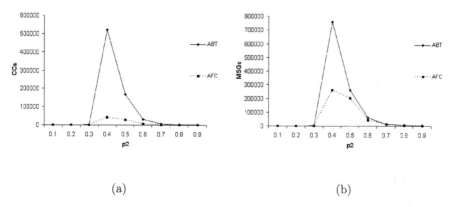

(a)   (b)

Fig. 11.1. (a) Number of nonconcurrent constraints checks in *AFC*, and in ABT, (b) total number of messages sent for both algorithms

Figure 11.1 presents a comparison of the computational effort performed by *AFC* and ABT on randomly generated DISCSPs. The advantage in non-concurrent constraints checks [Figure 11.1(a)] of *AFC* over ABT is quite large - *a factor of ten* - for the hard problem instances. The communication load, as measured by the total number of messages sent during search [Figure 11.1(b)], is also lower for *AFC* than for ABT, by a factor of 3 at the peak (see [44]).

11.1.2 Experimental evaluation of *ConcDB*

To investigate the effect of concurrency, one needs to compare the performance of concurrent search with and without splitting and dynamic splitting. To this end, the simplest concurrent search algorithm, *ConcBT*, was run in a 1-CPA version, 5-CPA version and a version which performs dynamic re-splitting (using a *step_limit* of 35). The *ConcBT* algorithm is used in this set instead of *ConcDB* to eliminate the effect of dynamic backtracking on the results. The 1-CPA version is completely sequential and serves as the baseline for comparison to the concurrent versions.

In the first set of experiments the density of the constraint networks is $p_1 = 0.7$. The value of the tightness, p_2 was varied between 0.1 and 0.9, to cover all range of problem difficulty. Results show averages over 50 runs.

Figure 11.2 shows the computational effort, the number of nonconcurrent constraint checks, for all three versions of *ConcBT*. It is easy to see that concurrency improves the search efficiency and that dynamic resplitting improves it further. For the harder problem instances the improvement is by a factor of 6 over the 1-CPA version and a factor of 3 over the 5-CPA version. Figure 11.3 shows the results in total number of messages sent. Clearly, the concurrent versions, either the 5-CPA version or the resplit one, circulate more CPAs in the network. However, the interesting result is that, even

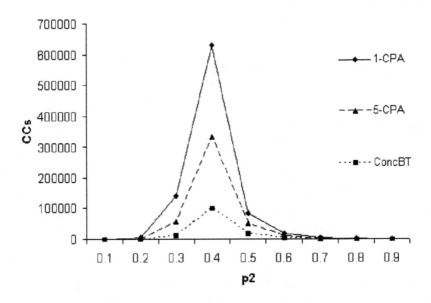

Fig. 11.2. Number of nonconcurrent constraint checks in different versions of *ConcBT*

though *ConcBT* with dynamic splitting increases the number of traversing CPAs during search, the effect on the total number of messages is negligible. The dynamic splitting *ConcBT* does send more messages concurrently but does so during a shorter period of time, resulting in a low amount of total communication.

In order to evaluate the performance of concurrent dynamic backtracking (*ConcDB*) it is compared to representatives of two families of algorithms. For sequential assignment DisCSP algorithms we select both *Conflict-based Back-jumping* (CBJ) [11, 68] and the *AFC* algorithm. The latter is an asynchronous and concurrent algorithm that performs assignments sequentially (see Chapter 6). CBJ is an improved version of synchronous backtracking [61], in which agents process *conflict sets* in order to backtrack directly to the culprit agent.

The family of asynchronous assignments is represented by asynchronous backtracking (ABT) [9, 61], again, the best version of ABT, reading whole mailboxes and keeping a polynomial number of NOGOODs (see Chapter 5). This forms the best performing version of ABT.

Figure 11.4 presents the number of nonconcurrent constraint checks performed by *ConcDB*, CBJ, *AFC*, and ABT on problems with low constraint density ($p_1 = 0.4$). For the harder problem instances, *ConcDB* outperforms

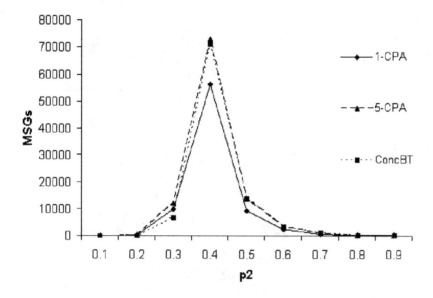

Fig. 11.3. Total number of messages sent in different versions of *ConcBT*

AFC by a factor of 1.5, ABT by a factor of 2.5 and CBJ by a factor of 3. Figure 11.5 presents the total number of messages sent by the algorithms in the same run. When it comes to network load the advantage of *ConcDB* over ABT and *AFC* is larger (a factor of 4). As expected, the total network load of the synchronous algorithm, which maintains a single message throughout the search, is the smallest. Still, the total number of messages sent by CBJ and *ConcDB* are very close.

11.2 Empirical Evaluation of Heuristic Ordering

Two sets of comparative experiments will be presented here. The first set will deal with distributed heuristics for sequentially assigning algorithms, like *AFC*. These heuristics were described in Sections 8.1, and 8.2. We will see that such heuristics improve the performance of even the simplest DISCSP algorithm to such an extent that it outperforms the best version of asynchronous backtracking. This was first noted in [11] and extended to *AFC* in [44].

The second set of experiments will deal with asynchronous heuristics and more specifically with the dynamically ordered ABT algorithm (*ABT_DO*). Here, the interesting finding is that successful asynchronous heuristics are in

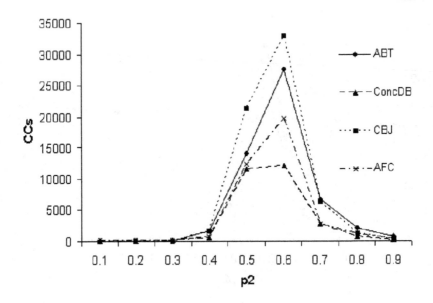

Fig. 11.4. Number of nonconcurrent constraint checks performed by ConcDB, ABT, and CBJ on low-density DisCSPs

general different from the centralized or sequential assignments versions. The best heuristic is found to be a NOGOOD-triggered ordering heuristic that outperforms the best version of static-ordered ABT by a large factor, especially on hard problem instances [74].

11.2.1 Evaluation of synchronous ordering heuristics

Figure 11.6 presents the number of nonconcurrent constraints checks performed by the AFC algorithm using different ordering heuristics on low density DisCSPs ($p_1 = 0.4$). All three ordering heuristics improve the performance of the statically ordered AFC. Figure 11.6 (b) presents a closer look at the difference between the different heuristics, removing the static AFC and scaling the heuristically ordered versions. The best performing heuristic is the minimal domain size (Min_Domain) heuristic. AFC using the Min_Domain heuristic performs half the NCCCs of AFC with the possible conflict (PC) heuristic and a third of the AFC using the Nogood-triggered (NG) heuristic (see Chapter 8). Figure 11.7 presents similar results for the measure of network load.

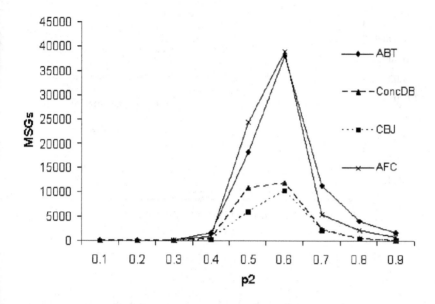

Fig. 11.5. Total number of messages sent by ConcDB, ABT, and CBJ on low-density DisCSPs

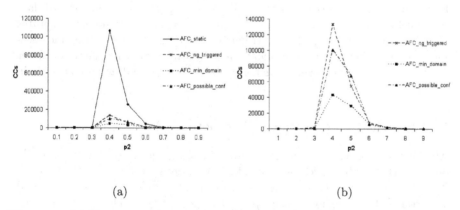

(a)   (b)

Fig. 11.6. (a) Nonconcurent constraints checks with different heuristics of *AFC*.
(b) Just the three ordering heuristics

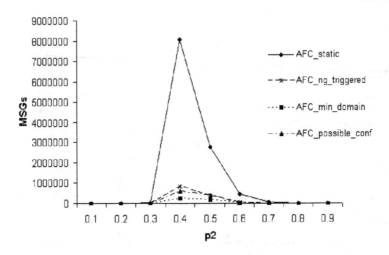

Fig. 11.7. Total number of messages sent by AFC with different ordering heuristics vs. static order ($p_1 = 0.4$)

The fact that the ratio of improvement of AFC over ABT grows with problem difficulty can be explained intuitively. Problem difficulty is known to be correlated with the number of solutions on random constraint networks [56]. Fewer solutions mean that a larger fraction of all partial assignments will fail. In asynchronous backtracking, each such "due to fail" assignment generates messages to multiple agents and triggers their further assignments and message passing. The above experiments demonstrate that when there are fewer solutions it is more efficient to generate consistent partial assignments, as in the AFC algorithm.

11.2.2 Evaluation of dynamically ordered ABT

All three sets of experiments for evaluating the performance of dynamically ordered ABT (ABT_DO) were conducted on networks with 20 agents ($n = 20$) each holding exactly one variable, 10 values for each variable ($k = 10$) and two values of constraints density $p_1 = 0.4$ and $p_1 = 0.7$. The tightness value p_2 is varied between 0.1 and 0.9 to cover all ranges of problem difficulty. For each pair of fixed density and tightness (p_1, p_2) 50 different random problems were solved by each algorithm and the results presented are an average of these 50 runs.

ABT_DO is compared to the run of standard ABT. For ordering variables in ABT_DO three different heuristics were used:

1. **Random:** each time an agent changes its assignment it randomly orders all agents with lower priorities in its *Current_order*.
2. **Domain-size:** this heuristic is inspired by the heuristics used for sequential assigning algorithms in [11]. Domain sizes are calculated based on the fact that each agent that performs an assignment includes its current domain size in the **order** message sent to all other agents. Every agent that replaces an assignment orders the lower priority agents according to their domain size from the smallest to the largest.
3. **Nogood-triggered:** agents change the order of the lower priority agents only when they receive a NOGOOD which eliminates their current assignment. In this case the agent moves the sender of the NOGOOD in front of all other lower priority agents. This heuristic was first used for dynamic backtracking in centralized CSPs by [23].

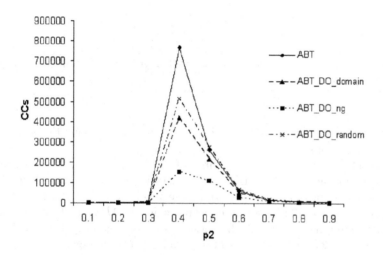

Fig. 11.8. Nonconcurrent constraints checks performed by ABT and *ABT_DO* using different ordering heuristics on low density DisCSPs ($p_1 = 0.4$).

Figure 11.8 presents the computational effort in number of nonconcurrent constraints checks to find a solution, performed by ABT and *ABT_DO* using the above three heuristics. The algorithms solve low-density DisCSPs with a density of $p_1 = 0.4$. *ABT_DO* with random ordering slightly improves the results of standard ABT. *ABT_DO* that uses domain sizes to order the lower priority agents performs slightly better than the random version. The largest improvement is gained by using the *Nogood-triggered* heuristic. For the hardest

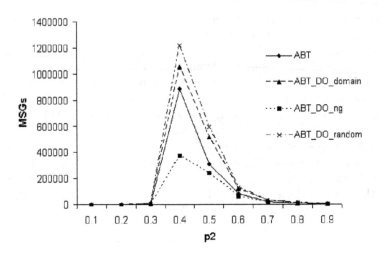

Fig. 11.9. Number of messages sent by ABT and ABT_DO on low density DisCSPs ($p_1 = 0.4$).

DisCSP instances, ABT_DO with the *Nogood-triggered* heuristic improves the performance of standard ABT by a factor of 4.

Figure 11.9 presents the total number of messages sent by the algorithms for the same problems. While ABT_DO with the random ordering heuristic shows a small improvement in the run time results over standard ABT, it sends more messages. This can be expected since in ABT_DO agents send additional **order** messages and **ok?** messages to all their neighbors while in standard ABT, **ok?** messages are sent only to lower priority agents (see Chapter 5 and Chapter 9). ABT_DO with domain size ordering sends more messages than standard ABT but fewer than the random ordering version. The really interesting result is that ABT_DO with the Nogood-*triggered* heuristic *sends fewer messages than ABT*. Counting the additional **ok?** messages (sent to higher priority agents) and the **order** messages, it still sends fewer messages than standard ABT on the hardest DisCSP instances.

In AFC agents assign their variables sequentially and perform consistency checks against the current partial assignment concurrently. Although the heuristics used by AFC are the same heuristics used by ABT_DO, the results are very different. All dynamic ordering heuristics used by AFC improve the run of static order AFC. The best heuristic is the *min-domain* heuristic (see Section 11.2.1). It is interesting to try and understand the difference between the behavior of asynchronous backtracking with dynamic ordering and that of sequential assignment DISCSP algorithms like asynchronous forward checking (AFC).

To achieve some understanding one needs to remember that agents in asynchronous backtracking constantly and asynchronously perform assignments against their current view of the system. The state of the system viewed by an agent includes its values, pruned by either NOGOODs or some current assignments of higher priority agents. In standard ABT a NOGOOD is discarded and its corresponding value is returned to the agent's current domain only when higher priority agents replace their assignments. In dynamic ordered ABT, NOGOODs can be discarded due to a change of order even if the assignments included in the NOGOOD are not changed. Consider an agent A_i that holds a NOGOOD ng which includes the assignment of a higher priority agent A_j. If agent A_j is moved to a lower priority than A_i, ng is no longer valid since values are discarded only when they conflict with assignments of higher priority agents.

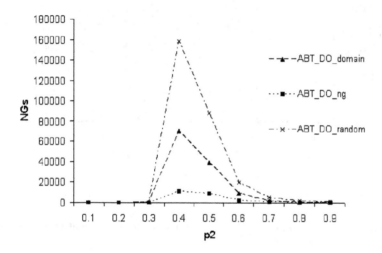

Fig. 11.10. Number of removed NOGOODs as a result of order changes by ABT_DO ($p_1 = 0.4$)

Another look at the tested heuristics with the above insight in mind reveals that both the *random* heuristic and the *min-domain* heuristic do not take this property into consideration and that reordering agents according to them may cause the loss of valid NOGOODs. In contrast, ABT_DO with the *Nogood-triggered* heuristic rarely removes NOGOODs due to changes of order. In ABT, an agent sends a NOGOOD to the lowest priority agent among the higher priority agents whose assignment is included in one of its NOGOODS (Chapter 5 [9]). This means that, if an agent A_i is moved by agent A_j to a place immediately following A_j, all the assignments of agents that were previously ordered between A_i and A_j are removed from A_i's NOGOODS. Since these assignments were not involved in the NOGOOD, all of A_i's previous NO-GOODS are still valid.

Figure 11.10 presents the total number of NOGOODS removed by *ABT_DO*, as a result of order changes. The *Nogood-triggered* heuristic looses a very small number of NOGOODS as a result of order changes. The number of NOGOODS removed by the random and the *min-domain* heuristic is much larger.

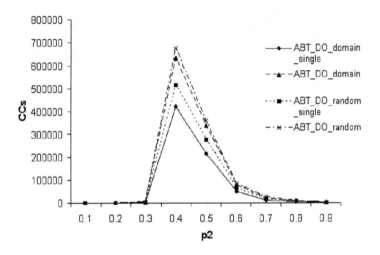

Fig. 11.11. Nonconcurrent constraints checks performed by different versions of the *ABT_DO* ordering heuristics ($p_1 = 0.4$)

In sequential assignment algorithms only the next variable to be assigned is selected by the heuristic. In *ABT_DO* all unassigned agents can be reordered. Figure 11.11 presents a comparison between two versions of the *random* and the *min-domain* heuristics. Each heuristic was performed in two different versions. In one, after each assignment all lower priority agents are reordered according to the heuristic, in the other only the agent which will have the highest priority among the lower priority agents is selected by the heuristic and the other agents keep their places from the previous heuristic (these heuristics are called *single* in the figures). The results are clearly in favor of the *single* version of the heuristics. Figure 11.12 presents a possible explanation for these results. It is clear that the *single* versions of the heuristics remove

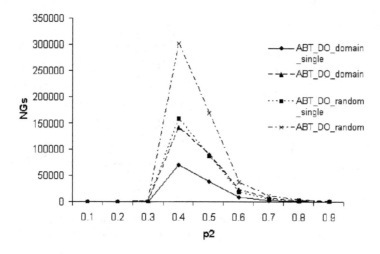

Fig. 11.12. Total number of NOGOODs that are removed as a result of order changes by *ABT_DO* with different versions of ordering heuristics ($p_1 = 0.4$)

fewer NOGOODs due to order changes than the heuristics that order all of the lower priority agents.

11.2.3 Retroactive ordering for ABT

The limited (parametrized) storage of NOGOODs of the retroactive ordered version of *ABT_DO* (Section 9.4) can be used to test several heuristic ideas. One aspect is to check the dependency of the performance on the size of the current domain of the moved agents. To this end one uses a retroactive heuristic in which agents are not allocated any additional NOGOOD storage. Agents include in their messages the size of their current domains. This information is stored in the agent's *Agent_views*. A NOGOOD generator moves itself to be in a higher position than the culprit agent but it moves in front of an agent *only if its current domain is smaller* than the domain of that agent. Otherwise, it places itself right after the culprit agent as in standard *ABT_DO*.

The left-hand side (LHS) of Figure 11.13 presents the results in NCCCs for *ABT_DO* and Retroactive *ABT_DO* with the above heuristic. The retroactive version of *ABT_DO* (depicted in the figures as *min-domain*) improves the run-time performance of *ABT_DO* (depicted as *ABT_DO_NG*). In order to emphasize the relation to the *Min-Domain* property, a third line in Figure 11.13 represents retroactive *ABT_DO* without checking the domain sizes (depicted in the figures as *After Second Last*). This version of retroactive

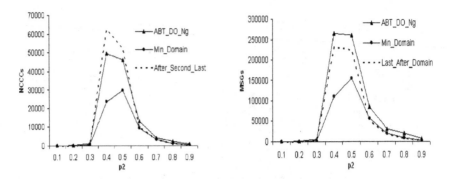

Fig. 11.13. Nonconcurrent constraint checks performed and messages sent by Retroactive ABT_DO and by ABT_DO on low-density DisCSPs ($p_1 = 0.4$)

ABT_DO was the slowest among the three. Similar results for the number of messages sent are presented on the right-hand side (RHS) of Figure 11.13. In the case of network load, both versions of *Retroactive ABT_DO* send less messages than standard ABT_DO.

In order to further demonstrate the dependency of the domain size of agents on the success of the selected heuristic, an additional experiment was performed. Here, the size limit for keeping NOGOODs is varied[1]. A NOGOOD generator which created a NOGOOD of length larger than k places itself right after the NOGOOD receiver as in standard ABT_DO. When the NOGOOD generator creates a NOGOOD smaller or equal to k, it places itself first in the priority order and sends the generated NOGOOD to all the participating agents. In the case of $k = n$ the resulting algorithm is exactly AWC. In the case of $k = 0$ the resulting algorithm is standard ABT_DO. The LHS of Figure 11.14 presents the number of $NCCCs$ performed by the algorithm with k equal to $0, 1, 3$ and n ($n = 15$). The results show similar performance when k is small. The performance of the algorithm deteriorates when $k = 3$ and the slowest performance is when $k = n$. Similar results for the total number of messages sent are presented on the RHS of Figure 11.14.

The fact that a larger storage which enables more flexibility of the heuristic actually causes a deterioration of the performance might come as a surprise. However, one must examine the effect of the specific heuristic used on the size of the domains of the agents which are moved up in the order of priorities. An agent creates a NOGOOD when its domain empties. After sending the NOGOOD it removes the assignment of the culprit agent from its *Agent_view* and returns to the domain only values whose eliminating NOGOOD included the removed assignment. When the agent is moved in front of other agents

---

[1] In this experiment the problems were smaller ($n = 15$) since the algorithms run slower.

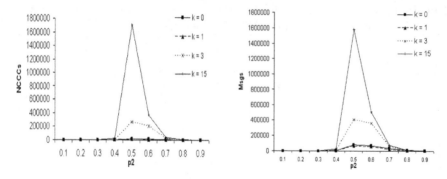

Fig. 11.14. Non concurrent constraint checks performed and messages sent by Retroactive ABT_DO with different limits on $Nogood$ size ($p_1 = 0.4$)

whose assignments were included in the generated NOGOOD it must return more values to its domain. These are the values whose explanation NOGOOD included the assignment of the agent which was passed. This of course does not happen for the case of a NOGOOD of size one and that is why for $k = 1$ we get better results. Thus, moving an agent as high as possible in the priority order actually results in moving upwards an agent with a larger domain.

The experiments demonstrate a clear relation between the heuristics and the *Min-Domain* property of the generated search tree. A well known fact from centralized CSP algorithms [16, 26] and from DISCSP algorithms with a sequential assignment protocol [11] is that the *Min-Domain* heuristic is very powerful on randomly generated problems. It is clear in the experiments that in most cases the *Nogood-triggered* heuristic of [71] moves to higher priority agents with smaller domains. This is because an agent whose domain was exhausted returns to its domain, after sending the NOGOOD, only the values in conflict with the assignment of the culprit agent. Thus, only a small number of values are returned to its domain. It is not surprising that this heuristic was found to be very successful [71, 72]. On the other hand, when an agent is moved to a higher position than the agents in the NOGOOD it discovered, it must return additional values to its domain. This contradicts the properties of the *min-domain* heuristic and was found to perform poorly in practice. The case of $k = 1$ did show an improvement since the last assignment in a detected NOGOOD is always removed from the *Agent_view* of the agent which found the NOGOOD.

In the best performing heuristic, agents are moved higher in the priority order as long as their domain size is smaller than the domains of the agents before them and as long as they do not pass the second last in the NOGOOD they have generated, which would result in returning more values to their domain. Since the agent moving to a higher position is not in conflict with the assignments of agents it has moved in front of, its move will not cause the loss of NOGOODs and therefore the information it holds on the size of the current domains of these agents remains valid. The retroactive ordering version has improved the results of [71, 72] by a factor of 2.

The Impact of Communication - Message Delays

The standard model of Distributed Constraints Satisfaction Problems has agents that are autonomous asynchronous entities. The actions of agents are triggered by messages that are passed among them. In real-world systems, messages do not arrive instantaneously but are delayed due to network properties. Delays can vary from network to network (or with time, in a single network) due to networks topologies, different hardware, and different protocols used. In order to investigate the impact of message delays on DISCSP algorithms, two essential requirements have to be satisfied:

- Means of controlling the amount and type of delays in the experimental set up.
- A common scale for message delays and the performance measures of distributed search algorithms.

The first study of the impact of message delays on DISCSP algorithms used randomly generated delays that were measured in real time of runs [19]. The results indicated a strong deterioration in the performance of ABT with random message delays. However, the scale of delays in [4, 19] dictated the measurement of performance in real time. While this is acceptable, it is highly implementation dependent. As explained in Chapter 11, the performance of distributed algorithms is measured by two standard means that are implementation independent. To achieve such measurement for distributed and concurrent algorithms, one must use a well-controlled environment in the form of a simulator. To simulate asynchronous agents, the simulator implements agents as *Java Threads*. Threads (agents) run asynchronously, exchanging messages by using a common mailer. After the algorithm is initiated, agents block on incoming message queues and become active when messages are received. The *Mailer* can simulate message delays, but, needs to be controlled by an algorithm that takes into account the concurrent time-keeping of the asynchronous system.

Concurrent steps of computation, in systems with no message delay, are counted by a method similar to that of [32, 45, 53]. As described in Chapter 10, every agent holds a counter of computation steps. Every message carries the value of the sending agent's counter. When an agent receives a message it updates its counter to the largest of its own counter and the counter value carried by the message. By reporting the cost of the search as the largest counter held by any agent at the end of the search, we achieve a measure of concurrent search effort that is similar to Lamport's logical time [32]. These concurrent counters that are stamped on all messages and, passed around, can serve the *Mailer* in monitoring system time and controlling message delays.

In systems with message delays, the measurement of concurrent run time (in the form of nonconcuurent constraints checks, NCCCs) is more complex. For the simplest possible algorithm, Synchronous Backtrack (*SBT*), the effect of message delay is very clear. The number of computation steps is not affected by message delays and the delay in every step of computation is the delay on the message that triggered it. Therefore, the total time of the algorithm run can be calculated as the total computation time plus the total delay time of messages. In the presence of concurrent computation, the time of message delays must be added to the total run time of the algorithm *only if no computation was performed concurrently*. To achieve this goal, the algorithm of the *Asynchronous Message-Delay Simulator* (*AMDS*) counts message delays in terms of computation steps and adds them to the accumulated run time when no computation is performed concurrently [72, 73].

In order to simulate message delays, all messages are passed by a dedicated *Mailer* thread. The mailer holds a counter of concurrent computation steps performed by agents in the system. This counter represents the logical time of the system and we refer to it as the *Logical Time Counter* (*LTC*). Every message delivered by the mailer to an agent carries the *LTC* value of its delivery to the receiving agent. To compute the logical time that includes message delays agents perform a similar computation to the one used when there are no message delays [45]. An agent that receives a message updates its own *LTC* to the larger of its own and the *LTC* on the message received. Then the agent performs the computation step, and sends its outgoing messages with the value of its *LTC* incremented by 1. The same mechanism can be used for computing the nonconcurrent *computational effort*, by counting nonconcurrent constraints checks. Agents add to the counter values in outgoing messages the number of constraints checks performed in the current step of computation.

The mailer simulates message delays in terms of concurrent computation steps. To do so it uses its own (global) *LTC*. When the mailer receives a message, it first checks if the *LTC* value that is carried by the message is larger than its own value. If so, it increments the value of the *LTC*. This generates the value of the global clock (of the Mailer) which is the largest of all the logical times of all agents. Next, a delay for the message (in number of steps) is selected. Different types of selection mechanisms can be used, from fixed delays, through random delays, to delays that depend on the actual load of the communication network [72]. To achieve delays that simulate dependency on network load, for example, one can assign message delays that are proportional to the size of the outgoing message queue.

12.1 Simulating Delayed Messages on DisCSPs

Algorithm 12.1: The Mailer algorithm

- **upon receiving message** *msg*:
  1. LTC ← max(LTC, msg.LTC)
  2. delay ← *choose_delay*
  3. msg.*delivery_time* ← msg.LTC + delay
  4. *outgoing_queue*.add(msg)
  5. *deliver_messages*
- **when there are no incoming messages and all agents are idle**
  1. LTC ← *outgoing_queue*.first_msg.LTC
  2. *deliver_messages*
- **deliver_messages**
  1. **foreach** (message m in outgoing queue)
  2.   **if** (*m.delivery_time* ≤ LTC)
  3.   deliver(m)

Let us go over the details of the *Mailer* algorithm in Algorithm 12.1, in order to understand the measurements performed by the simulator during run time. When the mailer receives a message, it first checks if the LTC value that is carried by the message is larger than its own value. If so, it increments the value of the LTC (line 1). In line 2 a delay for the message (in number of steps) is selected. Here, different types of selection mechanisms can be used, as mentioned above.

Each message is assigned a *delivery_time* which is the sum of the value of the message's LTC and the selected delay (in steps), and placed in the *outgoing_queue* (lines 3,4). The *outgoing_queue* is a priority queue in which the messages are sorted by *delivery_time*, so that the first message is the message with the lowest *delivery_time*. In order to preserve the assumption about ABT, that two messages between the same pair of agents must arrive in the same order they were sent, messages from agent A_i to agent A_j cannot be placed in the outgoing queue before messages which are already in the outgoing queue which were also sent from A_i to A_j. This property is essential to asynchronous backtracking, which is not correct without it (cf. [9]). The last line of the *Mailer*'s code calls method *deliver_messages*, which delivers all messages with *delivery_time* less or equal to the mailer's current LTC value to their destination agents.

When there are no incoming messages, and all agents are idle, if the *outgoing_queue* is not empty (otherwise the system is idle and a solution has been found) the mailer increases the value of the LTC to the value of the *delivery_time* of the first message in the outgoing queue and calls *deliver_messages*. This is a crucial step of the simulation algorithm. Consider the run of a synchronous search algorithm. For synchronous backtracking (SBT) [61], every delay needs the mechanism of updating the Mailer's LTC (line 1 of the second function of the code in Algorithm 12.1). This is because only one agent is computing at any given instance, in synchronous backtrack search.

The nonconcurrent run time reported by the algorithm is the largest LTC value that is held by any agent at the end of the algorithm's run. By incrementing the LTC only when messages carry LTCs with values larger than the mailer's LTC value, steps that were performed concurrently are not counted twice. This is an extension of Lamport's logical clocks algorithm [32], as proposed for DisCSPs by [45], and extended here for message delays.

A similar description holds for evaluating the algorithm run in nonconcurrent constraints checks. In this case the agents need to extend the value of their LTCs by the number of constraints checks they actually performed in each step. This enables a concurrent performance measure that incorporates the computational cost of the local step, which might be different in different algorithms. It also enables to evaluate algorithms in which agents perform computation which is not triggered or followed by a message.

12.1.1 Adjusting the measuring method for dynamic ordering

In asynchronous backtracking with dynamic agent ordering [74] as in the asynchronous weak commitment (AWC) search algorithm, agents hold in their *Agent_Views* assignments of both higher and lower priority agents. The agents check their current assignment only against assignments of agents with higher priority according to the current order. However, since the priority order is dynamic, an assignment of a lower priority agent which is currently irrelevant may become relevant as a result of a change in the order of priorities, thus such lower priority assignments are not discarded from the agent's *Agent_View*. The agents performing asynchronous backtracking with dynamic ordering (ABT_DO) or asynchronous weak commitment (AWC), send their assignments to all their neighbors (and not only to their current lower priority neighbors) for the same reason [61, 74].

Messages which carry the assignments of lower priority agents to higher priority agents do not trigger immediate computation since the assignment in the received message cannot rule out the local assignment even if they are in conflict.

A small change in the agents actions would adjust the measuring method of $AMDS$ presented above for counting nonconcurrent logic steps to deal with messages which do not trigger immediate computation, and their data is stored for later use. In order to preserve the concept of *nonconcurrent* logic steps, for every message received, before updating the local logic time counter

(LTC) the agent must make sure that the computation performed in order to produce the data carried by the message *could not have been performed* concurrently with the steps of computation it is about to perform. Another way to look at this is to ask if the computation steps about to be performed could have been performed if the message carrying the corresponding data was delayed. This can be done by the agents by delaying the update of their *LTC* in cases where the received *LTC* is larger. Instead the agents store the data in the message receive together with the corresponding *LTC*. When the stored data is first used for computation, the corresponding *LTC* is compared with the local *LTC* and the last is updated with the largest of the two.

12.2 Validity of *AMDS*

The validity of the proposed simulation algorithm can be established in two steps. First, its correspondence to runs of a *synchronous (cycle-counting) simulator* is presented. Understanding the nature of this correspondence, enables one to show that a corresponding synchronous cycle simulator cannot measure concurrent delayed steps and the *AMDS* is necessary.

In a *synchronous cycle simulator* (SCS) [61], each agent can read all messages that were sent to it in the previous cycle and perform a single computation step. The computation is followed by the sending of messages (which will be received in the next cycle). Agents can be idle in some cycles, if they do not receive a message which triggers a computation step. The cost of the algorithm run is the number of synchronous cycles performed until a solution is found or a nonsolution is declared (see [61]). Message delay can be simulated in such a synchronous simulator by delivering messages to agents several cycles after they were sent. Our first step is to show the correspondence of *AMDS* and an SCS.

Theorem 12.1. *Any run of AMDS can be simulated by a synchronous cycle simulator (SCS). Each cycle c_i of the SCS corresponds to an LTC value of AMDS.*

Proof. Every message m sent by an agent A_i to agent A_j, using the *AMDS*, can be assigned a value d which is the largest value between the *LTC* carried by m in the *AMDS* run and the value of the *LTC* held by A_j when it receives m. Running a synchronous cycle simulator (SCS) and assigning each message m with the value d calculated as described above, the message can be delivered to A_j in cycle d. The outcome of this special SCS is that every agent in every cycle c_i receives the same messages as the agents in the corresponding *AMDS* and the histories of all these messages are equivalent. This means that agents have the same knowledge about the other agents as the agents performing the corresponding steps in the *AMDS* run. Assuming that the algorithm is deterministic, each agent will perform the same computation and send the same messages. If the algorithm includes random choices the run can be simulated by recording $AMDS$ choices and forcing the same choice in the synchronous simulator run.   □

This theorem demonstrates that, for measuring the number of steps of computation, the asynchronous simulator is equivalent to a standard SCS *that does not wait for all agents* to complete their computation in a given cycle, in order to move to the next cycle. Message delays are simulated simply by the SCS delivering messages in delayed cycles.

The validity and importance of the asynchronous simulator can now be understood. Consider the important case where computational effort needs to be measured, in terms of constraints checks for example. At each cycle agents perform different amounts of computation, depending on the algorithm, the arrival of messages, etc. The SCS has no way to guess the amount of computation performed by each agent in any given step or cycle. It therefore cannot deliver the resulting message in the correct cycle (one that matches the correct amount of computation and waiting). The natural way to incorporate the computational cost into the performance measure is to clock the simulator by CCs (for example). But this is equivalent to using the $AMDS$ as proposed in section 12.1.

The $AMDS$ presented in Section 12.1 enables a deeper exploration of the behavior of different search algorithms for DisCSPs on systems with different message delays. Message delays emphasize the properties of families of algorithms which are not apparent when the algorithms are run in a system with perfect communication. Experimental evidence for such behavior was found recently for asynchronous backtracking algorithms [4, 54].

13

Message Delays and DisCSP Search Algorithms

The behavior of distributed search algorithms on DisCSPs can be studied on a set of three very different families of DisCSP algorithms. All search algorithms on DisCSPs can be divided into two families: *single search process* algorithms (SPAs) and *concurrent (multiple) search* process algorithms (CSAs). The only former experimental study of the performance of DisCSP algorithms compared two asynchronous single search algorithms [4].

The state of single process algorithms is defined by a *single tuple of assignments*, one for each agent. When this set of assignments is complete (containing assignments to all variables of all agents) and consistent, the SPA stops and reports a solution. A simple representation for the state of any *synchronous* SPA, like SBT [61] or CBJ [68], is a data structure that holds the *current partial assignment* of the search (CPA). Single search process algorithms can be asynchronous. In *asynchronous* backtracking (ABT) [9, 61], each agent holds its view of the current assignments of other agents in a single *Agent_View* (Chapter 5). When all agents are idle, all *Agent_Views* are consistent and a solution is reported [9, 61].

In concurrent search, multiple concurrent processes perform search on nonintersecting parts of the global search space of a DisCSP ([25, 55, 67]). All agents in a CSA participate in every search process, since each agent holds some variables of the search space. Each agent holds the current domains of its variables, for each of the search processes. Messages of CSAs carry the IDs of their related search process and the agents use the corresponding current domains for consistent assignments. The concurrent backtracking algorithm (*ConcBT*), distributes among agents a dynamically changing number of search processes [75] (see Chapter 7). Agents generate and terminate search processes dynamically during the run of the *ConcBT* algorithm. The concurrent dynamic backtracking (*ConcDB*) algorithm incorporates dynamic backtracking to the concurrent performing search processes. As a result, one search procedure can reveal a dead end of another concurrent search procedure and terminate it [75].

In interleaved asynchronous backtracking, agents participate in multiple processes of asynchronous backtracking. Each agent keeps a separate *Agent_View* for each search process in *IDIBT* [25]. The number of search processes is fixed by the first agent. The performance of concurrent asynchronous backtracking [25, 55] was tested and found to be ineffective for more than two concurrent search processes [25].

The general model of DisCSPs has variables owned by agents, who assign them values. The distinction between the two families of algorithms is in the number of concurrent assignments that agents maintain. In SPAs each agent can have no more than one assignment to its variable at any single instance. In multiple process algorithms (MPAs), on the other hand, agents maintain multiple concurrent assignments to their variable. To give an example, synchronous backtracking (SBT) is a single process algorithm. During search, a single CPA carries the assignments of some of the agents. The other agents which are waiting for the message with assignments to arrive are still unassigned. Therefore, each agent, in every step of the search, has either one assignment or none. Asynchronous backtracking (ABT) is also an SPA. All the variables in ABT have exactly one assignment at each instant of its run [9].

To maintain two concurrent assignments in a DisCSP, let us go back to Chapter 7. Think of the first agent as assigning two of its values to its variable. It then puts each assignment on a different message and initializes a backtracking process for each one. Each backtrack process traverses all agents, not in the same order, to accumulate assignments to all variables of all agents. All agents eventually receive two messages. One message has the first assignment for the first agent and the other has the second assignment that the first agent performed. Agents that receive a message either add their compatible assignment to the partial assignment already on the message or backtrack by sending the message back. All agents use a different current domain for each of the messages. It is easy to see that all agents react to the two messages in exactly the same way, assigning their variable to it or backtracking. This process stops when one of the messages accumulates a complete assignment and reports a solution or when both messages return to the first agent and find no more values to assign. In this case the two-process algorithm reports failure.

Several single process DisCSP search algorithms have appeared in the literature in the last decade: synchronous algorithms like synchronous backtrack (SBT) and conflict-based backjumping (CBJ) [61, 68]; asynchronous algorithms like asynchronous backtracking (ABT), asynchronous aggregations search (AAS) and asynchronous forward-checking (*AFC*) [44, 54]. In contrast, only a few multiple process DisCSP search algorithms appear in the literature [25, 55, 75]. The concurrent dynamic backtracking algorithm (*ConcDB*), with dynamic splitting of search processes, will be the representative of this family in the present study. *ConcDB* incorporates dynamic splitting, generating a variable number of search processes. Furthermore, the search processes cooporate in order to detect and terminate invalid active search processes (see Chapter 7).

The representative *synchronous* SPA will be the best of its kind, *synchronous conflict-based backJumping (CBJ)*. The synchronous (distributed) version of conflict based backjumping (CBJ) improves on simple synchronous backtrack (SBT) by using a method based on dynamic backtracking [23]. In the improved version, when an agent removes a value from its variable's domain, it stores the eliminating explanation (NOGOOD), i.e., the subset of the CPA that caused the removal. When a backtrack operation is performed, the agent resolves its NOGOODs, creating a conflict set which is used to determine the culprit agent to which the backtrack message will be sent. The resulting synchronous algorithm has the backjumping property (i.e., CBJ) [23]. When the CPA is received again, values whose eliminating NOGOODs are no longer consistent with the partial assignment on the CPA are returned to the agents' domain.

The CBJ algorithm is presented in Algorithm 13.1. In the main function, the first agent initializes the search by creating a CPA, assigning and sending it by using the function *assign_CPA* (lines 2-4). Lines 5-10 describe how agents respond to one of three types of messages:

1. *stop*: indicating that the search has ended
2. *CPA*: carrying a CPA forward
3. *backtrack*: carrying a CPA backwards, with an inconsistent assignment

Upon the reception of a stop message the agent simply stops the search by exiting the loop. When a CPA moving forward is received, the agent first calls function *refresh_domain*. This returns to the agent's *current_domain* values whose explanation is not included in the received CPA. Next, the agent calls function *assign_CPA*, attempting to assign its variable.

When a *backtrack* message is received, the agent calls function *remove_last_assignment* which removes the value assignment of the agent in the inconsistent CPA from its *current_domain*. It then stores it with the received CPA in the form of a NOGOOD. Finally, it replaces the CPA with a copy of the last CPA it sent, which holds the assignment it will try to extend and send forward. This takes place in the function *assign_CPA* that is called immediately after *remove_last_assignment*. When the agent fails to extend a CPA it calls the function *backtrack* whose first line resolves the inconsistent subset of the CPA (line 1). Then, a check is made whether the NOGOOD created is empty which will indicate the DISCSP has no solution (lines 2-4). If the NOGOOD found is not empty, it is sent to the agent with the lowest priority whose assignment is included in the NOGOOD (lines 6). This is standard dynamic backtracking [23].

13.1 The Impact of Message Delays

The network of constraints, in each of the experiments, is generated randomly by selecting the probability p_1 of a constraint among any pair of variables and

---

Algorithm 13.1: The distributed CBJ algorithm

- **CBJ**:
  1.done ← false
  2.if(first_agent)
  3. CPA ← create_CPA
  4.   assign_CPA
  5. while(**not** done)
  6.   **switch** msg.type
  7.   *stop*:done ← true
  8.   *backtrack*: remove_last_assignment
  9.   assign_CPA
  10. CPA:refresh_domain
  11.   assign_CPA
- **assign_CPA**:
  1. CPA ← assign_local
  2.   **if**(is_consistent(CPA))
  3.   **if**(is_full(CPA))
  4.   *report_solution*
  5.   stop
  6.   **else**
  7.   send(CPA, next)
  8.   **else**
  9.   *backtrack*
- **backtrack**:
  1. CPA ← *resolve_nogoods*
  2. **if**(*is_empty*(CPA))
  3.   CPA ← no_solution
  4.   stop
  5. **else**
  6.   send(*backtrack, CPA.last_asignee*)
- **remove_last_assignment**:
  1. store(CPA.last_assignment,CPA)
  2. CPA ← $\{last\_sent\_CPA\} \setminus \{last\_assignment\}$
  3. current_domain ← $\{current\_domain\} \setminus \{last\_assignment\}$
- **refresh_domain**:
  1. **for each** stored *Nogood sn*
  2.   **if**(not consistent(CPA,*sn*))
  3.   current_domain ← $\{current\_domain\} \cup \{sn.last\_assignment\}$
- **stop**:
  1. send(stop, *all_other_agents*)
  2. done ← true

the probability p_2, for the occurrence of a violation among two assignments of values to a constrained pair of variables. This set up is similar to that of our experimental evaluation of DISCSP algorithms in Chapter 11. The experiments with message delays were conducted on networks with 15 agents ($n = 15$) and 10 values ($k = 10$). Two density parameters were used, $p_1 = 0.4$ and $p_1 = 0.7$. The value of p_2 was varied between 0.1 to 0.9. This creates problems that cover a wide range of difficulty, from easy problem instances to instances that take several CPU minutes to solve (see Chapter 11). For every pair (p_1,p_2) in the experiments we present the average over 50 randomly generated instances.

In order to evaluate the algorithms, two measures of search effort are used. One counts the number of nonconcurrent constraint checks (NCCCs), to measure computational cost. This measures the combined path of computation, from beginning to end, in terms of constrait checks. The other measure used is the communication load in the form of the total number of messages sent [37]. In order to evaluate the number of nonconcurrent CCs including message delays, the $AMDS$ simulator is used.

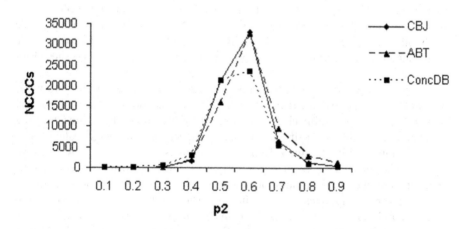

Fig. 13.1. Nonconcurrent constraint checks with no message delays ($p_1 = 0.4$)

In the first set of experiments the three algorithms are compared without any message delay. The results presented in Figures 13.1 and 13.3 show that the numbers of nonconcurrent constraint checks that the three algorithms perform are very similar, on systems with no message delays. ABT performs slightly fewer steps than CBJ and *ConcDB* performs slightly better than ABT. When it comes to network load, the results in Figures 13.2 and 13.4 show that, for the harder problem instances, agents in ABT send 4

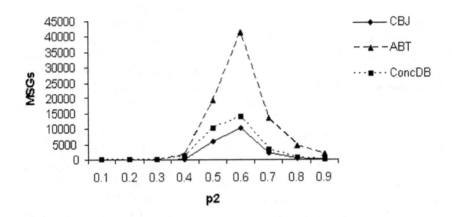

Fig. 13.2. Total number of messages with no message delays ($p_1 = 0.4$)

to 5 times *more messages* than sent by agents running CBJ and *ConcDB*. All four Figures, 13.1, 13.2, 13.3, and 13.4 clearly show the presence of a phase transition [65]. The comparison of CBJ and ABT demonstrates clearly the trade-off among single process DisCSP search algorithms. CBJ takes *more* nonconcurrent constraint checks (Figure 13.1) and sends *fewer* messages (Figure 13.2).

In the second set of experiments, messages were delayed randomly for 50-100 nonconcurrent constraint checks. Figure 13.5 presents the number of non concurrent constraint checks performed by the three algorithms running on sparse DisCSPs (density $p_1 = 0.4$) with random message delays. The most obvious result of Figure 13.5 is that CBJ is affected most by message delay. This could have been expected. Since CBJ performs no concurrent computation the total amount of message delay is added to the runtime of the algorithm. This gives a large effect on the run-time results. Figure 13.6 presents a closer look at the results of ABT and *ConcDB* in this run. While *ConcDB* performed about 40% more NCCCs than the number of NCCCs it performed with no message delays, ABT performes *three times more* NCCCs than it does for perfect communication.

Figure 13.7 presents the total number of messages sent by the three algorithms with random message delays. It is interesting to see that, while the total number of messages sent by CBJ and *ConcDB* is not affected by message delay, the number of messages sent by ABT grows by a factor of 2. Figures 13.8, 13.9 and 13.10 show similar results for denser DisCSPs ($p_1 = 0.7$).

The third set of experiments investigates the impact of the size and range of the random delays on the different algorithms. The effect of varying the

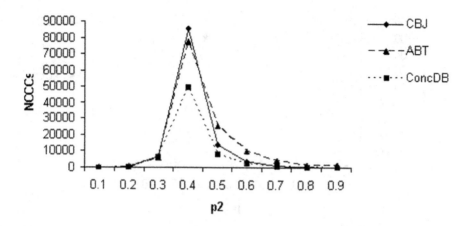

Fig. 13.3. Nonconcurrent constraint checks with no message delays ($p_1 = 0.7$)

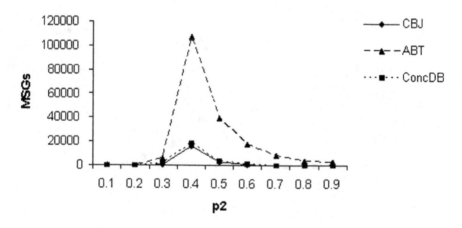

Fig. 13.4. Total number of messages with no message delays ($p_1 = 0.7$)

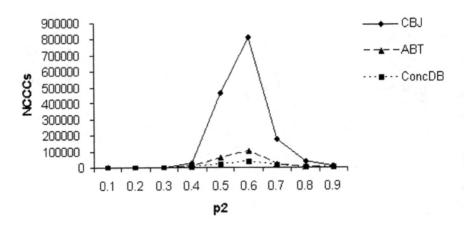

Fig. 13.5. Nonconcurrent constraint checks with random message delays ($p_1 = 0.4$)

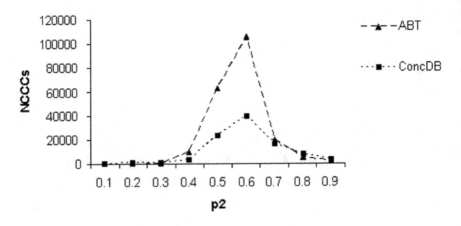

Fig. 13.6. A closer look at NCCCs performed by ABT and *ConcDB*, with random message delays ($p_1 = 0.4$)

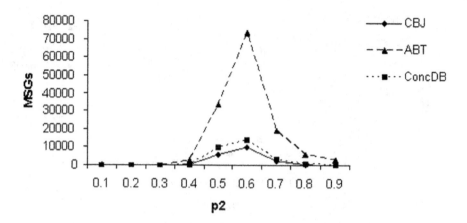

Fig. 13.7. Total number of messages with random message delays ($p_1 = 0.4$)

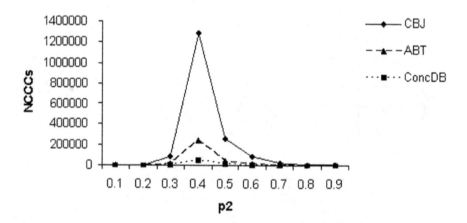

Fig. 13.8. Nonconcurrent constraint checks with random message delays ($p_1 = 0.7$)

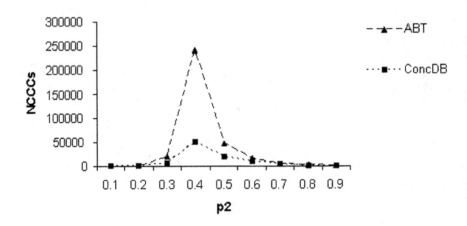

Fig. 13.9. A closer look on the NCCCs performed by of ABT and ConcDB, with random message delays ($p_1 = 0.7$)

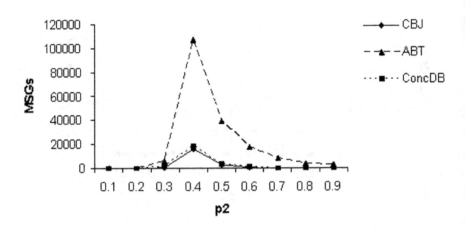

Fig. 13.10. Total number of messages with random message delays ($p_1 = 0.7$)

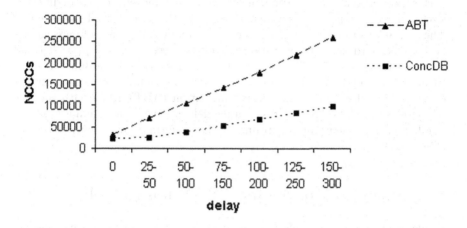

Fig. 13.11. Number of nonconcurrent CCs versus size of random message delays $(p_1 = 0.4)$

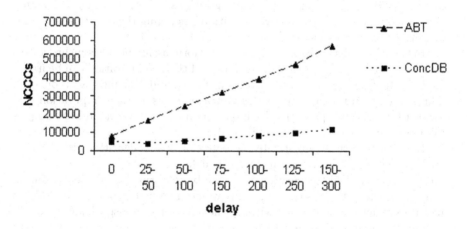

Fig. 13.12. Number of nonconcurrent CCs versus size of random message delays $(p_1 = 0.7)$

delay size on a sequential assignment (synchronous) single search algorithm is easy to understand. In order to investigate the behavior of algorithms which perform concurrent computation, in the presence of message delays of different sizes and range, experiments were performed for the harder problem instances. The algorithms were run with an increasing amount and range of message delay, on the hardest problem instances (tightness $p_2 = 0.6$ for $p_1 = 0.4$ and $p_2 = 0.4$ for $p_1 = 0.7$). The impact of random delays on the different algorithms is presented in Figures 13.11 and 13.12. The number of nonconcurrent constraint checks of the single search algorithm (ABT) grows with the size of the message delay. In contrast, larger delays have a small impact on the number of nonconcurrent constraint checks performed by concurrent search (*ConcDB*).

13.2 A summary of the Impact of Message Delays

While in systems with perfect communication, where there are no message delays, the number of synchronous steps of computation (on a synchronous simulator) is a good measure of the time of the algorithm run, the case is different on realistic systems with message delays. The number of nonconcurrent constraints checks has to take delays into account. When the number of nonconcurrent CCs is calculated, it reveals a large impact of message delay on the performance of single process algorithms. In other words, the actual time it would take CBJ to report a solution (including the delays of message) is much longer than that of *ConcDB* or ABT.

In asynchronous backtracking, agents perform assignments asynchronously. As a result of random message delays, some of their computation can be irrelevant due to inconsistent *Agent_Views* while the updating message is delayed. This can explain the large impact of message delays on the computation performed by ABT (cf. [4, 54]). The impact is not as strong as in synchronous CBJ (Figures 13.5, 13.7, 13.8, and 13.10).

In order to further investigate the behavior of the algorithms in the presence of message delays the simple method for counting nonconcurrent constraint checks of [45] (see Section 12.1) can be performed concurrently during the run of the *AMDS* simulator. This would give us the number of NCCCs which were actualy performed without the addition of messge delays to the final result. Figures 13.13 and 13.14 present the actual count of nonconcurrent constraints checks (without adding delays) performed by the agents during the algorithm run. As expected, CBJ performs exactly the same number of NCCCs as with no delays. The number of NCCCs performed by ABT in the presence of delays, *grows by a factor of 2*. This illuminates an important feature of the standard simulation of runs of DisCSP algorithms. Based on instantaneous arrival of messages, ABT reads multiple messages at each step. With random message delays, agents are more likely to respond to a single message, instead of all the messages sent in the former (ideal) cycle of computation. Messages in asynchronous backtracking are often conflicting. As a result, agents perform more unnecessary computation steps when responding to fewer messages in each cycle. The improvement that results from reading all incoming messages in each step [61], is no longer useful when messages have random delays. This can explain a similar result for ABT, on a different set of problems [4]. As can be seen in Figures 13.13 and 13.14, for a multiple search process algorithm, like *ConcDB*, the number of actual nonconcurrent CCs is not affected and even decreases by the delay of messages.

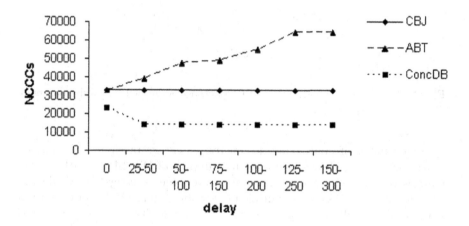

Fig. 13.13. Number of nonconcurrent CCs actualy performed versus size of random message delays ($p_1 = 0.4$)

To illuminate the robustness of *ConcDB* to message delay imagine the following example. Consider the case where *ConcDB* splits the search space multiple times and the number of CPAs is larger than the number of agents. In systems with no message delays this would mean that some of the CPAs are waiting in incoming queues, to be processed by the agents. This delays the search on the sub-search-spaces they represent. In systems with message delays, this potential waiting is caused by the system. By choosing the right *split_limit*, agents can be kept busy at all times, performing computation against consistent partial assignments. The experimental results presented in this chapter demonstrate that the above claim can be achieved.

In terms of network load, the results above show that asynchronous backtracking puts a heavy load on the network, which doubles in the case of message delays. The number of messages sent in concurrent search algorithms, is always much smaller and is affected only lightly by message delays.

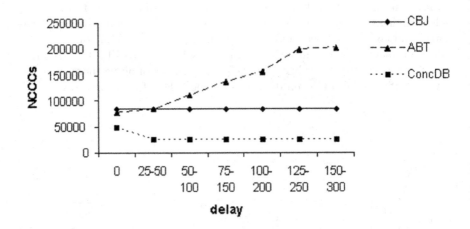

Fig. 13.14. Number of nonconcurrent CCs actualy performed versus size of random message delays ($p_1 = 0.7$)

The number of nonconcurrent constraints checks takes into account the impact of message delays on the actual runtime of DisCSP algorithms. Two families of DisCSP search algorithms have been investigated. Single process algorithms (SPAs) and multiple process algorithms (MPAs or concurrent search). The results imply that, single process algorithms (SPAs), are much more affected by message delays, than concurrent search. The number of NC-CCs grows linearly with message delay for completely synchronous algorithms like CBJ. The impact on asynchronous backtracking, (ABT), is large. Both the computational effort and the load on the network grow by a large factor, although the effect on run time is smaller than that of CBJ. This strengthens the results of [4].

Concurrent search shows the greatest robustness to message delays. This is connected to the fact that in concurrent search agents always perform computation against consistent partial assignments. Computation performed in one sub-search-space while others are delayed is not wasted as in asynchronous backtracking. The effect of message delay on concurrent search is minor in terms of nonconcurrent constraint checks as well as on its network load.

13.3 Message Delays and Dynamic Ordering

The impact of message delays can be tested on the ABT algorithm with and without dynamic agent ordering. Figure 13.15 presents the number of nonconcurrent constraints checks performed by ABT and dynamically ordered

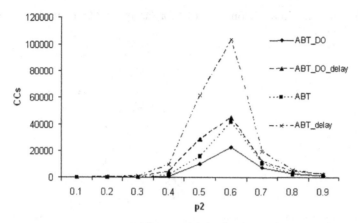

Fig. 13.15. Nonconcurrent constraint checks performed by ABT and ABT_DO with and without message delays (from [73])

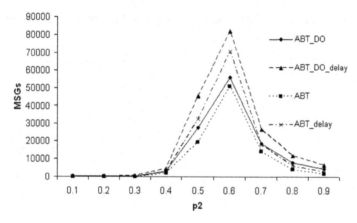

Fig. 13.16. Number of messages sent by ABT and ABT_DO with and without message delays (from [73])

ABT on systems with optimal communication (i.e., with no message delays) and on systems with random message delays between 50 and 100 CCs. It is apparent that the impact of meaasge delays on standard ABT is larger than on dynamically ordered ABT. Figure 13.16 presents the total number of messages sent by the agents performing the algorithms. The effect of message delays is similar on both algorithms. The number of messages increases by about 30%.

To test further the impact of message delays on dynamically ordered asynchronous backtracking, one can use the AWC algorithm (see Section 9.1). Experiments were performed on smaller systems with 10 agents since AWC does

not complete its runs in a reasonable time for larger problems in the presence
of message delays.

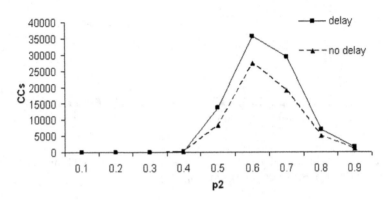

Fig. 13.17. Nonconcurrent constraint checks performed by AWC with and without
message delays ($p_1 = 0.4$)

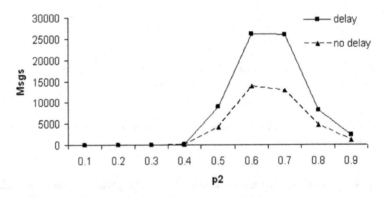

Fig. 13.18. Number of messages sent by AWC with and without message delays
($p_1 = 0.4$)

Figure 13.17 presents the number of nonconcurrent constraints checks performed by AWC on sparse systems ($p_1 = 0.4$). The factor of deterioration in
NCCCs for AWC is smaller than the factor for ABT and closer to the factor
of deterioration for *ABT_DO*. However, in the case of network load, as presented in Figure 13.18, the factor of deterioration in the presense of message
delays is much larger than for both versions of ABT.

Distributed Constraint Optimization Problems (DISCOPs)

Similarly to the transition from CSP to DISCSP, a DISCOP is a COP in which the variables are divided among a set of agents $A_1, A_2, ..., A_n$. Each agent knows only the constraints of its local variables. Again, it is often assumed that each agent holds exactly one variable, by the same reasoning used for the same assumption in DISCSPs (see Chapter 4). It is easy to see that agents that hold multiple variables can be constructed from single-variable agents in two general ways. One way is to define a composite assignment state for multiple-variable agents. Each such state is composed of assignments to all of the agent's variables. This will make agents have a large number of values, all combined assignments of an agent's variables. However, it clearly generates a single variable. The other form of generalizing a multiple-variable agent is to define virtual agents, each holding one of the variables of the agent. Thus, each agent in the distributed problem is a single-variable agent. Assuming only single-variable agents has been the practice of all researchers in the field (cf. [9, 47]).

Agents communicate by messages, trying to find a solution to the DISCOP. The same assumptions of DISCSPs are used: messages arrive in a finite time; in the order in which they were sent; a total ordering of the agents and variables is known to all agents; and the constraints are at most binary. These assumptions are commonly used for DISCSP and DISCOP algorithms [47, 61]. We will assume that each agent owns a single variable and thus use the terms "agent" and "variable" interchangeably. DISCOPs with all costs equaling either zero or one are called *MaxDisCSPs*, in accordance with *MaxCSPs* for the centralized case [33, 36].

MaxDisCSPs are DISCSPs in which the goal of the solving algorithm is to find a global assignment with a minimal number of violated constraints. For a soluble DISCSP this problem is equivalent and the solution has zero violations of constraints. For *unsolvable* DISCSPs the solving algorithm needs to scan the complete search space in order to find a global assignment with a minimal number of violated constraints. As was explained in Chapter 3, a natural algorithm for solving MaxCSPs is the branch & bound algorithm. Distributed versions of BnB will be discussed in the present chapter.

There are a few complete DisCOP algorithms that have been proposed in the literature. We will review most of them in the following sections. We choose to omit from this list of algorithms the algorithm ADOPT, and devote an entire chapter to it (Chapter 15) for several reasons. First, it is considered by many researchers as the leading DisCOP solver. Second, it is a complex asynchronous algorithm, and to fully understand it requires more than a single section. Third, we implemented this algorithm in our simulator (see [22, 72]), and explored its performance and behavior. In-depth understanding of this algorithm is a significant part of our comparative studies of the behavior of DisCOP algorithms, especially its detailed comparison to the AFB algorithm in Chapter 16 [22].

The rest of the chapter is divided as follows:

- In Section 14.1 an agent ordering of the form called "pseudo-tree" is described. This ordering is used by the DPOP algorithm as well as by the $ADOPT$ algorithm.

- The simplest algorithm for DisCOPs is the synchronous branch and bound (SBB) algorithm (Section 3.1). SBB is the extension of the BnB algorithm for COPs to the distributed world. This extension is similar to the way in which the backtracking algorithm for CSPs was extended into the synchronous backtracking (SBT) algorithm for DisCSPs (Chapter 4). The SBB algorithm is the first DisCOP algorithm to be described (Section 14.2).

- Section 14.3 presents a recent DisCOP algorithm - the Distributed Pseudo-tree Optimization algorithm (DPOP) [49]. The DPOP algorithm propagates information from lower priority to higher priority agents, until all information arrives at the highest priority agent, which then has enough information to immediately choose its optimal value. This value is informed to lower priority agents, which use it together with the information they previously propagated to also immediately choose their optimal value. DPOP is therefore a very special DisCOP algorithm that finds an optimal solution in two passes, but uses exponential size messages [49]. It is described in Section 14.3.

- For the sake of completeness, a brief description of the OptAPO algorithm is given in Section 14.4. OptAPO uses mediation to construct connected sub problems, which are solved in a centralized manner by a selected agent (the mediator), and then merged with other subproblem solutions to achieve a global solution.

14.1 Pseudo-trees

In a tree ordering, there is a single agent that is placed at the root. Each node agent has zero or more children; all agents except the root have a parent. A pseudo-tree ordering [20] is a tree ordering with the following unique property. If two agents share a constraint, then one of these agents is an ancestor of the other. This means that all constraints are either from parent to son (tree edges), or from an agent to one of its ancestors (back edges).

Pseudo-trees are useful for solving COPs because they allow splitting the problem into several smaller subproblems, solving the subproblems independently, and then merging the solution into a global solution. Given a node in the tree and the assignment of it and all of its ancestors, the subproblems rooted at this node's children can each be solved independently. If the assignments of the node and its ancestors are fixed, the optimal assignments of each subproblem are in fact the global optimal assignments. This is because constraints between subproblems cannot exist, as the constraints are only between a node and its descendants and ancestors.

As for how to find a pseudo-tree ordering, a simple solution is to build a depth first search tree (DFS tree) of the constraint graph. One can prove that a DFS tree is a pseudo-tree. However, this might not be the best pseudo-tree. A good pseudo-tree should have a low depth and a high width. Such a tree would include smaller sub problems to solve. Finding the optimal pseudo-tree among all possible trees is an NP-hard problem [28].

14.2 Synchronous Branch and Bound (SBB)

SBB [27, 47] is the extension of the BnB algorithm (for COPs) to an algorithm for DisCOPs. This is the simplest distributed version of the branch and bound algorithm (DisBnB). The framework of the algorithm is as follows. Only the agent holding the CPA message may perform computation. There is a single CPA message, containing a partial assignment. The CPA starts at the first agent, which assigns its first value to it and sends it to the second agent. Each agent that receives the CPA extends it by writing on it a value assignment to its variable, as well as the cost it incurred because of constraints with other assignments appearing in the received CPA. Whenever the CPA reaches a new full assignment at the last agent, the accumulated cost of the CPA is the cost of that full assignment. If this cost is smaller than the known upper bound, it is broadcast to all agents as the new upper bound. Each agent holding the CPA checks whether the CPA's accumulated cost is smaller than the upper bound. If this is false, it assigns the next value in its domain instead of the current value and checks again. An agent encountering an empty domain of values erases its assignment (and its cost) and sends the CPA back to the previous agent. When the domain of the first agent is exhausted, the last discovered full assignment is reported as the solution (this requires remembering what that assignment was, which can be done by the last agent).

The drawbacks of SBB are similar to the drawbacks of SBT in DisCSPs. It is a slow algorithm that only allows agents to perform computation while they hold the CPA message. There is only one such message in the system and most of the time the agents are idle, since another agent holds the CPA or the CPA is en route between two agents.

14.3 Distributed Pseudo-tree Optimization (DPOP)

```
 1: DPOP(X, D, R)
    Each agent X_i executes:
 2:
 3: Phase 1: pseudotree creation
 4: elect leader from all X_j ∈ X
 5: elected leader initiates pseudotree creation
 6: afterwards, X_i knows P(X_i), PP(X_i), C(X_i) and PC(X_i)
 7: Phase 2: UTIL message propagation
 8: if |Children(X_i)| == 0 (i.e. X_i is a leaf node) then
 9:    UTIL_{X_i}(P(X_i)) ← Compute_utils(P(X_i), PP(X_i))
10:    Send_message(P(X_i), UTIL_{X_i}(P(X_i)))
11: activate UTIL_Message_handler()
12: Phase 3: VALUE message propagation
13: activate VALUE_Message_handler()
14: END ALGORITHM
15:
16: UTIL_Message_handler(X_k, UTIL_{X_k}(X_i))
17: store UTIL_{X_k}(X_i)
18: if UTIL messages from all children arrived then
19:    if Parent(X_i)==null (that means X_i is the root) then
20:       v_i^* ← Choose_optimal(null)
21:       Send VALUE(X_i, v_i^*) to all C(X_i)
22:    else
23:       UTIL_{X_i}(P(X_i)) ← Compute_utils(P(X_i), PP(X_i))
24:       Send_message(P(X_i), UTIL_{X_i}(P(X_i)))
25: return
```

Fig. 14.1. The DPOP algorithm, part I - from [49]

The DPOP algorithm [49] is presented in Figures 14.1 and 14.2 (taken by permission from [49]) and is composed of three phases. The intuitive framework of each phase is as follows:

- In the first phase, a pseudo-tree ordering of the agents is constructed (see Section 14.1).
- In the second phase, UTIL messages are propagated from the leaves up to the root of the tree. A leaf agent that sends out a UTIL message, includes in it the best (lowest) cost it can achieve for each combination of value assignments of the agents it is constrained with. Agents that receive UTIL messages from down the tree use them to construct their own UTIL message, and report to their parent. UTIL messages take into account all constraining agents above them. In addition, all other agents mentioned

26:
27: **VALUE_Message_handler(**$VALUE^{X_i}_{P(X_i)}$**)**
28: add all $X_k \leftarrow v_k^* \in VALUE^{X_i}_{P(X_i)}$ to agent_view
29: $X_i \leftarrow v_i^* = Choose\_optimal(agent\_view)$
30: Send $VALUE^{X_i}_{X_i}$ to all $X_l \in C(X_i)$
31:
32: **Choose_optimal(agent_view)**
33:

$$v_i^* \leftarrow argmax_{v_i} \sum_{X_l \in C(X_i)} UTIL_{X_l}(v_i, agent\_view)$$

34: **return** v_i^*
35:
36: **Compute_utils(P(**X_i**), PP(**X_i**))**
37: **for all** combinations of values of $X_k \in PP(X_i)$ **do**
38:    let X_j be Parent(X_i)
39:    similarly to DTREE, compute a vector $UTIL_{X_i}(X_j)$
       of all $\{Util_{X_i}(v_i^*(v_j), v_j) | v_j \in Dom(X_j)\}$
40: assemble a hypercube $UTIL_{X_i}(X_j)$ out of all these
    vectors (totaling $|PP(X_i)| + 1$ dimensions).
41: **return** $UTIL_{X_i}(X_j)$

Fig. 14.2. The DPOP algorithm, part II - from [49]

in UTIL messages received from sons are also kept. For each combination of value assignments for all these agents, the lowest cost of the subtree rooted at the agent is selected. This means that agents must wait for all UTIL messages from all their sons before sending out their own UTIL message. Additionally, this means that the size of the message is potentially exponential. UTIL messages propagate until the root agent. The root agent can now combine the information from all UTIL messages of its successors, and determine the optimal value assignment to its variable. It can do so because the UTIL messages explicitly contain the optimal cost achieved for each of its value assignment, in each of its subtrees.

- Upon completion of the second phase of the algorithm the third phase of the algorithm begins the VALUE propagation. In this phase, the root agent assigns its optimal value, and informs its sons of this. The sons can now, using the UTIL information they previously computed, determine what value is optimal for their variable. They know the final value picked by their ancestors, and after assigning it, they too can inform their sons of their selected value in VALUE messages. This phase ends once all variables are assigned (i.e., VALUE messages have propagated to every leaf).

A major drawback of the DPOP algorithm is that it is fully synchronous. Agents must wait for all their sons to finish their computation before they may perform their own computation. However, there is a much more severe drawback to this algorithm, which is the size of the messages. Messages in DPOP may be exponentially large. For example, in a fully connected problem, a pseudo-tree would be a chain, and if there are 10 agents, then the UTIL message from the leaf agent to its parent would include its cost for each assignment combination of the other nine agents. If the domains are of size 10, then this message contains at least 10^9 such values [49].

In the two years since its first appearance much work has been published on the DPOP algorithm. It was empirically compared to the *ADOPT* algorithm in [50] and found to have better performance. Another way of dealing with exponential message size is to try and design approximations of pure DPOP. One such approximation was introduced in the form of $MB : DPOP$, a memory-bounded form of DPOP [50].

14.4 Optimal Asynchronous Partial Overlay (OptAPO)

A completely different DisCOP algorithm was proposed in 2004. The main idea of the Asynchronous Partial Overlay (APO) algorithm is to solve parts of the DisCOP problem and then merge the partial solutions into a global one [40]. The APO algorithm was proposed in two forms, one for satisfaction problems (e.g. DisCSPs) [39] and the other for optimization problems (DisCOPs). The optimizing version is called *OptAPO* [40]. OptAPO divides the agents into groups (initially of size one). Each group's sub-problem is solved optimally by the leader of the group (called the mediator) using a centralized BnB algorithm. Constraints with a cost greater than zero between solutions of neighboring groups cause these neighboring groups to merge into a single bigger group, which will be used in the next round. This growth of the group is actually performed in procedure *mediate*. As can be seen in Algorithm 14.2, this procedure is called when no conflict-free partial solution can be found (in procedure **check_ agent_ view** in Algorithm 14.1).

The algorithm terminates when there are no more violated constraints between groups, and each group's subproblem was optimally solved, which means a globally optimal solution was found. Most of the pseudo-code of OptAPO, as it appears in [40], is presented in Algorithm 14.1 and Algorithm 14.2. Due to the complexity of OptAPO, and the length of its pseudo-code, we will not explain this pseudo-code in detail. We refer the reader to the relevant paper [40] for a more comprehensive explanation. The following paragraphs describe intuitively the main ideas of the OptAPO algorithm.

OptAPO works by constructing a *good_ list* and maintaining a structure called the *agent_ view*. The agent view stores the names, values, domains, and constraints of agents in the environment that are linked to the owner of the agent view. The good_ list holds the names of the agents with whom the owner has identified either a direct or indirect constraint. As the problem solving unfolds, each agent tries to improve the value of the subproblem they

---

Algorithm 14.1: OptAPO - initialization and local resolution

---

procedure initialize
  $d_i \leftarrow random\ d \in D_i$;
  $p_i \leftarrow sizeof(neighbors) + 1$;
  $m_i \leftarrow$ **true**;
  $mediate \leftarrow$ **false**;
  add x_i to the *good_list*;
  send (**init**, $(x_i, p_i, d_i, m_i, D_i, C_i)$) to neighbors;
  $initList \leftarrow$ neighbors;
end initialize;

when received (**init**, $(x_j, p_j, d_j, m_j, D_j, C_j)$) **do**
  add $(x_j, p_j, d_j, m_j, D_j, C_j)$ to *agent_view*;
  if x_j is a neighbor of some $x_k \in good\_list$ **do**
    add x_j to the *good_list*;
    add all $x_l \in agent\_view \wedge x_l \notin good\_list$
      that can now be connected to the *good_list*;
    $p_i \leftarrow sizeof(good\_list)$;
  end if;
  if $x_j \notin initList$ **do**
    send (**init**, $(x_i, p_i, d_i, m_i, D_i, C_i)$) to x_j;
  else
    remove x_j from *initList*;
  end if;
  check_agent_view;
end do;

when received (**value?**, $(x_j, p_j, d_j, m_j, c_j)$) **do**
  update *agent_view* with $(x_j, p_j, d_j, m_j, c_j)$;
  check_agent_view;
end do;

procedure check_agent_view
  if $initList \neq \emptyset$ **or** $mediate \neq$ **false do**
    return;
  $m_i' \leftarrow hasConflict(x_i)$;
  if m_i' **and** $\neg \exists j(p_j > p_i \wedge m_j ==$ **true**) **do**
    if $\exists(d_i' \in D_i)(d_i' \cup agent\_view$ does not conflict)
      and d_i conflicts exclusively with lower priority neighbors **do**
      $d_i \leftarrow d_i'$;
      send (**ok?**, (x_i, p_i, d_i, m_i)) to all $x_j \in agent\_view$;
    else
      do mediate;
    end if;
  else if $m_i \neq m_i'$ **do**
    $m_i \leftarrow m_i'$;
    send (**ok?**, (x_i, p_i, d_i, m_i)) to all $x_j \in agent\_view$;
  end if;
end check_agent_view;

Algorithm 14.2: Mediating an OptAPO session

> **procedure mediate**
> $preferences \leftarrow \emptyset$;
> $counter \leftarrow 0$;
>   **for each** $x_j \in good\_list$ **do**
>   send (**evaluate?**, (x_i, p_i, m'_i)) to x_j;
> $counter{+}{+}$;
>   **end do**;
> $mediate \leftarrow$ **true**;
> **end mediate**;
>
> **when received** (**wait!**, (x_j, p_j)) **do**
> $counter{-}{-}$;
>   **if** $counter == 0$ **do choose_solution**;
> **end do**;
>
> **when received** (**evaluate!**, $(x_j, p_j, labeled\ D_j)$) **do**
>   record $(x_j, labeled\ D_j)$ in $preferences$;
> $counter{-}{-}$;
>   **if** $counter == 0$ **do choose_solution**;
> **end do**;
>
> **procedure choose_solution**
>   select a solution s using a branch and bound search that:
>   1. satisfies the constraints between agents in the $good\_list$
>   2. minimizes the violations for agents outside of the session
>   **if** $\neg\exists s$ that satisfies the constraints **do**
>   broadcast **no solution**;
>   **for each** $x_j \in agent\_view$ **do**
>   **if** $x_j \in preferences$ **do**
>   **if** $d'_j \in s$ violates an x_k **and** $x_k \notin agent\_view$ **do**
>   send (**init**, $(x_i, p_i, d_i, m_i, D_i, C_i)$) to x_k;
>   add x_k to $initList$;
>   **end if**;
>   send (**accept!**, $(d'_j, x_i, p_i, d_i, m_i)$) to x_j;
>   update $agent\_view$ for x_j;
>   **else**
>   send (**ok?**, (x_i, p_i, d_i, m_i)) to x_j;
>   **end if**;
>   **end do**;
> $mediate \leftarrow$ **false**;
>   **check_agent_view**;
> **end choose_solution**;

1

---

have centralized within their *good_list* or to justify its cost by identifying over-constrained structures in the constraint graph. To do this, agents take the role of the *Mediator* and initiate a mediation session with agents in their *good_list*. They compute the optimal value of their subproblem, and attempt to change the assignments of the variables within the session to achieve this optimal value. Whenever this cannot be achieved without causing a cost greater than zero for agents outside of the session, the mediator links with those agents to include them in the next session (adding to the *good_list*). In other words, the subproblem it is going to try to solve optimally in the next step of the OptAPO algorithm will also contain these additional agents. This process continues until each of the agents have justified the cost of their centralized subproblem and they have ensured that this subproblem contains all of the cost-bearing substructures that they need in order to be solved optimally.

OptAPO uses priorities to determine which agents should be mediators and which agents should join other agent's mediation session requests (this bears a close resemblance to leader election in a distributed environment [37]). The priorities are dynamically computed based on the size of the *good_list*, so that agents involved in larger subproblems have a higher priority than agents in smaller subproblems. The solving of a subproblem is done by the mediator agent alone, using a centralized algorithm such as branch and bound. This is possible since the agents involved in this subproblem send the mediator agent all their variable domains and constraints (in "init" messages).

An important observation about OptAPO is that the size of the subproblems increases with run time. Whenever there is a constraint of cost greater than zero between two agents belonging to two different subproblems, one of these agents joins the other's subproblem. The two mediators in charge of solving the two subproblems independently solve their subproblems optimally and have no way of coordinating the assignments to the two agents so that this constraint's cost would be zero and no such merging would take place. Furthermore, it is possible that a cost of zero between two constrained agents would be impossible due to the constraint definition. In general, the agents in small subproblems merge into the bigger subproblems and over time we get fewer groups of larger size. An extreme example is one in which for all constraints, all value combinations have a cost greater than zero. This would eventually lead to the creation of one big subproblem that contains all the agents, which will be solved centrally by a single agent.

The above observation emphasizes the main drawback of the OptAPO algorithm; its centralized solving. Solving a distributed problem via full centralization is always possible, but should not be done, for the reasons we listed in Chapter 4 such as privacy, lack of autonomy, and single point of failure. OptAPO does not fully centralize the problem, but instead attempts to identify clusters of highly constrained agents and only solve each small cluster centrally. These clusters might be small, but might also be large. This depends on the structure of the problem and the duration of the run time. For harder problems (highly constrained, that take a long time to solve) the clusters are expected to grow in size, up to the size of the entire problem.

15

Asynchronous Optimization for DisCOPs

Chapter 14 presented the distributed constraint optimization problem (DisCOP) as well as several solvers for it. One of the leading complete solvers for DisCOPs is the *ADOPT* algorithm by Modi et. al [47]. Its most important feature is the fact that it is inherently asynchronous. The synchronicity of *ADOPT* leads naturally to expecting superior (concurrent) performance to that of synchronous-assignments DisCOP algorithms. In many aspects the asynchronous aspects of *ADOPT* are analogous to those of ABT and raise similar expectations of performance. As we have seen for DisCSPs (Chapter 11), this is definitely not the case. Concurrent search algorithms that perform assignments synchronously outperform an inherently asynchronous algorithm like ABT by a large margin [44, 75].

Several improvements for *ADOPT* were proposed recently. Our goal in this chapter is not to present the best version of *ADOPT*, but rather to present and explain the *ADOPT* algorithm, as well as discuss several less noticeable aspects of the algorithm that were revealed during our implementation of it. These aspects include the following:

- Its unusual update of value assignments made by higher priority agents, that come from lower priority agents (see Section 15.5).
- Its use of pseudo-trees to enhance its performance, and its implications (see Section 15.5.2).
- The network load of *ADOPT*, and why it gets so large (see Section 15.5.3).

For simplicity, we deal only with DisCOPs in which each agent holds a single variable, and thus we use the terms agent and variable interchangeably.

ADOPT is a complex algorithm, with a large amount of pseudo-code [47]. Instead of explaining the lengthy code, let us try to understand the main ideas behind *ADOPT* in incremental steps. First, we will explain what are the upper and lower bounds that *ADOPT* uses, how are they computed and what they mean (Section 15.1). The basic value assignment logic of each agent will be explained in Section 15.2. The threshold mechanism used by *ADOPT* is added on top of the basic framework to improve performance (Section 15.3).

Following these preliminaries, the entire algorithm, as well as its termination mechanism, can be presented.

15.1 Lower and Upper Bounds in *ADOPT*

The basic framework of *ADOPT* relies on the computation of lower and upper bounds by each agent. The agents are pre-arranged (before the search) in a pseudo-tree ordering (see Section 14.1 for the definition of pseudo-trees). Each agent is responsible for computing bounds for the entire subproblem rooted at it, and reporting them to its parent. Here are some definitions that will help us understand what these bounds are:

- Agent priority - between two agents that share a constraint, the one further up the tree is said to be of higher priority.
- *CurrentContext* (or agentview) - a context is a partial assignment. Two contexts are compatible if they do not disagree on any variable assignment. The *CurrentContext* is the current agent's context of the assignments made by higher priorty agents.
- $\delta(d)$ is the *local cost* of the value $d \in D_i$. It is the added cost of constraints that apply to the assignment $X_i = d$ and all assignments in the *CurrentContext*.
- LB is the *lower bound* of the subproblem rooted at the current agent with respect to the *CurrentContext*. As explained in Chapter 3, the meaning of a lower bound is that, if a problem has a lower bound LB, any solution for it would cost *at least LB*.
- UB is the *upper bound* of the subproblem rooted at the current agent with respect to the *CurrentContext*. As explained in Chapter 3, the meaning of an upper bound is that, if a problem has an upper bound UB, a full assignment with cost smaller or equal to UB exists. In other words, a solution would cost *at most UB*.
- LB(d) is the *lower bound* of the subproblem rooted at the current agent with respect to both the *CurrentContext* and the assignment of d to the current agent.
- UB(d) is the *upper bound* of the subproblem rooted at the current agent with respect to both the *CurrentContext* and the assignment of d to the current agent.

From these definitions, we get the following two equalities:

1. LB $= min_{d \in D_i} LB(d)$ - since any solution to the subproblem in which the current agent assigns the value d would cost at least LB(d), and since this agent must assign one of its possible domain values $d \in D_i$, then the minimal value of all possible LB(d) is in fact the lower bound for the entire subproblem rooted at A_i.

2. $UB = min_{d \in D_i} UB(d)$ - The solution to the subproblem rooted at A_i, in which $A_i = d$ would cost at most UB(d). A solution to the entire subproblem rooted at A_i, would cost at most UB(d_1) if A_i assigns d_1, or would cost at most UB(d_2) if A_i assigns d_2, and so on. Therefore a solution to the entire subproblem rooted at A_i would cost at most UB $= min_{d \in D_i} UB(d)$.

In *ADOPT*, each agent receives the value assignments of higher priority agents via VALUE messages, and is responsible for computing lower and upper bounds (LB and UB) for the subproblem rooted at it. These bounds are continually refined over time, and are reported to the parent agent via COST messages. To compute these bounds all an agent needs are the lower and upper bounds received from its children, and to compute its local cost. The exact details of this computation will be explained at the end of this subsection. The algorithm is asynchronous, and therefore these bounds only need to be admissible. A lower bound of zero and an upper bound of infinity are always correct, so even in the lack of information the agent does not need to wait for messages and can report admissible bounds. If later more accurate information is received (from its sons) then the following COST messages that the parent will send will be more accurate.

The search process attempts to decrease the gap between the LB and the UB at each agent. The LB is increased and the UB decreases over time. If the lower bound and the upper bound are equal, it means that, for the given problem (or subproblem), any full assignment would cost at least as much as the lower bound, and that a full assignment of cost smaller or equal to the upper bound was found. Since the lower bound and upper bound are equal, that full assignment is an optimal solution.

15.1.1 Computing lower and upper bounds

Each agent keeps, for every value in its domain $d \in D_i$, and every child it has $x_l \in Children$, the following data structures:

- **context**(d, x_l) is the current context held by x_l as last reported.
- **lb**(d, x_l) is the lower bound reported by x_l for the subproblem rooted at x_l, based on the assignments in context(d, x_l) and the assignment of $X_i = d$.
- **ub**(d, x_l) is similarly defined for the upper bound.
- **t**(d, x_l) is the threshold assigned to child x_l will be explained in Section 15.3.

Whenever a VALUE message is received from a higher priority agent the *CurrentContext* is updated. All data structures which were based on some context(d, x_l) which is incompatible with the updated *CurrentContext* are reset.

When a COST message from a child A_l is received, it contains the child's LB, UB, and a copy of the *CurrentContext* of that child by which these bounds were computed. If the message's context is compatible with the *CurrentContext* (of A_i), then the lb(d, x_l), ub(d, x_l), and t(d, x_l) are updated with the received information. The combination of only saving COST information compatible with the *CurrentContext*, and resetting the data structures that contain information computed based on contexts which are incompatible with the *CurrentContext*, ensures that the information is always compatible with the *CurrentContext*.

Using this saved information, the agent can compute its LB and UB. In order to do so, it only needs to compute the LB(d) and UB(d) for every $d \in D_i$, since LB and UB can be computed from these.

LB(d) is a lower bound of the subproblem rooted at A_i with respect to the *CurrentContext*, and the assignment of d to the current agent A_i. We can see that LB(d) = $\delta(d) + \sum_{x_l \in Children} lb(d, x_l)$ is such a lower bound, as it includes the local cost of constraints between $A_i = d$ and past assignments in *CurrentContext*, and the sum of the lower bounds of each of the subproblems rooted at every child of A_i (these can be added since we are using pseudo-trees).

Similarly, UB(d) can be computed to be UB(d) = $\delta(d) + \sum_{x_l \in Children} ub(d, x_l)$. UB($d$) is the upper bound for the subproblem rooted at A_i with respect to the *CurrentContext* and the assignment of d to A_i. This means that a solution to this subproblem can be found with a cost no greater than UB(d). If a solution to each child's subproblem exists with cost no greater than $ub(d, x_l)$, then these solutions could be merged, and their costs added, into a global solution to the entire subproblem rooted at A_i, and together with the local cost of A_i, form an admissible upper bound for this entire subproblem.

15.2 Assigning Values

In the process of continuously attempting to increase the LB, each agent ensures that its current value assignment d, is one that yields the lowest LB(d) value (of all possible domain values $d \in D_i$). The agent informs its descendants of any assignment change it makes (via VALUE messages). Over time, the subproblem rooted at this agent is explored and LB(d) and UB(d) become tighter (the difference between them decreases).

Since the bounds for values are continuously refined as the search space is explored, the lower bound for the currently assigned value may increase. *ADOPT* is greedy in its value assignments. If the lower bound for the currently assigned value d_1, LB(d_1), is incremented and it is no longer the minimal LB(d), that agent changes its assignment to a value that does have the lowest lower bound. This leads to a different search space being explored, and over time more accurate bounds will be discovered. These may lead to another assignment change and so on. In other words, in *ADOPT* an agent changes its value assignment if the result of exploration of the current subproblem, which resulted in the lower bound for the current value assigned, is greater than the lower bound for another value. This type of exploration results in revisiting of values. For example an agent with two values may have assigned the first value, which had a lower bound of zero. Later it could find that the lower bound for this value is one, and this would cause it to switch its assignment to the second value. Later, the lower bound of this value could rise to two, which would cause the agent to switch back to the first value. Once the current value's lower and upper bound are equal, this value is the optimal value assignment for this agent. The agent will not switch its assignment an infinite number of times, since each assignment change is due to a $LB(d)$ increase from some value d, and $LB(d)$ is bounded by the optimal cost of the subproblem.

Similarly to ABT (see Chapter 5), each agent in $ADOPT$ keeps the assignment of higher priority agents, and only maintains the information relevant to their current assignment. When some higher priority agent informs an agent of an assignment change, the $CurrentContext$ of the agent becomes invalid, and must be updated, and all the information (lower and upper bounds) using this invalid context must be discarded. The alternative, keeping all obsolete data, would require exponential memory. An assignment change at an agent, results in *the need to discard all the lower and upper bounds computed/saved at descendant agents*.

In ABT, information was also discarded when the $Agent\_View$ was changed. However, it was not as important. In ABT, a previous combination of value assignments (of all higher priority agents) can never repeat itself. In $ADOPT$, there is a *revisiting of values*, and this situation can happen. The threshold mechanism addresses this issue and is described in Section 15.3.

To conclude, the basic framework of $ADOPT$ is as follows. Each agent assigns a value and informs its descendants via VALUE messages. Each agent also computes its LB and UB and reports them to its parent via COST messages. The bounds are reported constantly, without waiting for the entire search space to be explored and accurate bounds to be computed. These bounds are updated asynchronously over time. Using bounds from its children an agent can compute its own bounds and report them up the tree. Each agent attempts to pick the lowest-cost assignment it can, the one with the lowest lower bound. After assigning it, that subspace is explored and the lower bound increases. Once it increases enough, the agent finds a more promising value with a lower lower-bound and changes its assignment to that value. Changing the assignment, causes bounds computed further down the tree to be discarded as they are no longer relevant to the new context, and new bounds are gathered for the new assignment combination. The root agent cannot endlessly change its assignment since each such change is due to a lower bound increase, and this lower bound is bounded by the cost of the optimal solution. At some point it will stop changing its assignment. Now that the root's assignment is fixed, the assignments of all agents eventually become fixed and all agents find their assignment to result in an optimal solution.

Initialize

(1) $threshold \leftarrow 0; CurrentContext \leftarrow \{\};$

(2)   forall $d \in D_i, x_l \in Children$ do

(3) $lb(d, x_l) \leftarrow 0; t(d, x_l) \leftarrow 0;$

(4) $ub(d, x_l) \leftarrow Inf; context(d, x_l) \leftarrow \{\};$ enddo;

(5) $d_i \leftarrow d$ that minimizes $LB(d);$

(6)   **backTrack**;

when received (THRESHOLD, t, $context$)

(7)   if $context$ compatible with $CurrentContext$:

(8) $threshold \leftarrow t;$

(9)   **maintainThresholdInvariant**;

(10)   **backTrack**; endif;

when received (TERMINATE, $context$)

(11)   record TERMINATE received from parent;

(12) $CurrentContext \leftarrow context;$

(13)   **backTrack**;

when received (VALUE, (x_j, d_j))

(14)   if TERMINATE not received from parent:

(15)   add (x_j, d_j) to $CurrentContext;$

(16)   forall $d \in D_i, x_l \in Children$ do

(17)   if $context(d, x_l)$ incompatible with $CurrentContext$:

(18) $lb(d, x_l) \leftarrow 0; t(d, x_l) \leftarrow 0;$

(19) $ub(d, x_l) \leftarrow Inf; context(d, x_l) \leftarrow \{\};$ endif; enddo;

(20)   **maintainThresholdInvariant**;

(21)   **backTrack**; endif;

when received (COST, x_k, $context$, lb, ub)

(22) $d \leftarrow$ value of x_i in $context;$

(23)   remove (x_i, d) from $context;$

(24)   if TERMINATE not received from parent:

(25)   forall $(x_j, d_j) \in context$ and x_j is not my neighbor do

(26)   add (x_j, d_j) to $CurrentContext;$ enddo;

(27)   forall $d' \in D_i, x_l \in Children$ do

(28)   if $context(d', x_l)$ incompatible with $CurrentContext$:

(29) $lb(d', x_l) \leftarrow 0; t(d', x_l) \leftarrow 0;$

(30) $ub(d', x_l) \leftarrow Inf; context(d', x_l) \leftarrow \{\};$ endif; enddo; endif;

(31)   if $context$ compatible with $CurrentContext$:

(32) $lb(d, x_k) \leftarrow lb;$

(33) $ub(d, x_k) \leftarrow ub;$

(34) $context(d, x_k) \leftarrow context;$

(35)   **maintainChildThresholdInvariant**;

(36)   **maintainThresholdInvariant**; endif;

(37)   **backTrack**;

procedure **backTrack**

(38)   if $threshold == UB$:

(39) $d_i \leftarrow d$ that minimizes $UB(d);$

(40)   else if $LB(d_i) > threshold$:

(41) $d_i \leftarrow d$ that minimizes $LB(d);$ endif;

(42)   SEND (VALUE, (x_i, d_i))

(43)   to each lower priority neighbor;

(44)   **maintainAllocationInvariant**;

(45)   if $threshold == UB$:

(46)   if TERMINATE received from parent

(47)   or x_i is root:

(48)   SEND (TERMINATE,

(49) $CurrentContext \cup \{(x_i, d_i)\})$

(50)   to each child;

(51)   Terminate execution; endif; endif;

(52)   SEND (COST, x_i, $CurrentContext$, LB, UB)

        to parent;

Fig. 15.1. The main *ADOPT* procedures (from [47])

15.3 The Threshold Mechanism

In order to improve the performance of $ADOPT$, a *threshold mechanism* was introduced ($ADOPT$ was already presented with this improvement when it was presented in [46]). Each agent maintains a threshold value, which is initially zero. This value can either be set by that agent's parent via a THRESHOLD message, or set by the current agent itself. Intuitively, the threshold of an agent represents what a lower bound of the subproblem rooted at this agent is currently or was previously known. Because an agent cannot keep information not consistent with the $CurrentContext$, it must forget its LB value when a higher priority agent, like its parent, changes its assignment. However, if the parent agent later returns to its past assignment, then the previously discovered LB, saved at the parent, could be useful in speeding up the search at the son. The parent instructs the son to set its threshold value to the last LB the son reported. The child realizes it is revisiting a previously explored search-space, and knows not to swap its value assignment unless it exceeds that a previously discovered LB. Because it does not swap its assignment often, this allows the agents below it to explore the search space faster, without resetting their data structures on every assignment change. So, agents use the threshold value instead of the LB value in deciding when to swap their current assignment.

As we said, the threshold of an agent represents what the lower bound of the subproblem rooted at this agent is currently, or what was previously known to be the lower bound. To keep it accurate with the current LB, whenever the threshold is below the current LB, it is incremented by the agent to be equal to the LB.

In addition, as we will see, it is possible that an agent may receive a threshold from its parent that is too large. In such a case, the agent may discover that the UB is smaller than the threshold. This means that a solution can be reached with a cost of UB or less. Therefore, keeping the threshold (as an intuitive lower bound) higher than this cost will not help, and the threshold is reduced to be equal to the UB.

The above may become possible in a scenario in which an agent A_i reports its bound to its parent A_j. A_j changes his assignments a few times and eventually returns to a previously assigned value. Now, A_j directs A_i to set its threshold to some value t, which is the value that A_i previously reported to be its LB when A_j assigned the same value last time. A_i knows that it previously discovered that the lower bound for the subproblem rooted at it was t. Consider for example the situation in which A_i has two sons - A_{left} and A_{right}. A_i knows that the LB it computed before was composed of the sum of the lower bounds it received from both of its sons plus its local cost (see the equalities in Section 15.1). A_i's local cost computed now and computed back then is of course the same, as A_i's context is the same in both scenarios. However, A_i cannot know how much of t was from each son's LB, and cannot know what threshold to give them. As a result of this missing information,

A_i must use some heuristic, called the **threshold heuristic,** to divide t between its sons. A_i keeps a data structures $t(d, x_l)$ to hold the threshold value allocated to son x_l when A_i's assignment is d (see [47]).

Let us consider two possible cases. If A_i assigned a threshold **too small** to A_{left} (than what it would have assigned if it remembered what that son reported as its LB), then maybe A_{left} would not gain as much as it can to speed up its re-exploration. If its threshold were 0, which is equivalent to not using thresholds at all, this will imply some more thrashing during its exploration. However, A_{left} would always rediscover its previous LB and increase its threshold to match it.

If A_i assigned a threshold **too great** to A_{left}, then we seem to risk a non-optimal solution. A_{left} thinks that its previous LB had that value and may stay with a value that gives a cost greater than the originally discovered LB, but smaller than or equal to the given threshold. A_{left} would wrongly think that there is no reason to change it, as any value it picks would produce at least as much cost. If A_{left} is lucky, it may discover the UB to be smaller than the threshold and decrease it, but will not always be able to do so. The "salvation" comes from A_i, or more accurately, from A_{right}. If A_i assigned a threshold that is too high to A_{left} then it necessarily assigned a too small one to A_{right}. Given enough time, A_{right} would rediscover its LB and increment its threshold. The next COST message from A_{right} would contain this LB. Once A_i receives it, it will realize its error, and send a new THRESHOLD message to A_{left}, setting its threshold to a smaller value.

In practice, each agent in *ADOPT* continuously maintains three invariants to handle the thresholds to express the above behavior:

- **ThresholdInvariant**: LB $\leq$ *threshold* $\leq$ UB. The threshold on the cost of the subtree rooted at x_i cannot be less than its lower bound or greater than its upper bound.
- **AllocationInvariant**: for a current value $d \in D_i$,
  $threshold = \delta(d) + \sum_{x_l \in Children} t(d, x_l)$.
  The threshold on cost for x_i must equal the local cost of choosing d plus the sum of the thresholds allocated to x_i Šs children.
- **ChildThresholdInvariant**:
  $\forall d \in D_i, \forall x_l \in Children, lb(d, x_l) \leq t(d, x_l) \leq ub(d, x_l)$
  The threshold allocated to child x_l by parent x_i cannot be less than the lower bound or greater than the upper bound reported by x_l to x_i.

The procedures in Figure 15.2 show how these invariants are enforced.

15.4 *ADOPT* - Summary and Termination

The pseudo-code for the main *ADOPT* procedures, taken from [47], is shown in Figure 15.1. The computation of bounds is not included and was already explained in detail in the text. The algorithm starts by each agent performing

```
procedure maintainThresholdInvariant
```
(53) if $threshold < LB$
(54) $threshold \leftarrow LB$; **endif**
(55) if $threshold > UB$
(56) $threshold \leftarrow UB$; **endif**

%*note: procedure assumes ThresholdInvariant is satisfied*
```
procedure maintainAllocationInvariant
```
(57) **while** $threshold > \delta(d_i) + \sum_{x_l \in Children} t(d_i, x_l)$ **do**
(58)   choose $x_l \in Children$ where $ub(d_i, x_l) > t(d_i, x_l)$
(59)   increment $t(d_i, x_l)$; **enddo**
(60) **while** $threshold < \delta(d_i) + \sum_{x_l \in Children} t(d_i, x_l)$ **do**
(61)   choose $x_l \in Children$ where $t(d_i, x_l) > lb(d_i, x_l)$
(62)   decrement $t(d_i, x_l)$; **enddo**
(63) SEND (**THRESHOLD**, $t(d_i, x_l)$, *CurrentContext*)
          to each child x_l


```
procedure maintainChildThresholdInvariant
```
(64) **forall** $d \in D_i, x_l \in Children$ **do**
(65)   **while** $lb(d, x_l) > t(d, x_l)$ **do**
(66)   increment $t(d, x_l)$; **enddo;endo**
(67) **forall** $d \in D_i, x_l \in Children$ **do**
(68)   **while** $t(d, x_l) > ub(d, x_l)$ **do**
(69)   decrement $t(d, x_l)$; **enddo;enddo**

Fig. 15.2. Procedures for updating thresholds in *ADOPT* [47]

the *initialize* procedure, which initializes all its data structures and assigns some value. Then the procedure *backtrack* is called. Unfortunately, the *backtrack* procedure was poorly named. There is no relation between this procedure and the traditional definition of backtracking. This *backtrack* procedure checks if the current value assignment should be changed, and if so, changes it. Next, VALUE messages containing the current assigned value are sent to all lower priority neighbors (descendants in the tree). A COST message with the agent's UB, LB, and *CurrentContext* are sent to its parent. This procedure is performed not only after initialization, but also following every message received.

The *when received THRESHOLD* procedure sets the agent's threshold to the threshold sent by the parent, makes sure the threshold invariants are maintained, and calls the backtrack procedure.

The *when received VALUE* procedure simply updates the *CurrentContext* with the value assignment, re-initializes data structures that are no longer valid due to this update, and calls the backtrack procedure.

The *when received COST* procedure takes the context by which the LB and UB in the message were computed, uses it to update its *CurrentContext* with the assignments of agents that are of higher priority but not directly constrained with this agent (which means they do not send VALUE messages to this agent), then re-initializes data structures that are no longer valid due to this update. If the message's context is compatible with this agent's *CurrentContext*, the information on the message is saved in the lb(), ub() and context() data structures. This may break the threshold invariants so they must be re-enforced. Finally, the backtrack procedure is called.

Termination of *ADOPT*

The termination of *ADOPT* starts at the root and goes down the tree from top to bottom. When the root's threshold (which is also equal to its LB since it has no parent to change it) equals UB, the cost of the solution is known, and a value that gave such a LB (which equals UB) is picked. The root then sends the TERMINATE message to its sons along with its assignment and terminates (see line 47 in Figure 15.1). An agent which received a TERMINATE message from its parent records it in the *when received TERMINATE* procedure, saves the assignments of terminated agents in its *CurrentContext* and calls the backtrack procedure. Now every such agent is like the root, it cannot receive messages from higher in the tree, and its *CurrentContext* is fixed forever (updating it from any further VALUE or COST messages is disabled in these procedures). Just as the root eventually reached the state UB = LB = threshold, so will this agent, and the process will repeat itself until all agents terminate.

It is important to note that, even though the parent terminated, this does not mean that the search is over for the son. It is quite possible that the parent had a value d_1 just before it terminated, but then terminated after assigning d_2, causing its son to lose all its saved bounds (as the context is now different). The son agent must re-search its search-space, incrementing lower bounds of its values again from zero, until it solves the subproblem and knows which of its values should be picked to result in an optimal solution, and then terminate.

15.5 Special (and Surprising) Features of *ADOPT*

ADOPT is a very complex and difficult to follow algorithm. Its complexity is probably related to the difficulty of running an asynchronous distributed branch and bound algorithm. The maintenance of upper and lower bounds for all agents asynchronously and the need for the asynchronous combination of such local bounds to result in a correct algorithm that terminates, needs some very complex mechanisms. Other DISCOP algorithms that were described in Chapter 14 are much simpler at the cost of elegance. DPOP is completely synchronized and uses exponential size messages in the worst case (see Section 14.3). OptAPO becomes more and more centralized as its mediators accumulate larger mediation sessions and solve them centrally (Section 14.4). As we will see in Chapter 16, an asynchronous (though sequential assignment) algorithm can be designed for DISCOPs - the *Asynchronous Forward Bounding (AFB)* algorithm. It will be shown to be of a superior performance to *ADOPT*.

Due to *ADOPT*'s complex structure and behavior, several interesting phenomena can be shown to exist during its run. These are unexpected behaviors that will be described in the next three subsections. The first behavioral feature is just surprising. The second, dependence on the structure of the pseudo-tree, points to a possible drawback of the use of pseudo-trees. The third and most important behavior feature of *ADOPT* is the fact that it can potentially exchange an exponential number of messages. This is a very dangerous property and will be clearly identified in Section 15.5.3.

15.5.1 Updating context from lower priority agents

An important issue with *ADOPT* that might be easily overlooked was mentioned in Section 15.4 when the procedure that handles COST messages was described. The *CurrentContext* of the current agent is updated (partly at least) from a COST message it received from its son down the tree. This goes against the general idea of all asynchronous backtracking algorithms (like ABT), that agents update their context by messages that originate with higher priority agents. Let us present and explain briefly the logic behind this abnormal updating.

Since in *ADOPT* agents only communicate with their parents or neighbors (in the constraint graph), it is possible for an agent that is below another agent in the tree not to receive VALUE messages from its ancestor (as these two agents are not constrained directly).

Consider the example in Figure 15.3. It is easy to see that A_3 does not receive VALUE messages from A_1 directly, but A_5 does. When A_5 reports its LB and UB in a COST message, it computes those bounds based on its *CurrentContext* at the time, which includes some assignment of A_1. Different assignments of A_1 may produce a different LB and UB in A_5. When receiving the COST message from A_5, A_3 must keep the context in which they were computed, and in fact it updates its own *CurrentContext* to contain the assignment of A_1 included in the received context. Imagine, for example, that A_4 and A_1 are also constrained (not as shown in the figure). In such a case, A_1 would report VALUE messages to A_4 as well. In principle, A_4 may report COST messages to A_3 that are based on some **other** value of A_1. This can happen if the VALUE message to A_4 is slightly delayed, and A_4 reports its COST based on the previous assignment. Naturally the bounds from the two sons A_4 and A_5 cannot be added if they are based on contexts in which the assignment of A_1 is different.

A_3 cannot know which assignment of A_1 is more correct (more up-to-date). It has no choice but to assume that A_1 has changed its value assignment, and update its *CurrentContext* with every COST message it receives. Until the updated value of A_1 arrives at A_4, it would continuously receive COST from both A_4 and A_5 and would alternate its context.

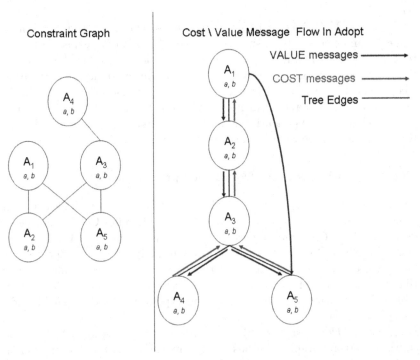

Fig. 15.3. An illustration of the VALUE and COST message flow in *ADOPT*. On the left is a constraint problem, on the right a schema of messages sent by *ADOPT* when solving the problem.

15.5.2 Pseudo-trees and concurrency of computation

The use of pseudo-trees is targeted at enhancing performance of distributed search. However, it turns out to have an effect on concurrency in *ADOPT* (as well as on other algorithms that are based on pseudo-trees).

Pseudo-trees, as described in Chapter 14, are a powerful ordering method for enchancing performance. They enable a division of the problem into several subproblems which can be solved independently. The solutions of all these subproblems can be merged to produce a globally optimal solution. *ADOPT* takes advantage of this concurrency since each agent informs all its constrained descendants of its value assignments. A parent agent enables its children to independently solve their individual subproblems in a recursive manner. The lower and upper bounds they will report back can be merged (added) into a bound for the parent agent itself.

This type of division produces some concurrency. While one child is working on solving its subproblem, its sibling can independently work on its own subproblem. A good pseudo-tree is one that is very wide and shallow. This creates the maximal number of subproblems that can be independently solved. Each of these subproblem can be optimally solved fairly quickly since it is relatively small.

Let us take an extreme example to demonstrate the principle. In a constraint graph that looks like a star, a single agent in the middle is constrained with all other agents, and those are the only constraints in the graph. If the pseudo-tree would put that central agent as root, and all other agents as its children we would get a tree of depth 2. Once the first agent picks its assignment, all other agents can quickly compute the optimal value for themselves. However, if we were to pick a different pseudo-tree, say one that looks like a chain, then it would be harder to solve. Value changes at agents would invalidate contexts below them, which may cause them to switch assignments, causing more contexts below to become invalid, and so on. This ordering gives far worse performance, even though it is still a pseudo-tree.

In other words, while many pseudo-trees exist, clearly some are better than others. Unfortunately, there is an exponential number of pseudo-trees (in the worst case), and the problem of finding the best one is considered to be NP-hard [28]. Regardless of the method used to build the pseudo-tree, the density of the constraint networks limits the possible trees. The higher the density, the more constraints exist in the network, and the deeper the optimal pseudo-tree becomes. In the extreme case of fully connected constraint problems ($p_1 = 1.0$), any pseudo-tree must in fact be a chain. This is easily proven, since any tree with a node with two or more sons would not be a pseudo-tree. Any two siblings are constrained (since $p_1 = 1$) and obviously there is no path from root to leaf that covers them both. Therefore, every pseudo-tree for this problem must have a branching factor of no more than one, or in other words, it is a chain.

To conclude, *ADOPT* uses pseudo-trees to enhance its concurrency. Finding the optimal pseudo-tree can be hard. Furthermore, even the optimal tree cannot always guarantee a great deal of concurrency. Even its optimal form is dependent upon the constraint density of the problem. This important fact about *ADOPT*'s concurrent behavior will be easy to see in the comparative empirical study of *ADOPT* and *AFB* in Chapter 16, where *ADOPT* will perform very badly on hard instances of DisCOPs.

15.5.3 Network load of *ADOPT*

During empirical evaluations of *ADOPT* the network load, in the form of the total number of messages sent, grows at a high exponential rate. This was not reported in the original *ADOPT* paper [46]. This exponential growth can be explained by the fact that in *ADOPT*, after receiving a message of any type, the agent processes that message's contents (regardless of the type of message) and then calls the *backtrack* procedure. In this procedure, the agent may or may not swap its value assignment, and then send both VALUE messages to its lower priority neighbors and a COST message to its parent. Therefore, following every message received, an average of two or more messages (COST upwards, VALUE downwards) are sent. Even agents that are at the top (root) or bottom (leafs) of the tree send a single message (either COST or VALUE) following every message received.

It seems obvious that over time the number of messages in the system would grow and at an exponential rate. Some agents replace one message in the system with another, and other agents replace one message by several new messages. One may hope that simply eliminating duplicate messages sent in sequence by the same agent would solve this. However, if an agent does **not** send a VALUE or a COST message because its previous message of that type contained the exact same information, the algorithm becomes incorrect.

For example, in Figure 15.3, imagine that A_5 learns of a new value assignment that was made by A_1. Assume that agent A_2 does not receive this message due to a delay in the message pipeline between A_1 and A_2. A_5 would send a COST message to A_3, which in turn would send a COST message to A_2. This COST message would contain information computed based on the new value assigned by A_1, but A_2 would discard it as it is not consistent with its context. When A_2 learns of the new value of A_1, it may decide not to change its value, and if it does not send a VALUE message to A_3, then A_3 would not resend the needed COST message. In summary, identical messages must always be sent and cannot be discarded. Consequently, *the total number of messages is expected to grow exponentially during the run of the ADOPT algorithm.*

Asynchronous Forward-Bounding

The *Asynchronous Forward Bounding (AFB)* algorithm for DISCOPs was published in its full form in [22]. The algorithm incorporates concepts and techniques from two former algorithms.

- AFB uses the idea of *asynchronous lookahead* of the *AFC* algorithm (see Chapter 6). It uses a CPA messages framework and time-stamping of messages.
- The core of the *AFB* search process is based on the general branch and bound algorithm. This makes it a COP solver (see Chapter 3).

As before, for simplicity of exposition we only handle DISCOPs in which each agent has a single variable.

16.1 AFB - Overview

The *AFB* algorithm passes a single, most up-to-date current partial assignment among the agents. Agents assign their variables only when they hold the up-to-date CPA. The CPA is a unique message that is passed between agents, and carries the partial assignment that agents attempt to extend into a complete and optimal solution by assigning their variables on it. The CPA also carries the accumulated cost of constraints between all assignments it contains, as well as a unique time stamp.

Only one agent performs an assignment on a CPA at any time. Copies of the CPA are sent forward to unassigned agents and are concurrently processed by multiple agents. Each unassigned agent computes a lower bound on the cost of assigning a value to its variable, and sends this bound back to the agent which performed the assignment. The assigning agent uses these bounds to prune subspaces of the search space which do not contain a full assignment with a cost lower than the best full assignment found so far.

More specifically, every agent that adds its assignment to the CPA sends forward copies of the CPA, in messages we term *FB_CPA*, to all agents whose assignments are not yet on the CPA. An agent receiving an *FB_CPA* message computes a lower bound on the cost increment caused by adding an assignment to its variable. This estimated cost is sent back to the agent who sent the *FB_CPA* message via *FB_ESTIMATE* messages. The computation of this bound is detailed in Section 16.2.

16.2 Lower Bound Estimation for the Cost Increment

The computation of the lower bound on the cost increment caused by adding an assignment to the agent's local variable is done as follows.

Denote by $cost((i,v), (j,u))$ the cost of assigning $A_i = v$ and $A_j = u$. For each agent A_i and each value in its domain $v \in D_i$, we denote the minimal cost of the assignment (i,v) incurred by an agent A_j by $h_j(v) = min_{u \in D_j}(cost((i,v),(j,u)))$. We define $h(v)$, the total cost of assigning the value v, to be the sum of $h_j(v)$ over all $j > i$. Intuitively, $h(v)$ is a lower bound on the cost of constraints involving the assignment $A_i = v$ and all agents A_j such that $j > i$. Note that this bound can be computed once per agent, since it is independent of the assignments of higher priority agents.

An agent A_i which receives an *FB_CPA* message can compute for every $v \in D_i$ both the cost increment of assigning v as its value, i.e., the sum of the cost of the conflicts v has with the assignments included in the CPA, and $h(v)$. The sum of these is denoted by $f(v)$. The lowest calculated $f(v)$ among all values $v \in D_i$ is chosen to be the lower bound estimation on the cost increment by agent A_i.

Figure 16.1 presents a constraint network in which A_1 already assigned the value v_1 and A_2, A_3, A_4 are unassigned. Let us assume that the cost of every constraint is one. The cost of v_3 will increase by one due to its constraint with the current assignment, thus $f(v_3) = 1$. Since v_4 is constrained with both v_8 and v_9, assigning this value will trigger a cost increment when A_4 performs an assignment. Therefore $h(v_4) = 1$ is an admissible lower bound of the cost of the constraints between this value and lower priority agents. Since v_4 does not conflict with assignments on the CPA, $f(v_4) = 1$ as well. $f(v_5) = 3$ because this assignment conflicts with the assignment on the CPA and in addition conflicts with all the values of the two remaining agents.

Since $h(v)$ takes into account only constraints of A_i with lower priority agents (A_j s.t. $j > i$), unassigned lower priority agents do not need to estimate their cost of constraints with A_i. Therefore, these estimations can be accumulated and summed up by the agent which initiated the forward bounding process to compute a lower bound on the cost of a complete assignment extended from the CPA. Thus, asynchronous forward bounding enables early detection of partial assignments that cannot be extended into complete assignments with a cost smaller than the known upper bound, and to initiate backtracks as early as possible.

Algorithm 16.1: Main procedures of the AFB algorithm

procedure **init**:
1. $B \leftarrow \infty$
2. **if** $(A_i = A_1)$
3. $generate\_CPA()$
4. $assign\_CPA()$

when received (**FB_CPA**, A_j, PA)
5. $f \leftarrow$ estimation based on the received PA.
6. send $(FB\_ESTIMATE, f, PA, A_i)$ to A_j

when received (**CPA_MSG**, PA)
7. $CPA \leftarrow PA$
8. $TempCPA \leftarrow PA$
9. **if** $TempCPA$ contains an assignment to A_i, remove it
10. **if** $(TempCPA.cost \geq B)$
11.   backtrack()
12. **else**
13. $assign\_CPA()$

when received (**FB_ESTIMATE**, estimate, PA , A_j)
14. save estimate
15. **if** (CPA.cost + all saved estimates) $\geq B$)
16. $assign\_CPA()$

when received (**NEW_SOLUTION**, PA)
17. $B\_CPA \leftarrow PA$
18. $B \leftarrow PA.cost$

procedure **assign_CPA**:
19. clear estimations
20. **if** CPA contains an assignment $A_i = w$, remove it
21. iterate (from last assigned value) over D_i until found
    $v \in D_i$ s.t. $CPA.cost + f(v) < B$
22. **if** no such value exists
23.   backtrack()
24. **else**
25.   assign $A_i = v$
26.   **if** CPA is a full assignment
27.   broadcast (**NEW_SOLUTION**, CPA)
28. $B \leftarrow CPA.cost$
29. $assign\_CPA()$
30.   **else**
31.   send(**CPA_MSG**, CPA) to A_{i+1}
32.   **forall** $j > i$
33.   send(**FB_CPA**, A_i, CPA) to A_j

procedure **backtrack**:
34. clear estimates
35. **if** $(A_i = A_1)$
36.   broadcast(**TERMINATE**)
37. **else**
38.   send(**CPA_MSG**, CPA) to A_{i-1}

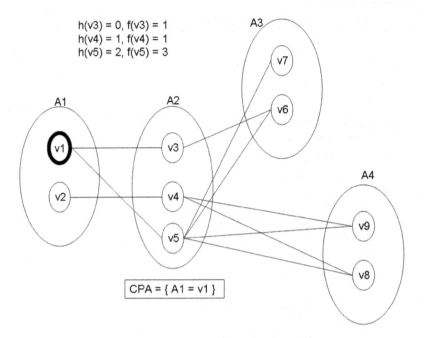

h(v3) = 0, f(v3) = 1
h(v4) = 1, f(v4) = 1
h(v5) = 2, f(v5) = 3

Fig. 16.1. A simple DisCOP, demonstration

16.3 AFB - Algorithm Description

The AFB algorithm is run on each of the agents in the DISCOP. Each agent first calls the procedure *init* and then responds to messages until it receives a TERMINATE message. The algorithm is presented in Algorithm 16.1. The computation of bounds, and the time-stamping mechanism are not shown, as they are explained in the text.

In the initialization, each agent updates B to be the cost of the best full assignment found so far and, since no such assignment was found, it is set to infinity (line 1). Only the first agent (A_1) creates an empty CPA and then begins the search process by calling **assign_CPA** (lines 3-4), in order to find a value assignment for its variable.

An agent receiving a CPA (when received **CPA_MSG**), first makes sure it is relevant. The time stamp mechanism by [48] is used to determine the relevance of the CPA (for more details on this mechanism see Section 16.4).

If the CPA's time stamp reveals that it is not the most up-to-date CPA, the message is discarded. In such a case, the agent processing the message has already received a message implying that an assignment of some agent which has a higher priority than itself has been changed. When the message is not discarded, the agent saves the received PA in its local CPA variable (line 7). Then the agent checks that the received PA (without an assignment to its own variable) does not exceed the allowed cost B (lines 8-10). If it does not exceed the bound, it tries to assign a value to its variable (or replace its existing assignment if it has one already) by calling **assign_CPA** (line 13). If the bound is exceeded, a backtrack is initiated (line 11) and the CPA is sent to a higher priority agent since the cost is already too high (even without an assignment to its variable).

Procedure **assign_CPA** attempts to find a value assignment for the current agent within the bounds of the current CPA. First, estimates related to prior assignments are cleared (line 19). Next, the agent attempts to assign every value in its domain it did not already try. If the CPA arrived without an assignment to its variable, it tries every value in its domain. Otherwise, the search for such a value is continued from the value following the last assigned value. The assigned value must be such that the sum of the cost of the CPA and the lower bound of the cost increment caused by the assignment will not exceed the upper bound B (lines 20-22). If no such value is found, the assignment of some higher priority agent must be altered, and so backtrack is called (line 23). Otherwise, the agent assigns the selected value on the CPA.

When the agent is the last agent (A_n), a complete assignment has been reached with an accumulated cost lower than B, and it is broadcasted to all agents (line 27). This broadcast will inform the agents of the new bound for the cost of a full assignment, and cause them to update their upper bound B.

The agent holding the CPA (A_n) continues the search by updating its bound B and calling **assign_CPA** (line 29). The current value will not be picked by this call, since the CPA's cost with this assignment is now equal to B, and the procedure demands the cost to be lower than B. So the agent will continue the search, testing other values, and backtracking if they do not lead to further improvement.

When the agent holding the CPA is not the last agent (line 30), the CPA is sent forward to the next unassigned agent, for additional value assignment (line 31). Concurrently, forward bounding requests (i.e., FB_CPA messages) are sent to all lower priority agents (lines 32-33).

An agent receiving a forward bounding request (when received **FB_CPA**) from agent A_j, again uses the time-stamp mechanism to ignore irrelevant messages. Only if the message is relevant, does the agent compute its estimate (lower bound) of the cost incurred by the lowest cost assignment to its variable (line 5). The exact computation of this estimation was described above [it is the minimal $f(v)$ over all $v \in D_i$]. This estimation is then attached to the message and sent back to the sender as an **FB_ESTIMATE** message.

An agent receiving a bound estimation (when received **FB_ESTIMATE**) from a lower priority agent A_j (in response to a forward bounding message) ignores it if it is an estimate to an already abandoned partial assignment (identified by using the time-stamp mechanism). Otherwise, it saves this estimate (line 14) and checks if this new estimate causes the current partial assignment to exceed the bound B (line 15). In such a case, the agent calls

assign_CPA (line 16) in order to change its value assignment (or backtrack if a valid assignment cannot be found).

The call to **backtrack** is made whenever the current agent cannot find a valid value (i.e., below the bound B). In such a case, the agent clears its saved estimates, and sends the CPA backwards to agent A_{i-1} (line 38). If the agent is the first agent (with nowhere to backtrack to), the terminate broadcast ends the search process in all agents (line 36). The algorithm then reports that the optimal solution has a cost of B, and the full assignment with such a cost is B_CPA.

16.4 The Time-Stamp Mechanism

As mentioned previously, AFB uses the time-stamp mechanism of [48] to determine the relevance of the CPA. The requirements from this mechanism are that, given two messages with two different partial assignments, it must determine which one of them is obsolete. An obsolete partial assignment is one that was abandoned by the search process because one of the assigned agents has changed its assignment. This requirement is accomplished by the time-stamping mechanism in the following manner. Each agent keeps a local running-assignment counter. Whenever it performs an assignment it increments its local counter. Whenever it sends a message containing its assignment, the agent copies its current counter onto the message. Each message holds a vector of time stamps, containing the counters of the agents it passed through. The i-th element of the vector corresponds to A_i's counter. This vector is in fact the time stamp. A lexicographical comparison of two such vectors will reveal which time stamp is more up-to-date.

Each agent saves a copy of what it knows to be the most up-to-date time stamp. When receiving a new message with a newer time stamp, the agent updates its local saved best time stamp. Suppose agent A_i receives a message with a time stamp that is lexicographically smaller than the locally saved best, by comparing the first $i-1$ elements of the vector. This means that the message was based on a combination of assignments which was already abandoned and this message is discarded. Only when the message's time stamp in the first $i-1$ elemental is equal or greater than the locally saved best time stamp is the message processed further.

The vector's counters might appear to require a lot of space, as the number of assignments can grow exponentially in the number of agents. However, if the agent (A_i) resets its local counter to zero each time the assignments of higher priority agents are altered, the counters will remain small (log of the size of the value domain).

16.5 AFB - Proof of Correctness

In order to prove correctness for AFB two claims must be established. First, that the algorithm terminates and second that when the algorithm terminates its global upper bound B is the cost of the optimal solution. To prove termination one can show that the AFB algorithm never goes into an endless loop. To prove the last statement it is enough to show that the same partial assignment cannot be generated more than once.

Lemma 16.5.1 *The AFB algorithm never generates two identical CPAs.*

Assume by negation that A_i is the highest priority agent (first in the order of assignments) that generates a partial assignment CPA for the second time. The replacement of an assignment can only be triggered by one of two messages arriving at A_i from a lower priority agent A_j ($j > i$); either a backtrack CPA message, or an $FB\_ESTIMATE$ message. In the first case the next assignment on the CPA will be generated by the procedure **assign_CPA**. Each of the values in the domain of A_i is considered exactly once. When the agent's domain is exhausted the agent backtracks and under the above assumption will never receive the same partial assignment again. If the received message is an estimate that clashes with the upper bound (e.g., the second case), a new CPA is generated. The generated CPA is a clone of the last CPA the agent received from a higher priority agent. Only values which were not considered on the previous CPA are left in its current domain. Therefore, the situation with the new CPA is similar to the first case. Termination follows immediately from Lemma 16.5.1.

Next we prove that, upon termination, the complete assignment, corresponding to the optimal solution, is in B_CPA (see Algorithm 16.1). There is only one point of termination for the AFB algorithm, in procedure **backtrack**. So, one needs to prove that during search no partial assignment that can lead to a solution of lower cost than B is discarded. But, this fact is immediate, because the only place in the code where values are discarded is in the third line of procedure **assign_CPA** (line 21). Within this procedure, values are discarded only when the calculated lower bound of the value being considered is higher than the current bound on the cost of a global solution. Clearly, this cannot lead to a discarding of a lower cost global solution.

One still needs to show that whenever the algorithm calls the procedure **assign_CPA**, it does not loose a potential lower cost solution. There are altogether four places in the algorithm where a call to procedure **assign_CPA** is made. One is in procedure *init*, which is irrelevant. The three relevant calls are in the code performed when receiving a CPA or receiving an $FB\_ESTIMATE$, and in the procedure **assign_CPA** itself.

The third case is trivially correct. Before calling the procedure the global bound B is updated and the corresponding complete solution is stored. Consequently, the current solution is not lost. The first two calls (see Algorithm 16.1) appear in the last lines of the procedures processing the two messages. When processing an $FB\_ESTIMATE$ message, the call to **assign_CPA** happens after the lower bound of the current value has been tested to exceed the global bound B (line 15). This is correct, since the current partial solution cannot be extended to a lower cost solution. The last call to **assign_CPA** occurs in the last line of processing a received CPA message. Clearly, this call extends a shorter partial solution and does not discard a value of the current agent. This completes the correctness proof of the AFB algorithm.   □

16.6 Concurrency in AFB

At any point in time during the run of AFB, there is a single most-up-to-date CPA in the system. Each agent adds an assignment when it holds it, so assignments are performed sequentially. One might think that this would necessarily result in poor performance, as the search process does not try to take advantage of the existing multiple computational resources available to it. The concurrency of AFB comes from the use of the forward-bounding mechanism. While the CPA is held by one agent, many copies of it are sent forward, and a collection of agents concurrently compute lower bounds for that CPA. When the CPA advances to the next agent, again this process repeats, and so the unassigned agents are constantly kept working, either when they receive the CPA, or when they need to compute bounds for some other partial assignment.

This approach is quite different from that used by asynchronous assignments algorithms such as $ADOPT$ or ABT. In these algorithms the search process attempts to perform assignments concurrently by the collection of agents. Since many agents are assigning their variables simultaneously, there is a probability that must be handled by the algorithm, that the current agent's view of assignments made by other agents is incorrect. This is due to the fact that agents concurrently alter their assignments. The algorithm must be able to deal with this uncertainty.

One can say about the advantage of asynchronous assignments algorithms, that either the agent's information is accurate and not waiting for a sequential process to reach the current agent is saving time, or the agent's information is inaccurate and its previous computation will not be useful once the updated information arrives. So it may appear that asynchronous assignments algorithms would be better than sequential assignment algorithms. However, asynchronously assigning algorithms must also deal with inconsistencies caused by message delay. For example, if several higher priority agents change their assignments at some lower priority agent, only some of the messages are received (the others are delayed) and computation is done based on an inconsistent agent view. This type of scenario, which has computation based on an inconsistent partial assignment, is completely avoided in sequential assigning algorithms.

To conclude, The AFB algorithm includes concurrent computation by multiple agents without having to deal with the uncertainty that comes with asynchronous assignments. Each agent that receives a message containing a partial assignment knows with certainty that the given partial assignment is the one it was supposes to receive, and not a result of a network delay inconsistency. Therefore, AFB has both concurrent computation and the certainty of working with consistent partial assignments.

Extending AFB - BackJumping

In this chapter we present the AFB-BJ algorithm. AFB-BJ is an extension of the AFB algorithm that incorporates a backjumping mechanism for improved performance. Sometimes during the run of the AFB search, the CPA is backtracked to some agent A_i after it was determined to be a dead end. A_i then attempts to replace its assignment with another assignment, and if successful passes the CPA to the next agent A_{i+1}. A_i would repeat this process whenever the CPA is backtracked from A_{i+1}, until it has attempted to extend the CPA with every value in its domain of values, and only when it has tested them all would it backtrack the CPA to A_{i-1}. The proposed mechanism for backjumping allows agents such as A_{i+1} to detect situations in which the CPA can be sent directly to agents prior to A_i without missing out on potential solutions. As can be seen from the above description, this avoids useless computation, as A_i explores its remaining values.

Backjumping is widely used in CSP algorithms. The conflict-based backjumping algorithm (CBJ) [51] is a proven example of a speed up mechanism for centralized CSPs [14]. In CBJ, conflict sets hold the culprit variables responsible for the elimination of values from each variable's current domain. When backtracking is required, these conflict sets can be used to identify the culprit variables responsible for the dead end, and therefore allow backjumping directly to the latest variable that was assigned among those variables. Graph-based backjumping [16] is another form of backjumping, in which backjumping possibilities are inferred from the constraint graph.

Recently, conflict-based backjumping was also applied to $MAX\text{-}CSPs$ [76]. The extension of backjumping to optimization problems is not trivial, since culprit variables are harder to detect. When accumulating explanations for eliminated values in constrained optimization problems, many values involved in some constraints might be part of the optimal solution. Bounds for each value as well as the current lower and upper bounds must be used to detect the culprit variables. To the best of the author's knowleddge, no other DISCOP algorithm to date uses any form of backjumping mechanism.

17.1 Adding Value Ordering Heuristics

Before adding a backjump mechanism, one first needs to add a value ordering heuristic. A value ordering heuristic is a heuristic for reordering the domain values of agents. Since agents pick their next assignment to be the next untested value in their value domain, ordering these values in different ways has the potential to produce different performances, as shown for example in [14]. A good value ordering heuristic for AFB is called $min\text{-}cost$ and the resulting version of the algorithm is called accordingly $AFB\text{-}minC$. The $min\text{-}cost$ heuristic arranges the values of an agent by the cost of each value with respect to the assignments of higher priority agents on the CPA. Each agent performs this reordering whenever it needs to perform an assignment. Since the ordering cannot change without a change in the assignment of higher priority agents, no reordering is performed as long as these assignments remain fixed. Once an updated CPA arrives, containing new assignments for higher priority agents, the agent reorders its values and the ordering remains until the next time higher priority agents change assignments (in other words, until a backtrack is performed).

Since AFB does not assume any special ordering of the values, it remains correct and complete with any specific ordering. To see why the algorithm remains correct, observe that an obsolete ordering is in a one-to-one correspondence to a time stamped CPA, i.e., to an assignment of higher priority agents. Any message received that is related to an obsolete ordering and is discarded is also related to an obsolete time stamped CPA. As long as the current CPA remains valid, the value ordering is fixed and there is no possibility of missing exploration of values due to reordering during search.

17.2 Backjumping - Key Concepts

In both centralized and distributed CSPs, backjumping can be accomplished by maintaining data structures that will allow an agent to deduce who is the latest agent (in the order in which assignments were made) whose changed assignment could possibly lead to a solution. Once such an agent is found, the assignments of all following agents are unmade and the search process backjumps to that agent [23, 44, 51].

A similar process can be designed for branch and bound based solvers for COPs and DisCOPs. Consider a sequence of assignments by the agents A_1, A_2, A_3, A_4, A_5 where A_5 determined that none of its possible value assignments can lead to a full assignment with a cost lower than the cost of the best full assignment found so far. Clearly, A_5 must backtrack.

In chronological backtracking, the search process would simply return to the previous agent, namely A_4, and have it change its assignment. However, A_5 can sometimes determine that no value change of A_4 would suffice to reach a full assignment of a lower cost. Intuitively, A_5 can safely backjump to A_3, if it can compute a lower bound on the cost of a full assignment extended from the assignments of A_1, A_2, and A_3, and show that this bound is greater or equal to the cost of the best full assignment found so far. This is the intuitive basis of how backjumping can be added to AFB.

More formally, let us consider a state in which A_i decides to backtrack, and the cost of the best full assignment found so far is B (i.e., B is the upper bound of the current state of the search). The current partial assignment includes the assignments of agents $A_1, ..., A_{i-1}$.

Definition 17.1. *$CPA[1..k]$ is the set of assignments made by agents $A_1, ..., A_k$ in the current partial assignment. We define $CPA[1..0] = \{\}$.*

Definition 17.2. *$FA[k]$ is the set of all **full** assignments, which include all the assignments appearing in $CPA[1..k]$. For example, $FA[2]$ contains all full assignments in which both A_1 and A_2 have the same value assignments as they do in the current partial assignment. Naturally, $FA[0]$ is the set of all possible full assignments.*

Upon a backtrack operation, instead of simply backtracking to the previous agent, A_i performs the following actions. It computes a lower bound on the cost of any full assignment in $FA[i-2]$. If this bound is smaller than B, it backtracks to A_{i-1} just like it would do in chronological backtracking. However, if this bound is greater or equal to B, then backtracking to A_{i-1} would do little good. No value change of A_{i-1} alone could result in a full assignment of cost lower than B. As a result, A_i knows it can safely backjump to A_{i-2}. It may be possible for A_i to backjump even further, depending on the lower bound on the cost of any full assignment in $FA[i-3]$. If this bound is smaller than B, it backjumps to A_{i-2}. Otherwise, it knows it can safely backjump to A_{i-3}. Similar checks can be made about the necessity to backjump further.

The backjumping procedure relies on the computation of lower bounds for sets of full assignments ($FA[k]$). Next, we will show how can A_i compute such lower bounds. Let us define the notions of past, local and future costs in Definitions 17.3, 17.4, and 17.5.

Definition 17.3. *PC (past costs) is a vector of size $n+1$, in which the $k-th$ element $(0 \leq k \leq n)$ is equal to the cost of $CPA[1..k]$.*

Definition 17.4. *$LC(v)$ (local costs) is a vector of size $n+1$ computed by A_i and held by it, in which the $k-th$ element $(0 \leq k \leq n)$ is*

$$LC(v)[k] = \sum_{(A_j, v_j) \in CPA \ s.t. \ j \leq k} cost(A_i = v, A_j = v_j)$$

Since the CPA held by A_i only includes assignments of $A_1, ..., A_{i-1}$, it follows that

$$(\forall j \geq i) LC(v)[i-1] = LC(v)[j]$$

Intuitively, $LC(v)[i]$ is the accumulated cost of the value v of A_i, with respect to all assignments in $CPA[1..i]$.

Definition 17.5. $FC_j(v)$ *(future costs) is a vector of size $n+1$ in which the $k-th$ element $(0 \leq k \leq n)$ contains a lower bound on the cost of assigning a value to A_j with respect to the partial assignment CPA[1..k]. Assume that this structure is held by agent A_i. If $k \geq i$, then CPA[1..k] contains the assignment $A_i = v$. For $k < i$ the value v of A_i is irrelevant as it does not appear in CPA[1..k].*

The above vectors provide additive lower bounds on full assignments that start with the current CPA up to k, FA[k]. PC[k] is the exact cost of the first k assignments, LC(v)[k] is the exact cost of the assignment $A_i = v$, and $\sum_{j>i} FC_j(v)[k]$ is a lower bound on the assignments of $A_{i+1}, ..., A_n$. Therefore, the sum

$$\mathbf{FALB}(v)[k] = LC(v)[k] + PC[k] + \sum_{j>i} FC_j(v)[k]$$

is a *full assignment lower bound* on the cost of any full assignment extended from CPA[1..k] in which $A_i = v$.

FA[k] contains all full assignments extended from CPA[1..k], and is not limited to assignments in which $A_i = v$. If we go over all FALB(v)[k], for all possible values $v \in D_i$ we produce a lower bound on any assignment in FA[k].

Definition 17.6. $FALB[k] = \min_{v \in D_i}(FALB(v)[k])$.
FALB[k] is a lower bound on the cost of any full assignment that is extended from CPA[1..k].

In a distributed branch and bound algorithm, this bound is computed by A_i. PC, the cost of previous agents, is sent along with their value assignment messages to A_i. LC(v), the cost of assigning v to A_i, can be computed by A_i. A_i requests all agents ordered after it, A_j $(j > i)$, to compute FC$_j$ and send the results back to A_i. This is part of the *AFB* mechanism for forward bounding, as explained in Chapter 16. In the *AFB* algorithm [22] A_i already requests unassigned agents to compute lower bounds on the CPA and send back the results. The additional bounds needed for backjumping can easily be added to the existing *AFB* framework.

17.3 A Backjumping Example

To demonstrate the backjumping possibility, consider the DISCOP in Figure 17.1. Let us assume that the search begins with A_1 assigning **a** as its value and sending the CPA forward to A_2. A_2, A_3, A_4, and A_5 all assign the value **a** and we get a full assignment with cost 12. The search continues, and after fully exploring the sub space in which $A_1 = a, A_2 = a$, the best assignment found is $A_1 = a, A_2 = a, A_3 = b, A_4 = a, A_5 = b$ with a total cost of $B = 6$. Assume that A_3 is now holding the CPA after receiving it from

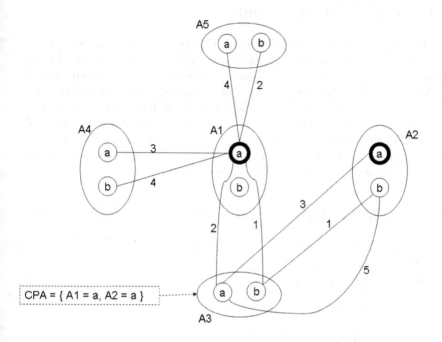

Fig. 17.1. An example DisCOP for backjumping

some future agent (A_4 or A_5). A_3 has exhausted its value domain and must backtrack. It computes:

$$FALB(a)[1] = PC[1] + LC(a)[1] + (FC_4(a)[1] + FC_5(a)[1])$$

$$= 0 + 2 + (3 + 2) = 7$$

$$FALB(b)[1] = PC[1] + LC(b)[1] + (FC_4(b)[1] + FC_5(b)[1])$$

$$= 0 + 1 + (3 + 2) = 6$$

$$FALB[1] = min(FALB(a)[1], FLAB(b)[1]) = 6$$

$FALB[1] \geq B$, therefore A_3 knows that any full assignment extended from $\{A_1 = a\}$ would cost at least 6. A full assignment with that cost was already discovered, so there is no need to explore the rest of this sub-space, and it can safely backjump the search process back to A_1, to change its value to **b**. Backtracking to A_2 leaves the search process within the $\{A_1 = a\}$ sub space, which A_3 knows cannot lead to a full assignment with a lower cost.

17.4 The AFB-BJ Algorithm

The *AFB-BJ* algorithm is run on each of the agents in the DISCOP. Each agent first calls the procedure **init** and then responds to messages until it receives a TERMINATE message. The algorithm is presented in Algorithm 17.1 and Algorithm 17.2. As in pure *AFB*, a time-stamping mechanism is used on all messages. Timestamping is used to determine which messages are relevant and which are obsolete. For simplicity, we choose to omit the description of this mechanism from the pseudo-code, referring the reader to the description in Chapter 16. For the same reason we choose to omit the pseudo-code detailing the calculation of LC, PC, FC, and FALB.

Algorithm 17.1: Initialization and message-handling procedures of AFB-BJ

---

procedure **init**:
1. $B \leftarrow \infty$
2. **if** $(A_i = A_1)$
3.   *generate_CPA()*
4.   *assign_CPA()*

when received (**FB_CPA**, A_j, PA)
5. $V \leftarrow$ estimation vector for each PA[1..k] $(0 \leq k \leq n)$
6. send $(FB\_ESTIMATE, V, PA, A_i)$ to A_j

when received (**CPA_MSG**, PA, A_j)
7. $CPA \leftarrow PA$
8. $TempCPA \leftarrow PA$
9. **if** $(j = i - 1)$
10. $\forall j$ re-initialize $FC_j(v)$
11.   reorder domain values $v \in D_i$ by LC(v)[i] (from low to high)
12. **if** $(TempCPA$ contains an assignment to $A_i)$ remove it
13. **if** $(TempCPA.cost \geq B)$
14.   backtrack()
15. **else**
16.   *assign_CPA()*

when received (**FB_ESTIMATE**, V, PA , A_j)
17. $FC_j(v) \leftarrow V$
18. **if** (FALB(v)[i] $\geq B$)
19.   *assign_CPA()*

when received (**NEW_SOLUTION**, PA)
20. $B\_CPA \leftarrow PA$
21. $B \leftarrow PA.cost$

Algorithm 17.2: The assigning and backtracking procedures of AFB-BJ

---

procedure **assign_CPA**:
22. **if** CPA contains an assignment $A_i = w$, remove it
23. iterate (from last assigned value) over D_i until the first value satisfying
    $v \in D_i$ s.t. $CPA.cost + f(v) < B$
24. **if** no such value exists
25.   backtrack()
26. **else**
27.   assign $A_i = v$
28.   **if** CPA is a full assignment
29.   broadcast (**NEW_SOLUTION**, CPA)
30. $B \leftarrow CPA.cost$
31. $assign\_CPA()$
32.   **else**
33.   send(**CPA_MSG**, CPA, A_i) to A_{i+1}
34.   **forall** $j > i$
35.   send(**FB_CPA**, A_i, CPA) to A_j

procedure **backtrack**:
36. **if** $(A_i = A_1)$
37.   broadcast(**TERMINATE**)
38. **else**
39.   j $\leftarrow$ backtrackTo()
40.   remove assignments of $A_{j+1}, .., A_i$ from CPA
41.   send(**CPA_MSG**, CPA, A_i) to A_j

function **backtrackTo**:
42. **for** $j = i - 1$ **downto** 1
43.   **foreach** $v \in D_i$
44.   **if** (FALB(v)[j-1] + (PC[j] - PC[j-1]) < B)
45.   **return** j
46. broadcast(**TERMINATE**)

The algorithm starts by each agent calling **init** and then awaiting messages until termination. At first, each agent updates B to be the cost of the best full assignment found so far and, since no such assignment was found, it is set to infinity (line 1). Only the first agent (A_1) creates an empty CPA and then begins the search process by calling **assign_CPA** (lines 3-4), in order to find a value assignment for its variable.

An agent receiving a CPA (when received **CPA_MSG**), checks the time stamp associated with it. An out-of-date CPA is discarded. When the message is not discarded, the agent saves the received PA in its local CPA variable (line 7). If the CPA was received from a higher priority agent, the estimations of future agents in FC_j are no longer relevant and are discarded, and the domain values must be reordered by their updated cost (lines 9-11). Then, the agent attempts to assign its next value by calling **assign_CPA** (line 16) or to backtrack if needed (line 14).

Procedure **assign_CPA** attempts to find a value assignment for the current agent. The assigned value must be such that the sum of the cost of the CPA and the lower bound of the cost increment caused by the assignment will not exceed the upper bound B (lines 23). If no such value is found, the assignment of some higher priority agent must be altered, so backtrack is called (line 25). When a full assignment is found which is better than the best full assignment known so far, it is broadcast to all agents (line 29). After succeeding to assign a value, the CPA is sent forward to the next unassigned agent (line 33). Concurrently, forward-bounding requests (i.e., FB_CPA messages) are sent to all lower priority agents (lines 34-35).

An agent receiving a bound estimation (when received **FB_ESTIMATE**) from a lower priority agent A_j (in response to a forward bounding message) ignores it if it is an estimate to an already abandoned partial assignment (identified using the time stamp mechanism). Otherwise, it saves this estimate (line 17) and checks if this new estimate causes the current partial assignment to exceed the bound B (line 18). In such a case, the agent calls **assign_CPA** (line 19) in order to change its value assignment (or backtrack if a valid assignment cannot be found).

The call to **backtrack** is made whenever the current agent cannot find a valid value (i.e., below the bound B). In such a case, the agent calls **backtrackTo()** to compute to which agent the CPA should be sent, and backtracks the search process (by sending the CPA) back to that agent. If the agent is the first agent (with nowhere to backtrack to), the terminate broadcast ends the search process in all agents (line 37). The algorithm then reports that the optimal solution has a cost of B, and that the full assignment corresponding to this cost is B_CPA.

The function **backtrackTo()** computes to which agent the CPA should be sent. This is the kernel of the backjumping (BJ) mechanism. It goes over all candidates, from $j-1$ down to 1, looking for the first agent it finds that has a chance of reaching a full assignment with a lower cost than B. FALB$(v)[j\text{-}1]$ is a lower bound on the cost of a full assignment extended from CPA$[1..j\text{-}1]$, and PC$[j]$-PC$[j\text{-}1]$ is the cost added to that CPA by A_j's assignment. Since A_j picked the lowest cost value in its domain (its domain was ordered in line 11), the addition of these two components produces a more accurate lower bound on the cost of a full assignment extended from CPA$[1..j\text{-}1]$. If this bound is not smaller than B, then surely any combination of assignments made by A_j and any following agent could only raise the cost, which is already too high. In case even backjumping back to A_1 does not prove helpful, the search process is terminated (line 46).

17.5 AFB-BJ - Proof of Correctness

In order to prove the correctness of the AFB_BJ algorithm we first prove the correctness of the proposed backjumping method and then show that its combination with AFB does not violate AFB's correctness as proven in Section 16.5.

In order to prove the correctness of the backjumping method one need only show that none of the agents' assignments that the algorithm backjumps over can lead to a solution with a lower cost than the current upper bound. The condition for performing backjumping over A_j (line 44) is that the lower bound on the cost of a full assignment extended from the assignments of $A_1 \dots A_{j-1}$ and of the assignment cost of A_j exceeds the global upper bound B. Since A_j picked the lowest cost value in its remaining domain (as the domain is ordered), extending the assignments of $A_1 \dots A_{j-1}$ must lead to a cost greater than or equal to B. Therefore, backjumping to A_{j-1} cannot discard any potentially lower cost solutions. This completes the correctness proof of the $AFB - BJ$ backjumping [e.g., function **backtrackTo()**] method.

Assuming the correctness of AFB as proven in Section 16.5, in order to prove the correctness of the composite algorithm $AFB\text{-}BJ$ it is enough to prove the consistency of the lower bounds computed by the agents in $AFB\text{-}BJ$. The lower bounds computed by $AFB\text{-}BJ$ include FC, LC, and PC as described in Section 17.2. PC is contained in the CPA, and is updated by any agent that receives it and adds an assignment (not shown in the code). $LC(v)$ is computed by the current agent A_i whenever it assigns v as its value assignment. FC_j is computed by A_j in line 5 (in Algorithm 17.1), and is sent back to A_i in line 6. A_i receives and saves this in line 17. The lower bounds contained inside these vectors are correct because PC was exactly calculated when holding the CPA, LC was exactly calculated by the current agent A_i, and the bounds in FC_j are the same bounds computed in AFB which were proven to be correct lower bounds for the assignment of A_j in Section 16.5. The FC_j bounds are accurate and based on the current partial assignment since the time stamp mechanism prevents processing of bounds which are based on an obsolete CPA. Whenever the CPA is altered by some higher priority agent, the previous bounds are cleared (line 10 of Algorithm 17.1). $\qquad\square$

Empirical Evaluation of DisCOP algorithms

To evaluate DISCOP algorithms the simplest approach is to build on experience from centralized COPs (see Chapter 3). Centralized constraints optimization problems are many times evaluated on *Max-CSPs* [33, 36]. The distributed version of *Max-CSPs* are termed $MaxDisCSP$ and are DISCOPs for which all costs are either zero or one. These problems can be randomly generated similarly to randomly generated CSPs by selecting the number of agents n (each with a single variable). Each variable is given a domain of fixed size k. A probability p_1 is set and is used to decide on the existence of a constraint between any pair of agents (this sets an average constraint density). For each constraint between two agents, each pair of value assignments is assigned a cost of 1 with a fixed probability of p_2. By keeping the same n, k, p_1 and varying p_2, one generates a set of random problems with increasingly tighter constraints. This family of $MaxCSPs$ were used to evaluate lookahead search algorithms for centralized COPs in [33, 36].

When evaluating distributed algorithms it is best to simulate the distributed system. Running experiments on multiple machines is both costly and has the disadvantage that the possibility of repeating experiments under the exact same conditions is nonexistent. The simulator uses threads, where each thread plays the role of a single agent, and the agents (threads) exchange messages using standard Java routines. We use an asynchronous simulator, placing no limitation on the execution of the agents (with no need to wait for the next cycle to read the next message, each agent works at its own pace). This method faithfully measures the concurrent run of asynchronous algorithms (see Chapter 10).

It is important to note here that DISCOP algorithms have been empirically evaluated on very small and easy problems. In the main paper on *ADOPT* [47] the algorithm is tested on 3-coloring problems, where the independent variable is the number of agents. In other words, *the difficulty of the problems remains fixed*. In addition, the measurement of the algorithm's performance uses the number of cycles on a *synchronous simulator*. As was shown in Chapter 10, this is a very problematic measure that does not capture the concurrent performance of DISCOP algorithms. In the main paper on the DPOP algorithm [49] (in Section 14.4) the algorithm is tested on small instances of the *meetings scheduling problem (MSP)*, which again is far from a hard instance of DISCOPs. In the following section the *AFB* algorithm (in both versions) is compared to *ADOPT* and all algorithms are tested on a large family of *MaxDisCSP* problems. The combination of a wide range of difficulty of DISCOPs, an asynchronous simulator, and concurrent performance measures, contribute to the importance of this experimental evaluation [22].

18.1 Empirical Evaluation of AFB and AFB-BJ

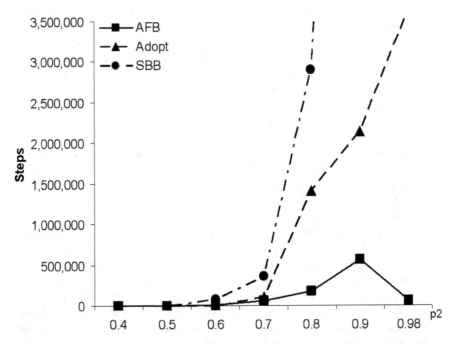

Fig. 18.1. Total non-concurrent computational steps by AFB, *ADOPT* and SBB on low-density (p_1=0.4) MaxDisCSPs

All experiments were performed on a simulator in which agents are simulated by threads which communicate only through message passing. The distributed optimization problems used in all of the presented experiments are random *MaxDisCSPs*. The network of constraints in each of the experiments is generated randomly by selecting the probability p_1 of a constraint among any pair of variables and the probability p_2, for the occurrence of a violation (a nonzero cost) among two assignments of values to a constrained pair of variables. Such uniform random constraints networks of n variables, d values in each domain, a constraints density of p_1, and tightness p_2 are commonly used in experimental evaluations of CSP algorithms (cf. [52]). *MaxCSPs* are commonly used in experimental evaluations of constraint optimization problems (COPs) [36]. Other experimental evaluations of DISCOPs include graph coloring problems [47, 66], which are a subclass of *MaxDisCSP*.

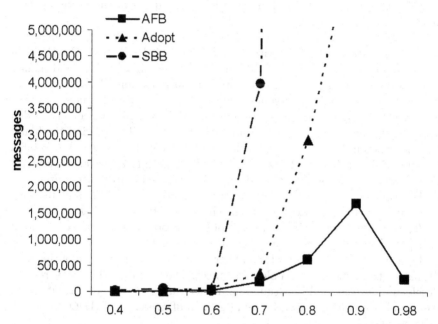

Fig. 18.2. Total number of messages sent by $AFB, ADOPT$ and SBB on low-density (p_1=0.4) MaxDisCSP

In order to evaluate the performance of distributed algorithms, two independent measures of performance are used: run time, in the form of nonconcurrent steps of computation, and communication load, in the form of the total number of messages sent [37]. We use the method described in Chapter 10 and Chapter 11 for counting nonconcurrent computational steps.

The first set of experiments compares the performance of $ADOPT$, SBB and AFB. Figure 18.1 presents the average run time in number of nonconcurrent computation steps, on randomly generated MaxDisCSPs with $n = 10$ agents, domain size $k = 10$, and a relatively low constraint tightness of $p_1 = 0.4$. Figure 18.2 compares the same algorithms on the same problem instances by the total number of messages sent. From these figures it is clear that the $ADOPT$ outperforms the basic algorithm (synchronous) SBB, in accordance with the experimental evaluation reported in [47]. It is also clear that AFB outperforms $ADOPT$, especially for the very tight (high-p_2) problems. This is true for both of the performance measures.

The second set of experiments includes the $ADOPT$ algorithm and three versions of the AFB algorithm: AFB, AFB-$minC$ - a variation of AFB which includes dynamic ordering of values based on minimal cost (with the current CPA), and AFB-BJ which is the composite backjumping and forward-bounding algorithm. AFB-BJ uses the same value ordering heuristic as AFB-$minC$. This was selected in order to show that the improved performance of AFB-BJ is a result of the backjumping feature and not of the value ordering heuristic.

Figure 18.3 presents the average run time in number of nonconcurrent computation steps, of all algorithms: $ADOPT$, AFB, AFB-$minC$ and AFB-BJ, on MaxDisCSPs with $n = 10$ agents, domain size $k = 10$, and a high constraint density of $p_1 = 0.7$. Asynchronous optimization ($ADOPT$) is much slower than the standard version of AFB. Also clear from this figure, is that the value ordering heuristic greatly improves AFB's performance. The added backjumping improves the performance much further. The RHS of the figure provides a zoom in of the section of the graph between $p_2 = 0.9$ and $p_2 = 0.98$. For such tight problems, $ADOPT$ did not terminate in a reasonable amount of time and was simply terminated (and thus is missing from the graph).

For tightness values that are higher than $p_2 > 0.9$ AFB and its variants demonstrate a phase transition. This phase transition behavior of the AFB algorithms is very similar to that of lookahead algorithms on centralized $MaxCSP$s [33, 36] that was described in Section 3.4.

Figure 18.4 presents the total number of messages sent by each of the algorithms for the same set of problem instances. The results of this measurement closely match the results of run time, as measured by nonconcurrent steps. We can also see the exponential rapid growth of messages of $ADOPT$, which was described in Section 15.5.3.

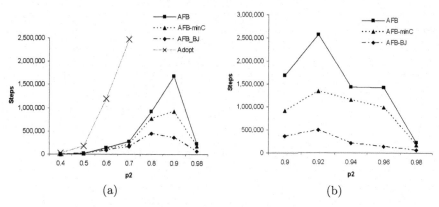

(a)   (b)

Fig. 18.3. (a) Number of nonconcurrent steps performed by $ADOPT$, AFB, AFB-$minC$, and AFB-BJ for high-density MaxDisCSP ($p_1 = 0.7$). (b) A closer look at $p_2 > 0.9$

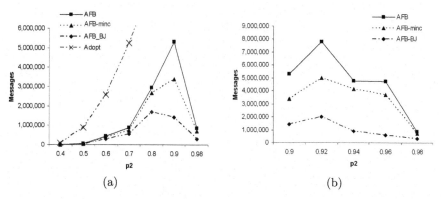

(a)   (b)

Fig. 18.4. (a) Number of messages sent by $ADOPT$, AFB, AFB-$minC$, and AFB-BJ for high-density MaxDisCSPs ($p_1 = 0.7$). (b) A closer look at $p_2 > 0.9$

References

[1] M.S. Affane and H. Bennaceur. A weighted arc consistency technique for max-csp. In *Proc. 13th Europ. Conf. on Artific. Intell. (ECAI-98)*, pages 209–213, 1998.

[2] Andrew B. Baker. The hazards of fancy backtracking. In *Proc. 12th Nat. Conf. Artificial Intelligence (AAAI-94)*, pages 288–293, Seattle, WA, USA, July 1994.

[3] R. Bejar, B. Krishnamachari, C. Gomes, and B. Selman. Distributed constraint satisfaction in a wireless sensor tracking system. In *Proc. Workshop on Distributed Constraint Reasoning, IJCAI01*, 2001.

[4] R. Bejar, C. Domshlak, C. Fernandez, K. Gomes, B. Krishnamachari, B.Selman, and M.Valls. Sensor networks and distributed csp: communication, computation and complexity. *Artificial Intelligence*, 161:1-2:117–148, January 2005.

[5] C. Bessiere and J. Regin. Refining the basic constraint propagation algorithm. In *Proc. IJCAI-01*, pages 309–315, 2001.

[6] C. Bessiere and J.C. Regin. Using bidirectionality to speed up arc-consistency processing. *Constraint Processing (LNCS 923)*, pages 157–169, 1995.

[7] C. Bessiere and J.C. Regin. Mac and combined heuristics: two reasons to forsake fc (and cbj?) on hard problems. In *Proc. CP 96*, pages 61–75, Cambridge MA, 1996.

[8] C. Bessiere, A. Maestre, and P. Messeguer. Distributed dynamic backtracking. In *Proc. Workshop on Distributed Constraints (in IJCAI-01)*, 2001.

[9] C. Bessiere, A. Maestre, I. Brito, and P. Meseguer. Asynchronous backtracking without adding links: a new member in the abt family. *Artificial Intelligence*, 161:1-2:7–24, January 2005.

[10] I. Brito and P. Meseguer. Distributed forward checking. In *Proc. CP-2003*, pages 801–806, September, Ireland, 2003.

[11] I. Brito and P. Meseguer. Synchronous, asynchronous and hybrid algorithms for discsp. In *Workshop on Distributed Constraints Reasoning(DCR-04) CP-2004*, Toronto, September 2004.

[12] B.J. Clement and A.C. Barrett. Space applications for distributed constraint reasoning. In *Proc. 6th workshop on Distributed Constraints Reasoning (DCR-05)*, Edinburgh, 2005.

[13] R. Dechter and D. Frost. Backjump-based backtracking for constraint satisfaction problems. *Artificial Intelligence*, 136:2:147–188, April 2002.

[14] R. Dechter and D. Frost. Backjump-based backtracking for constraint satisfaction problems. *Artificial Intelligence*, 136:147–188, 2002.

[15] R. Dechter and J. Pearl. Network-based heuristics for constraint satisfaction problems. *Artificial Intelligence*, 34:1–38, 1988.

[16] Rina Dechter. *Constraint Processing*. Morgan Kaufman, 2003.

[17] J. P. Modi (ed.). Distributed constraints reasoning - 2004. In *Proc. 5th Workshop on Distributed Constraints Reasoning (DCR-04)*, Toronto, 2004.

[18] M. Yokoo et. al. Distributed constraint satisfaction for formalizing distributed problem solving. In *IEEE Intern. Conf. Distrb. Comp. Sys.*, pages 614 – 621, 1992.

[19] C. Fernandez, R. Bejar, B. Krishnamachari, and K. Gomes. Communication and computation in distributed csp algorithms. In *Proc. CP2002*, pages 664–679, Ithaca, NY, USA, July 2002.

[20] E. C. Freuder and M. J. Quinn. Taking advantage of stable sets of variables in constraint satisfaction problems. In *Proc. IJCAI-85*, pages 1076–1078, Los Angeles, USA, 1985.

[21] Eugene C. Freuder. A sufficient condition for backtrack-bounded search. *Journal of ACM*, 32:755–761, 1985.

[22] A. Gershman, A. Meisels, and R. Zivan. Asynchronous forward-bounding for distributed constraints optimization. In *Proc. ECAI-06*, pages 103–107, Lago di Garda, August 2006.

[23] M. L. Ginsberg. Dynamic backtracking. *J. of Artificial Intelligence Research*, 1:25–46, 1993.

[24] Y. Hamadi. Distributed interleaved parallel and cooperative search in constraint satisfaction networks. In *Proc. IAT-01*, Singappore, 2001.

[25] Y. Hamadi. Interleaved backtracking in distributed constraint networks. *Intern. Jou. AI Tools*, 11:167–188, 2002.

[26] R. M. Haralick and G. L. Elliott. Increasing tree search efficiency for constraint satisfaction problems. *Artificial Intelligence*, 14:263–313, 1980.

[27] Katsutoshi Hirayama and Makoto Yokoo. Distributed partial constraint satisfaction problem. In *Proc. CP-97*, pages 222–236, 1997.

[28] R. J. Bayardo Jr. and D. P. Miranker. On the space-time trade-off in solving constraint satisfaction problems. In *Proc. IJCAI-95*, pages 558–562, 1995.

[29] N. Jussien, R. Debruyne, and P. Boizumault. Maintaining arc-consistency within dynamic backtracking. In *Principles and Practice of Constraint Programming (CP 2000)*, pages 249–261, Singapore, 2000.

[30] E. Kaplansky and A. Meisels. Scheduling agents - distributed employee timetabling. *Ann. of Operations Research*, 2007.

[31] G. Kondrak and P. van Beek. A theoretical evaluation of selected backtracking algorithms. *Artificial Intelligence*, 21:365–387, 1997.

[32] L. Lamport. Time, clocks, and the ordering of events in distributed system. *Communication of the ACM*, 2:95–114, April 1978.

[33] J. Larrosa and P. Meseguer. Phase transition in max-csp. In *Proc. 12th European Conference on Artificial Intelligence (ECAI-96)*, pages 190–194, Budapest, Hungary, 1996.

[34] J. Larrosa and P. Meseguer. Partition-based lower bound for max-csp. In *Proc. Constraints Processing 1999 (CP-99)*, pages 303–315, Alexandria, Virginia, 1999.

[35] J. Larrosa and T. Schiex. The quest of the best form of local consistency for weighted csp. In *Proc. International Joint Conference on Artificial Intelligence (IJCAI-03)*, pages 239–244, Acapulco, Mexico, P2003.

[36] J. Larrosa and T. Schiex. Solving weighted csp by maintaining arc consistency. *Artificial Intelligence*, 159:1–26, 2004.

[37] N.A. Lynch. *Distributed Algorithms*. Morgan Kaufmann Series, 1997.

[38] R. T. Maheswaran, M. Tambe, E. Bowring, J. P. Pearce, and P. Varakantham. Taking dcop to the real world: Efficient complete solutions for distributed multi-event scheduling. In *Proc. 3rd Intern. Joint Conf. on Autonomous Agents & Multi-Agent Systems (AAMAS-04)*, pages 310–317, NY, New York, 2004.

[39] R. Mailler and V. R. Lesser. Asynchronous partial overlay: A new algorithm for solving distributed constraint satisfaction problems. *J. Artif. Intell. Res. (JAIR)*, 25:529–576, 2006.

[40] R. Mailler and V.R. Lesser. Solving distributed constraint optimization problems using cooperative mediation. In *AAMAS-04*, pages 438–445, 2004.

[41] A. Meisels and E. Kaplansky. Iterative restart techniques for solving timetabling problems. *Europ. Jou. OR*, 153:41–50, 2003.

[42] A. Meisels and O. Lavee. Using additional information in discsp search. In *Proc. 5th workshop on distributed constraints reasoning, DCR-04*, Toronto, 2004.

[43] A. Meisels and A. Schaerf. Modelling and solving employee timetabling problems. *Annal. Math. and AI*, 39:41–59, 2003.

[44] A. Meisels and R. Zivan. Asynchronous forward-checking for distributed csps. *Constraints*, 16:132–156, 2006.

[45] A. Meisels, I. Razgon, E. Kaplansky, and R. Zivan. Comparing performance of distributed constraints processing algorithms. In *Proc. AAMAS-2002 Workshop on Distributed Constraint Reasoning DCR*, pages 86–93, Bologna, July 2002.

[46] J. Modi, W. Shen, M. Tambe, and M. Yokoo. An asynchronous complete method for distributed constraints optimization. In *Proc. Suton. Agents and Multi-agent Sys.*, 2003.

[47] P.J. Modi, W. Shen, M. Tambe, and M. Yokoo. Adopt: asynchronous distributed constraints optimization with quality guarantees. *Artificial Intelligence*, 161:1-2:149–180, January 2005.

[48] T. Nguyen, D. Sam-Hroud, and B. Faltings. Dynamic distributed backjumping. In *Proc. 5th workshop on distributed constraints reasoning DCR-04*, pages 46–61, Toronto, September 2004.

[49] A. Petcu and B. Faltings. A scalable method for multiagent constraint optimization. In *Proc. IJCAI-05*, pages 266–271, Edinburgh, Scotland, UK, 2005.

[50] A. Petcu and B. Faltings. Mb-dpop: A new memory-bounded algorithm for distributed optimization. In *Proc. 20th Intern. Joint Conf. on Artif. Intell. (IJCAI-07)*, pages 1452–1457, Hyderabad, India, 2007.

[51] P. Prosser. Hybrid algorithms for the constraint satisfaction problem. *Computational Intelligence*, 9:268–299, 1993.

[52] P. Prosser. An empirical study of phase transitions in binary constraint satisfaction problems. *Artificial Intelligence*, 81:81–109, 1996.

[53] M.C. Silaghi. *Asynchronously Solving Problems with Privacy Requirements*. PhD thesis, Swiss Federal Institute of Technology (EPFL), 2002.

[54] M.C. Silaghi and B. Faltings. Asynchronous aggregation and consistency in distributed constraint satisfaction. *Artificial Intelligence*, 161:1-2:25–54, January 2005.

[55] M.C. Silaghi and B. Faltings. Parallel proposals in asynchronous search. Technical Report 01/#371, EPFL, August 2001. http://liawww.epfl.ch/cgi-bin/Pubs/recherche.

[56] B.M. Smith and M. Dyer. Locating the phase transition in binary constraint satisfaction problems. *Artificial Intelligence*, 81:155 – 181, 1996.

[57] G. Solotorevsky, E. Gudes, and A. Meisels. Modeling and solving distributed constraint satisfaction problems (dcsps). In *Constraint Processing-96, (short paper)*, pages 561–2, Cambridge, Massachusetts, USA, October 1996.

[58] E. Tsang. *Foundations of Constraint Satisfaction*. Academic Press, 1993.

[59] R.J. Wallace and E. Freuder. Constraint-based multi-agent meeting scheduling: effects of agent heterogeneity on performance and privacy loss. In *Proc. 3rd workshop on distributed constraint reasoning, DCR-02*, pages 176–182, Bologna, 2002.

[60] R.J. Wallace and E. Freuder. Constraint-based reasoning and privacy/efficiency tradeoffs in multi-agent problem solving. *Artificial Intelligence*, 161:1-2:209–228, January 2005.

[61] M. Yokoo. Algorithms for distributed constraint satisfaction problems: A review. *Autonomous Agents & Multi-Agent Sys.*, 3:198–212, 2000.

[62] M. Yokoo. Asynchronous weak-commitment search for solving distributed constraint satisfaction problems. In *Proc. 1st Intrnat. Conf. on Const. Progr.*, pages 88 – 102, Cassis, France, 1995.

[63] M. Yokoo and K. Hirayama. *Distributed Constraint Satisfaction Problems*. Springer Verlag, 2000.

[64] M. Yokoo, E.H. Durfee, T. Ishida, and K. Kuwabara. Distributed constraint satisfaction problem: Formalization and algorithms. *IEEE Trans. on Data and Kn. Eng.*, 10:673–685, 1998.

[65] M. Yokoo, K. Hirayama, and K. Sycara. The phase transition in distributed constraint satisfaction problems: First results. In *Proc. CP-2000*, pages 515–519, Singapore, 2000.

[66] W. Zhang, Z. Xing, G. Wang, and L. Wittenburg. Distributed stochastic search and distributed breakout: properties, comparishon and applications to constraints optimization problems in sensor networks. *Artificial Intelligence*, 161:1-2:55–88, January 2005.

[67] R. Zivan and A. Meisels. Parallel backtrack search on discsps. In *Proc. AAMAS-2002 Workshop on Distributed Constraint Reasoning DCR*, Bologna, July 2002.

[68] R. Zivan and A. Meisels. Synchronous vs. asynchronous search on discsps. In *Proc. 1st European Workshop on Multi Agent System, EUMAS*, Oxford, December 2003.

[69] R. Zivan and A. Meisels. Concurrent backtrack search for discsps. In *Proc. FLAIRS-04*, pages 776–81, Miami Florida, May 2004.

[70] R. Zivan and A. Meisels. Concurrent dynamic backtracking for distributed csps. In *CP-2004*, pages 782–7, Toronto, 2004.

[71] R. Zivan and A. Meisels. Dynamic ordering for asynchronous backtracking on discsps. In *CP-2005*, pages 32–46, Sigtes (Barcelona), Spain, 2005.

[72] R. Zivan and A. Meisels. Message delay and discsp search algorithms. *Annals of Mathematics and Artificial Intelligence (AMAI)*, 46:415–439, 2006.

[73] R. Zivan and A. Meisels. Message delay and asynchronous discsp search. *Archives of Control*, 16:221–242, 2006.

[74] R. Zivan and A. Meisels. Dynamic ordering for asynchronous backtracking on discsps. *Constraints*, 11:179–197, 2006.

[75] R. Zivan and A. Meisels. Concurrent search for distributed csps. *Artificial Intelligence*, 170:440–461, 2006.

[76] R. Zivan and A. Meisels. Conflict directed backjumping for maxcsps. In *Workshop on Heuristic Search, Memory-based Heuristics and Their Applications , AAAI-2006*, Boston, 2006.

[77] R. Zivan, M. Zazon, and A. Meisels. Min-domain ordering for asynchronous backtracking. In *Proc. Constraints Processing 2007 (CP-07)*, Providence, RI, September, 2007.

Index